THIS LIGHT CALLED DARKNESS

A RAVEN CHRONICLES

ANTHOLOGY,

SELECTED WORK 1997–2005

Other Raven books and publications

Poem of Stone and Bone, The Iconography of James W. Washington Jr.
in Fourteen Stanzas and Thirty-One Days
Paperback ISBN 978-1-7354780-2-9
  by Carletta Carrington Wilson

Words From the Café, an anthology, 2nd Edition
Paperback ISBN 978-0-9979468-9-5
  Edited by Anna Bálint, photographs by Willie J. Pugh

Dogzes and Katzes
Paperback ISBN 978-1-7354780-1-2
  Drawings by Elizabeth (Detonator Beth) Lawrence
  Edited by Phoebe Bosché, Scott Martin

Spirits of the Ordinary, A Tale of Casas Grandes, 2nd Edition
eBook, ISBN 987-0-9979468-6-4
Paperback, ISBN 987-0-9979468-8-8
  Fiction by Kathleen Alcalá

Take a Stand: Art Against Hate, A Raven Chronicles Anthology
(Winner of the 2021 Washington State Book Award for Poetry)
ISBN 978-0-9979468-7-1
  Edited by Anna Bálint, Phoebe Bosché, Thomas Hubbard

Stealing Light, A Raven Chronicles Anthology,
  Selected Work 1991-1996
ISBN 978-0-9979468-5-7
  Edited by Kathleen Alcalá, Phoebe Bosché, Paul Hunter,
  Stephanie Lawyer

Raven Chronicles Journal, Vol. 26, Last Call
ISBN 978-0-9979468-4-0
  Edited by Kathleen Alcalá, Anna Bálint, Phoebe Bosché,
  Gary Copeland Lilley, Priscilla Long

Raven Chronicles Journal, Vol. 25, Balancing Acts
ISBN 978-0-9979468-3-3
  Edited by Anna Bálint, Phoebe Bosché, Matt Briggs,
  Paul Hunter, Doug Johnson

Raven Chronicles Journal, Vol. 24, HOME
ISBN 978-0-9979468-2-6
  Edited by Kathleen Alcalá, Anna Bálint, Phoebe Bosché,
  Paul Hunter, Stephanie Lawyer

This Light Called Darkness

A Raven Chronicles

Anthology,

Selected Work 1997–2005

Editors

Kathleen Alcalá

Phoebe Bosché

Paul Hunter

Anna Odessa Linzer

Raven Chronicles Press
Seattle, Washington

RAVEN CHRONICLES PRESS

Copyright © 2023

Printed in the United States of America
Raven Chronicles Press
First Edition, Copyright © 2023

ISBN: 978-1-7354780-4-3
Library of Congress Control Number: 2022951959

Cover: *Late November, Refuge*, National Elk Refuge,
Jackson, Wyoming, 2021, photograph by Claudia Mauro.
Book Design: Phoebe Bosché, Adobe Jenson Pro (text), and (display).
Graphics & Cover Design: Scott Martin.

Established in 1991, *The Raven Chronicles* is a Seattle-based
literary organization that publishes and promotes artistic work
and community events that embody the cultural diversity and
multitude of imaginations of writers and artists living in the
Pacific Northwest and other regions of the United States.

Raven Chronicles Press
15528 12th Avenue NE
Shoreline, Washington 98155-6226
editors@ravenchronicles.org
https://www.ravenchronicles.org

This anthology is dedicated to all our colleagues—
writers, artists, teachers, mentors, friends—
whose work is included in this anthology,
including those who are no longer with us:

Waverly Fitzgerald
Murray Gordon
Robert Gregory
Marion Kimes
Jeanne Ruth (Ackley) Lohmann
Jo Nelson
David Warren Paul
Nancy Redwine
Judith Roche
Joan Angevine Swift
David Lloyd Whited
Bill Yake

Raven with Berries, photograph by Kathleen Gunton

TABLE OF CONTENTS

LIST OF ARTISTS AND ILLUSTRATORS
Pages art/illustrations appear on:

Alfredo Arreguín: 175, 375, 418
Anna Bálint: 32
Toni Lee Bennett: 178
Anita K. Boyle: 351
Matt Briggs: 31: 1997 cover; 65: 1998 cover
Michelle Brooks: 300
Manit Chaotragoongit: 272, 335, 358
Joel A. Derefield: 155: 2000 cover
Nancy D. Donnelly: 216, 230
Anita Endrezze: 313
Genda J. Guilmet: 53: 1997-98 cover; 82, 247, 326
Kathleen Gunton: 6
Jeff Niles Hacking: 160
Mike Hess: 290
Judy Horn: 116-117: 1999 cover
Paul Hunter: 164: 2001 cover
Irene H. Kuniyuki: 225: 2002-03 cover
Clare McLean: 127: 1999-2000 cover
Scott Martin: 41, 255: 2003 cover; 339: 2004-05 cover
Claudia Mauro: cover photograph
Whitney Pastorek: 256, 262
Polly Purvis: 18, 321: 2004 cover
Joel Sackett: 88-89: 1999 cover; 97
Stephanie Shachat: 320: 2004 cover
Judith Skillman: 44
Martha Studt: 25: 1997 cover
Peggy Sullivan: 147
Mark Sullo: 60, 194, 205: 2002 cover
Gail E. Tremblay: 281: 2003-04 cover
Carl Van Vechten: 134
Andrew Wesner: 346
Gloria White Calico: 70
Carletta Carrington Wilson: 165: 2001 cover
Bill Yake: 414

Foreword

Calling on the Light

This Light Called Darkness is the second anthology in the Raven Chronicles Press series featuring some of the outstanding work that appeared in *Raven Chronicles Magazine*—a nonprofit, independent publishing and cultural organization, based in Seattle, that soared for twenty-seven years, 1991 to 2018. Through forty-eight issues in twenty-six magazine-format volumes, Raven brought together flocks of writers in the Pacific Northwest / Salish Sea region and beyond, for readings, workshops, cultural celebrations, and the occasional march or demonstration. I love the story of the origin of *Raven Chronicles*, as recounted on the Raven website:

> *Raven Chronicles* began in 1991, when Kathleen Alcalá and Philip Red Eagle guest-edited several King County Arts Commission Newsletters. They realized that there was a lack of diverse, multicultural writing being published in Seattle and the Northwest region in general. They thought: let's start our own magazine!

> We chose the name *Raven* because—as we learned from Upper Skagit storyteller Vi Hilbert (now deceased)—in northern Northwest Coast mythology Raven is a powerful figure who transforms the world, by accident or on purpose, yet he is also a trickster, a shape-shifter who is mischievous, often selfish, but brings light to the world. We added *Chronicles* because we intended the magazine to be a chronicle of how time passes, *chronos*, and us with it.

Over the past several years—having published the last few numbers of the magazine in book format, culminating in the "Last Call" final issue in summer 2018—*Raven Chronicles* has migrated to book publishing. As Raven Chronicles Press, it continues to publish work that embodies the cultural diversity of writers and artists living in the Pacific Northwest and beyond.

Volumes appearing so far include the long-awaited second edition of Bainbridge Island-based writer Kathleen Alcalá's acclaimed *Spirits of the Ordinary: a Tale of Casas Grandes* (2021), a novel which interweaves linked narratives based on the lore of Alcalá's ancestors in northern Mexico of the 1870s; and Carletta Carrington Wilson's forthcoming hybrid volume, *Poem of Stone and Bone: The Iconography of James W. Washington Jr. in Fourteen Stanzas and Thirty-One Days*, which documents four site-specific installations that poet, visual artist, librarian, and arts activist Wilson created in 2011 on the Seattle property of noted African American sculptor James W. Washington, Jr.

So far, anthologies that curate at the intersection of arts and activism prevail in the output of Raven Chronicles Press, including *Words From the Café* (2016), edited by poet, writer, editor, and cultural activist Anna Bálint, illustrated with photographs by Willie Pugh, and featuring writing by people in recovery from trauma, addiction, mental illness, and homelessness—courageous individuals with whom Bálint has worked in classes, workshops, and support circles at Seattle's Recovery Cáfe, where she founded the Safe Place Writing Circle. Most recent, and so far the most acclaimed of these anthologies, is *Take a Stand: Art Against Hate*, edited by Anna Bálint, Phoebe Bosché, and Thomas Hubbard (2020). Winner of the 2021 Washington State Book Award for Poetry, this anthology features work in response and resistance to the dangerous and deluded regime of the (fortunately) former Hater-in-Chief, and it serves as a sort of peace march in print form—a proactively humanitarian and nonviolent campaign for justice that poets, writers, artists, and activists have undertaken in support of the struggles embodied in the writings and depicted in the photos and artwork displayed in its pages.

Among Raven's current projects, including this present volume, is to compile and make available in book form the finest work that has appeared in *Raven Chronicles Magazine* over the decades. The first anthology, *Stealing Light: A Raven Chronicles Anthology, Selected Work 1991-1996*—published in 2018 and edited by Kathleen Alcalá, Phoebe Bosché, Paul Hunter, and Stephanie Lawyer, with Matt Briggs and Tiffany Midge—brings together in one volume the poems, essays, fiction, interviews, and storytelling of ninety-two writers, and the artwork / illustrations of twenty-six artists from the magazine's first five years. The title, of course, refers to the Coast Salish stories of Raven the trickster stealing light, but also bringing it to humans.

This Light Called Darkness, the second volume to collect work from *Raven Chronicles Magazine*, covers the years 1997–2005, from Volume 7, Number 1 (Summer 1997) to Volume 11, Number 3 (2004-2005), and in its title extends the motif of light and darkness from the previous volume's title, with a glance toward paradox: in what sense can light be darkness? What impressed me about the poems, interviews, short stories, essays, and nonfiction narratives presented here was the quality of mystery, that brilliant shadow or light gleaming out of darkness that pervaded so much of the writing. After I was asked to write a foreword for this volume, I found myself devouring the entire manuscript, drawn into an engagement with the writing that made many words seem to rise off the page and glow with an urgency that kept me reading.

A few pieces haunted me. Nancy Redwine's story, "The Accident," enters the mind of a woman crushed by a falling redwood tree, and the interior monologue re-visitation of her life and loves over the days she is dying—the flashes of insight in darkness she achieves in this liminal state:

> I saw everything through the branches of the tree. Everything was broken and framed in its own raggedness. The light lifted up the edges of my vision so that what grew up from under the severed places was illuminated . . . I saw how being broken was the most important thing that could happen to anyone.

Two stories with lively language and hearty humor that I could not stop reading were Anna Mockler's "Painting Wallpaper" and Deborah Parks-Satterfield's "Lula." Mockler is particularly good at vivid listing:

> In twenty years since I left my parents' house, seventeen and friendly, I'd lived in five major cities and thirty-one apartments, a number inflated by the years I crashed around on many beds and sofas, with and without: sensitive black Irish carpenters, handsome piano-tuning poets, tall scholars who could really dance, men of no profession who were good to climb trees with by moonlight, comics who turned out to be drug dealers, cabdrivers who turned out to be drug addicts, former newsmen who tap danced as they pushed cable cars around the lazy Susan terminal.

And Parks-Satterfield creates in Lula a larger-than-life "Hellspawn" of a woman who knows what she wants and goes for it: "No sweet words for Lula. She'd take ya man, take ya woman, take ya food off the table. She could steal the sweetness out of a cookie and not break it." Among other high-energy transgressions, Lula purloins—with her loins!—one Mr. Jacobs from his wife: a romantic heist that crosses the boundaries of life and death . . . and propriety! Read the story to see what I mean!

There is work that awakens social concerns: "Get to Know Your Jacket" by Murray Gordon, a poem in which each part of this item of clothing is connected to the name of an underpaid textile worker with an immigrant name who executes that act of assembly on sleeve or shoulder seam or pocket. There is powerful writing in the wake of 9/11: David Warren Paul's narrative "A Better Way," about acts of support for the Idriss Mosque in North Seattle in the face of threats of violence and vengeance upon the members of the local Islamic community. The poem "At the Reading" by Robert Gregory, haunts us obliquely as snow blowing past the window behind the reader grows quietly ominous, carrying what seem to be "ragged torn fragments / of paper and skin."

Other pieces about reading conjure Seattle's tutelary poet, Richard Hugo. Bobby Anderson's "Writing a Place in the City" relates how discovered connections with Hugo's rough, working-class upbringing allowed his work to serve as a mentor and way-shower for this writer at a troubled time in his youth. And Joan Swift's poignant poem, "The Readings at Richard Hugo House," regrets "the trout we never caught," recalling how Hugo once invited her to fish with him on his beloved Lake Kapowsin. "I didn't go," she admits, and now it's too late, the chance has passed with Hugo's passing: "Now you're too big to catch in anyone's net, // out there on some migration all of us will make . . ."

Two other pieces I have to mention both evoke the power of place and of objects inherent to their place. Avital Gad-Cykman's "Cycle of Seasons," set in the harsh, arid *sertão* of northeastern Brazil, with its elements of magical realism, brings two outsiders together in the brilliant desert colors and giddy promise of this region. And Anita Endrezze's compelling story, "The Medicine Bundle," follows the trajectory of a stolen Kiowa medicine bag and its sacred contents, among them a mysterious symbol, representing "lightning or an arrow or a cosmic music note or a tree branch divided by the sky." None of the non-Native people who try to appropriate this symbol as it passes magically from one to the next—across continents and countries and the cupidity of corporate brandings—can fathom its uncanny power, and they all are vanquished by this symbol in ways ironically appropriate to their individual delusions and vanities. Like Raven, with his mythical trickster spirit, this Kiowa symbol steals the light of self-awareness from those who have none, and brings the light of understanding to us readers who seek to respect the identities and heritage of others. And as we read *This Light Called Darkness*, we find ourselves compelled to call upon the light of our own spirit to appreciate and resonate with the multiplicity of voices speaking here, showing us the way.

—*Carolyne Wright*
In North Seattle: the traditional Duwamish/
Coast Salish homeland, November 2022

Mask, Coast Salish Pow Wow, Seattle, 1999, photograph by Polly Purvis

Introductions

Kathleen Alcalá: Reading back through these essays, poems, translations, and short stories is like watching my literary life flash before my eyes.

How we debated including some works. How we tried to balance inherently political work with sheer beauty. I miss those who have moved on from the northwest, some to foreign countries, some to a higher plane. Do these works reflect the societal tone of that time? Our preoccupations before our brains were taken over by social media? I think we were saner then.

> Creamy, brown-speckled-caps with firm stems, smelling of pine and dark rich earth. Cooked in butter. Steamed in rice or soup. Frozen and hoarded like gold coins locked deep in icy safes. Sent by some to far away Hawaii, California, the East Coast—to be opened and relished by a black-haired, brown-eyed people.

From Sharon Hashimoto's "The Mushroom Man," a short story grounded in the International District of Seattle and the working-class concerns of an immigrant population, to David W. Paul's, "A Better Way," which details his compassionate reaction to the attempted setting on fire of a mosque near his home, we celebrate the eccentricities, relationships, and hostilities of our friends and characters.

And then this, by Kathleen Walsh Spencer:

Army Nurses, Vietnam, 1966

After the Vietnam Women's Memorial,
Washington, D.C., Glenna Goodacre, Sculptor

Too exhausted to swat the flies
that buzz their hair, three nurses
sit back to back on sandbags
to rest, to wait for the wounded

soldier to be choppered out, handed
over to the *USS Sanctuary* floating off Vietnam.

Among the bamboo trees of Phu Non, Vietnam,
one of the nurses holds the flyer,
stretches her arm, reaches her hand
across his chest: a pieta of nurse
and soldier, her limbs wound
around him to contain this awkward package
slipping from her grasp.

War and its aftermath seem to be rising again, invading our lives and our dreams. In Ukraine, women are undergoing training to fly drones in this nightmarish war with Russia. The words from this earlier war reverberate in the shattered air of today.

The work in this set of Raven Chronicles magazines highlights our tentative purchase on the land and landscape, mixed in with stories from all over the world. This international flavor gradually increases with each issue, reflecting our evolving relationship with the internet, the shrinking of the world literary stage to bring strangers into our intimate circle of tree huggers.

If you have work in these Raven issues, thank you. Rest assured that your words still matter. If the work in this anthology is new to you, I encourage you to browse through and take the time to savor a gem or two each evening, for many evenings to come.

Anna Odessa Linzer: Given that Raven's wing is in this wild endeavor, it is little wonder that there is some mystery and some magic in Raven Chronicles. How Phoebe Bosché and Phil Red-Eagle and Kathleen Alcalá found each and flew together in this literary journey, bringing so many of us along through the years, remains a bit of a mystery to me. Was it hatched at the 1992 Returning the Gift Native American Writers' Festival in Norman, Oklahoma? Was it there in that same place and time that I also first met Phoebe and Phil? The place where somehow Phoebe solicited from me a piece on the festival and I sent her entries from my diary that began with flying to Oklahoma, sitting next to a woman who was a cop who delivered prisoners to the prison where

Leonard Peltier was locked up, and, as I listened to her rant, I had to grip the back of the seat in front of me "to keep myself in control and to help lift the plane up through the clouds." Until I was there in Norman, surrounded by so many voices. Was it that magic time in Oklahoma that Raven first flew? That place that was a "whirlwind, a storm of poems, angry words, beautiful tears, laughter, ancient languages, songs, drumming, and tender conversation in a good place where being an Indian and being a writer is celebrated, is the very center."

Because so suddenly it was all magic. Back in the Northwest there were readings at bookstores in Seattle—some fine stores gone now or moved—and on Bainbridge Island, editors' meetings at Elliott Bay Book Company in Pioneer Square and in cafes, picnics, and gathering at my home in Indianola and in other homes in Seattle, more Native Writers conferences in Neah Bay, in Indianola, and in Taos. All the while packages of manuscripts seemingly from everywhere flew into my Post Office box, delighting and perplexing me for hours into the night.

I am sure that there are explanations for the mystery and magic of Raven Chronicles. Or maybe there are not. I like to believe that the real magic came from the three original Ravens, and that some of us were wonderfully swept up in the mystery and magic and were lucky enough to add our voices.

Paul Hunter: It is no easy task to put together an anthology, to see and sense it as a whole, especially one like *This Light Called Darkness*. Beneath the canopy of its lovely enigmatic title, the pages sway and jostle, their leaves dance with voices that do not argue or compete, as they might in some other magazines. These voices seem almost to settle into each other, shuffle their order as one thumbs through the pages and they naturally touch. These leaves might well be accretions—as if leaves or growth rings on a living tree. Just under the bark of the cover there surges a common life, where the pieces fed of the same sap feel like family, open and honest, as each seems to say "What about this too? And now what of this?" as it adds its song or story, its deepest and boldest questions and wonderings to the pile.

Working on the first anthology I had felt that the poems were first to arrive in those early issues. They announced their subjects and asserted their voices, while the more everyday and prosaic parts of the issues—the stories and essays, reviews and commentary, took more time to show up at the party. Reading works for this second anthology, covering the years from 1997 to 2005, I was struck by the wide range of prose voices that had found their way to the Raven table. These works felt less explanatory, their styles clearer and more assured. It seemed a sign that, for this reader at least, the magazine seemed to be maturing into its role as a broader organ or vehicle of community. That these artists were reading each other, taking one another seriously, and were comfortable being aboard and sharing the ride.

Then one other thought occurred to me. Writers need community, common places where they can find light, warmth, and nourishment. But this impulse to locate oneself in community really runs deeper than public spaces, eateries and watering holes, bus stops and park benches, even homeless encampments. What we really seek, whether we acknowledge it or not, is the shelter and clothing and sustenance for which we have only one word, whether we've felt it often for ourselves or not—and that is home. The magic of this magazine has lain in plain sight for decades, and is the reason it has gotten some of the finest work by artists from an ever-widening circle. They turned this way, and have kept turning this way, kept this publication in mind like its other readers have, because through thick and thin what it offered felt sustaining and welcoming—felt like home. Try it and see if you don't agree.

Philip H. Red Eagle and his merry crew in Tacoma published three *South Sound Editions of Raven Chronicles Magazine*: Vol. 7, No. 3, with managing editors Jean Musser and Kelly Richstein; Vol. 8 No. 3, with editors Karen Havnaer, Dotti Krist, Gina Leach, and Matt Cygny; and Vol. 9, No. 3, with editors Allen Braden, Sharon Carter, Matt Cygny, Karen Havnaer, Ian Lamberton, and Dotti Krist. They published work by dozens and dozens of writers and artists, including an interview with local hero, Jesuit Priest William J. (Bix) Bichsel, who was serving prison time for protesting the School of the Americas at Ft. Benning, Georgia; several poems from Deborah A. Miranda's award-winning poetry book *Indian Cartography*; and dedications/memorials to several mentors/writers we have lost: Tom Heidlebaugh, E.K. Caldwell, and Vicki L. Sears.

Phoebe Bosché: The thing I love about putting together Raven anthologies is that it's like time travel—without leaving my office or backyard. For most of the years 1995–2005 we produced 2–4 magazines a year, each with a theme and a whole lot of features, not always the same ones: Spoken Word; Rants, Raves & Reviews; Raven Notes; East of Eden (South Sound Edition); Beyond Borders; Scribes (Richard Hugo House Young Writers); Food & Culture; etc. We loved giving so many distinct voices the freedom to engage with readers and fellow writers. Many, many of the writers whose work we chose had never had work published before; several were high school students.

This is the second of four planned anthologies: selected work from all the *Raven Chronicles Magazines/Journals* we published up until 2018. As was the case with the first anthology, *Stealing Light*, many writers, whose work we chose to represent the magazine their work appeared in, are no longer with us: dead or missing in action. And, as the years pass, the list gets longer. Goodbye Waverly, Murray, Robert, Marion, Jeanne Ruth, Jo, David, Nancy, Judith, Joan, David Lloyd, and Bill (Yake, who died during the final month of finishing this anthology), . We don't have you, dear friends and colleagues, but we have your work. Here.

Raven is known also for the artwork we publish, and one of our most published artists is dear friend, Alfredo Arreguín. Alfredo loves his corvids, and he tells us: "Oh my dear amigos, los Cuervos / crows, that have been my companions since childhood! I have happy memories of crows following me and my friends to the forests outside my city of birth, Morelia, Michoacán, Mexico, where we played Tarzan. These mysterious black birds would accompany me on my morning walks around Green Lake, in Seattle, Washington, and inspired me to paint a large canvas that I named *A Murder of Crows*. That painting appeared on the cover of *Raven Chronicles* with a poem by my friend, the poet Tess Gallagher, in 1991. [This was Raven's first magazine.] I salute and appreciate these magnificent birds, and propose a toast with a small glass of Tequila Cuervo!"

Here's a toast to all the writers and artists in *This Light Called Darkness*. And to you, dear reader. *Gozar!*

"... in that secret place between memory
and promise that is always
ripe with summer."

—Anna Odessa Linzer

I

Volume 7, Number 1, Summer 1997

Raven Presents   *$3*

The Girl Who Always Thought It Was Summer

Work By
Annie Hansen ◆ John Willson
Sharon Hashimoto

The girl in the cloud dress, pencil drawing,
by Martha Studt (1983)

The Mushroom Man

Sharon Hashimoto

Labor Day weekend.

And the air is rich with golden leaves that ride upon the wind. Dusty, sun-dried browns turn mushy, muddy wet black with hazy fog and misty rain. On cool clear nights the moon hangs low, glowing cheddar cheese yellow. And V-shaped flights of birds point arrows to the south.

Labor Day weekend, and the whispers begin.

Port Townsend. Shelton. Cascades.

Whispers that echo like wind through the trees, raining secrets that soak deep into the mind. Whispers that pour like rivers from overflowing mouths down Rainier Avenue and Jackson, Empire Way and Genesee. Whispers that speak of mushrooms.

"Last year, we only found about two dozen . . ."

". . . hope it rains . . . much too dry . . ."

"The Ogawas went last week . . ."

"Uwajimaya is selling them at five dollars a pound!"

Creamy, brown-speckled caps with firm stems, smelling of pine and dark rich earth. Cooked in butter. Steamed in rice or soup. Frozen and hoarded like gold coins locked deep in icy safes. Sent by some to far away Hawaii, California, the East Coast—to be opened and relished by a black-haired, brown-eyed people. Found even in lean years, in ample abundance, by Osam.

"Osam? Tall, skinny . . . with horn rim glasses?"

"Didn't he work for the City?"

"You know, Toshio's middle son."

"He found how many?!" they would exclaim, their voices rising on the last note and lingering on the air with the tone of gentle wind chimes. "Where?" they would murmur, jealous of his riches, "Where does he go?"

And he would nod, smile, and say nothing while passing out generous quantities to friends and families who knew better than to ask. Too many battles had been waged over "secret locations." Too many whispers and secrets had built walls between friends, made enemies among families.

Sure-footed Osam, whose journeying feet travelled far, past dull red mushrooms with shiny tops and fragile porcelain-white mushrooms that dipped in the center. Keen eyes would spot treasure hidden beneath a mottled forest floor. And clever fingers would probe deep beneath tree roots to expose tender young buds.

Sam to some. Osam to others. Papa to me.

He was a centipede of tall long legs that walked swiftly down the rain-drenched streets of Seattle. Towering stilts that wandered deep into the woods, over decaying logs and padded softly over brown-green moss. Legs I used to hug tight and smile at the face that floated among the clouds above mine. Sweat and grass and the odor of trees and branches and the creek about him. That was Papa. Against the cool rubber of his boots, I would always smell mushrooms.

He was mountains and magic and memories—a mystery in the fine chain that bound me to him, and to Grandma and Grandpa. Sometimes he was sad and sometimes he was old, his eyes hungering for something distant, far-off. And watching him dreamily patch his worn faded boots, I would think questions at him, never daring to ask out loud. Where do the mountains begin, where do they end? Papa, do you know? How do you get there from here? Then feeling my eyes upon him, he would look up and push his glasses back up his narrow nose. His thin, even voice still tinged with smoky thoughts would remind me that homework must be done before bed.

A quiet man. A comfortable man. A quiet and comfortable house.

But some nights I would wake, snapped out of sleep like a rubber band. Listening to the house waiting, like the silence before a thunderstorm. Smothered and imprisoned between blankets and sheets, I would lie, feeling the tension run like electricity throughout the house. Then, just after midnight. Hushed, rough-edged voices would claw the night. The edge of a broken glass, it cut and made my dreams bleed into the dark.

Mama and Papa. Mostly Mama. Talking in broken Japanese. Whispers in bits of English.

"... don't like you going by yourself. Why can't you take somebody with you?"

"Dare?"

"Davey ... Sam ... Big Joe ..."

"... hanashimasu ..."

"Yes, about my secre ..."

"Shush! You'll wake the children!"

And the ricocheting emotions would bounce off the walls, always returning to me as I hid, buried in my bed, feeling the shadows hovering near. Then I would dream of dark clammy places that would yield to sweaty sheets and pillows thrown in fear upon the floor. Even morning sunlight and skies of robin egg blue would not chase away the autumn feelings in the air.

"Where does Papa go?" I once asked Mama as she packed a chicken-filled Tupperware and a thermos into a sturdy cardboard box.

"Tomorrow? East to Mercer Island, all the way down I-90. To Easton, I think. To the Olympics, maybe, on Sunday. And back to work on Monday."

"Olympics. Easton." I murmured softly.

"What's that?"

I watched her carefully as she fitted paper plates and napkins beside the thermos. "Do we get to go?"

"Linda's going to Sally's birthday party tomorrow and you have a piano lesson."

"When do we get to go?"

And Mama stopped her quick, butterfly-like movements to stare at me. She frowned and her eyebrows were straight lines across her forehead. "When do we get to go?" her quiet voice mocked mine. "When he asks."

She sat down heavily in the kitchen chair that wobbled because one leg had been bent, then sent me to the basement shelves for a can of olives. Anxious to escape her mood, I tramped half-running down the steps, jumping the fourth stair to the bottom.

"Please walk up the, stairs," she shouted down to me.

"Yes Mama."

But I knew she was remembering . . .

Butter and heavily-scented pine cut fresh that evening had run like bright streamers of heavenly aromas that lit up the house. Papa had smiled and bubbled, a bright yellow balloon, as he carried in four boxes of freshly picked mushrooms.

"So many . . ." Mama had whispered, her voice filtered softly around, through, and under the mountains of mushrooms. Quickly she had rolled up her sleeves, sorting the young buds from the wormy, blossomed mushrooms. I had watched her washing, cutting, dicing, cooking, freezing mushrooms in a thousand and one ways.

Puzzle pieces, I had thought to myself. Each gently gathered and somehow fitted into the quiet man leaning with one hip against the kitchen table. Part Mama. Part me and Linda, Grandma and Grandpa. Forests filled with pieces.

"Matsutake . . ." I had whispered. Mushroom man. Grown wild. Hidden in dark burrows beneath fallen trees. Dormant, but full of quiet secrets that touched me like the flying seasons. I had smiled up at Papa, not seeing the awful grayness creep into my father's face as his hands fluttered upwards to his chest before collapsing on the floor . . .

Winds blow chill on September days and the bright fall sun no longer warms my face and arms. The rain falls soft like chilly, early morning dreams and half-recalled memories that I try to forget. Falling leaves drift like Papa's rising voice, arguing with the doctor, with Mama, with the strange voices that called to him from the past. That sometimes call to me.

Sometimes I sit in Papa's dusty room where he hung his compass and hip boots from a long nail pounded deep into the wall. The feet of his boots always swing when I enter searching for the light switch above the naval clock that used to keep perfect time. Sunlight has dulled the calendar painting of green grass in a green Japan with temples and women in kimonos. A picture of a very young Mama, and Papa as a young man with old eyes, is pinned to the wall. They stand before a row of dilapidated houses painted like neglected crops in a barren land. Mama says it was taken in Heart Mountain, that she remembers little of it. I look at her eyes in the picture and see how they have faded and dulled since then. Haunted eyes, I think to myself.

I remember Papa, sitting bent in his chair, after his illness and the sudden quietness that filled the house. Of the smell of mushrooms that lingered for days. Of Mama's thin and worried face.

One Saturday I will always relive. Half-waking before the sun rose and listening for the birds that were no longer there, flown south to warm sunny lands. Wondering what had wakened me, I yawned and eased onto my side, heard the bed creak quietly beneath me. Mind drifting, I lay muffled in the soft sounds of the early darkness. But distantly I heard again the soft shuffle of boots on hardwood floors and the final sound of a door closing, and came suddenly awake.

I remember that evening and the phone ringing. Twice long, one short. Mama crying softly in her bed. Uncle Jinx and Aunt Fumi speaking with quick looks to the neighbors:

"His heart. It was his heart."

"...but where?"

"The south slope of Mount Rainier. Deep inside. Past the lumber roads and trails."

"She begged him not to go ..."

"...so stupid ... so stubborn ..."

"Greedy?"

"What then?"

"Maybe ... I don't know."

Labor Day weekend, and the whispers begin. 📖

II

Volume 7, Number 2, Summer/Fall 1997

Cover design & graphics by Matt Briggs

Chief Sealth Trail, Pea Patch, Seattle, 2017, photograph by Anna Bálint

Orogeny

Pamela Moore Dionne

Paradox and illusion define this coast
built by the subduction of Juan de Fuca plate.
This is the birthplace of mountainous rock
where magnetic reversals align
themselves against the pole's forces
and we struggle to define history.

While we walk, I analogize history
as struggle: a beating against the coast
of our beings, our internal forces
dragged down by sinking plates,
morphosed dense material fighting to align
and not to align, like this rock.

Walking a rhythmic heel-toe, I rock
back and forth between geologic history
and my own. My body aligns
itself with the waves along this coast.
I try to think about tectonic plates,
avoid all reference to internal forces.

But these are not to be denied, these forces
that push against what I want to know, that rock
my belief, leaving me with an empty plate,
making me face my history, our history,
unable any longer simply to coast
on an ignorance of what does not align.

And then I see it. There is a line
beyond which we have crossed. It forces
collisions and collapse. We cannot coast

safely past this rough rock
because it is made of habit and history.
It is the stuff of which we have filled our plates.

This story is dark with lithograph plates
that do not equally align.
We have printed an orogenic history
full of anticlines and stratified forces.
This shifting sandstone is the rock
that built our coast.

We must leave the coast, trudge the uplifted plate
where a horseshoe of rock moves solidly along a line.
We must attend these forces and shape our own history.

The Mind of the West

Eric Lee Christensen

At a Christmas party in Idaho a couple of years ago, I met a farmer who asked me what I do for a living. When I told him that I work for the Department of Energy, he sneered, "A beer-a-crat!" His tone left no doubt that he considered bureaucrats to be on a par with horse thieves and politicians.

Only later did I learn that this man was a dairy farmer, and therefore should have been overjoyed at the existence of bureaucrats, a small army of whom operate solely for the benefit of the dairy industry. Indeed, dairy farmers receive federal largesse on a scale that rivals nearly any other special interest.

On any given day in the West, one might have a similar experience—a farmer, rancher, miner, or some other person whose livelihood depends on, or at least is greatly enhanced by, government handouts, loudly, and without apparent irony, denouncing government in all its forms. How can so many Westerners harbor such fervid anti-government feelings in a region whose economy depends so heavily for, to name but a few programs, crop and water subsidies, below-cost sale of resources from federal lands, military spending, and rural electrification?

The answer is suggested in W.J. Cash's *The Mind of the South*, a classic study of another region where the dominant mythology powerfully distorts economic and social reality, often beyond recognition. Although Cash's work is now more than a half-century old, it still provides a remarkably useful model of Southern thinking, or at least the thinking of typical white Southerners of the lower and middle classes. This model parallels strikingly the traditional mindset of many Westerners, and the bitter lessons of Southern history likewise offers disturbing parallels to the history of the West.

In Cash's view, the first element of the Southern mind is the "savage ideal," an extreme and violent form of individualism borne of conditions on the frontier and rekindled by the Civil War, which forced the South to rebuild its ruined economy in frontier-like conditions. The parallels to the Western mind, where frontier never lurks far below the surface, are obvious.

The West's frontier mentality is exemplified by the strange case of Claude Dallas, a sociopathic hermit who murdered two Idaho Fish and Game officers in cold blood when they caught him poaching deer. Rather than being vilified as a killer of peace officers and a thief of public resources, as he deserved to be, Dallas became something of a folk hero who, by living off the land in isolated wilderness, embodied the symbolism of the long-lost mythical Western frontier. His murder of the Fish and Game officers was excused, and even celebrated, as the proper response to authorities who threatened to bring him into the modern world with limits on individual freedom.

In Cash's South, the savage ideal is overlain with a healthy layer of historical mythology, in which the antebellum South is transmogrified into a "Cloud-Cuckoo-Land" of white-mansioned caricature, in which every man owned a manor house, a thousand acres of cotton land, and two hundred slaves. The gods of the Southern pantheon—Robert E. Lee, Stonewall Jackson, Nathan Bedford Forrest—achieved immortality in valiant, if futile defense of these mythological values against the depredations of the Yankee in the Great Lost Cause of the Civil War (or, as it is often styled in the South, "The War of Northern Aggression"). In Cash's Cloud-Cuckoo-Land, every young Southern boy dreams of what it must have been like to follow General Pickett across that wide Pennsylvania wheatfield on a steamy July day in 1863 as the High Tide of the Confederacy crashed against the rocks of the Yankee war machine. Indeed, Cash describes Margaret Mitchell's sentimental novel Gone With The Wind as "a sort of new confession of the Southern faith."

The fountainhead of these historical myths, of course, is the most powerful myth of all, White Supremacy, which gave rise to the South's most indefensible institution, slavery, and, after the war, to Jim Crow, the Klan, and George Wallace.

The West has its own mythology, what we might call "The Myth of the Marlboro Man," that functions in much the same way as the "Cloud-Cuckoo-Land" myth. The Western mythology, much embellished by dime-store novels and Sunday afternoon cinema, is peopled by a larger-than-life group of rugged and solitary pioneers, animated by White Supremacy's first corollary, Manifest Destiny, who, sweeping westward in an irresistible wave, wrested the land from brutal savages and unforgiving Nature, making it safe for the creation of a nation of super-individualist yeoman farmers and ranchers.

Thus, every young Western boy dreams of what it must have been like to stand shoulder-to-shoulder with Custer at Little Big Horn, gallantly facing the unstoppable Savage tide. Or even more fancifully, he dreams that he is John Wayne, galloping full-speed across the silver screen toward the black-hatted bad guys, six-gun blazing in one hand, Winchester rifle blazing in the other, reins in his teeth, Stetson miraculously clinging to his head.

Both sets of regional myths seriously distort historical reality. Thus, as Cash points out, only a tiny percentage of Southerners ever belonged to the antebellum aristocracy. A white Southerner's ancestors were much more likely to be poor tenant farmers, or even poorer sharecroppers, living as near-serfs in the quasi-feudal world of the Southern plantation, or poor settlers relegated to small farms on the marginal soils forsaken by the planters. Similarly, a Westerner's forebears, if they lived in the West at all, were unlikely to have fit the Marlboro Man image. Rather, they were much more likely to be among the chronically underpaid hirelings who operated the mines and railroads owned by Eastern or European capitalists, or to be factory hands seeking refuge from the Dust Bowl at mills attracted by the New Deal's cheap hydropower.

These regional mindsets also produce devastating practical effects. For many Westerners, the ideology of the super-individualist is so strong that they simply cannot appreciate the beauty of the land around them. Secretary Bruce Babbit, surely a true son of the West, states, "I grew up imprisoned in the mythology of the individualistic West. I was surrounded by the stories and mythology of individuals who had conquered the West . . . I grew up in a culture . . . that was deaf to the sound, the mystery and the romance of the land." Thus, much of what makes the West unique and supports the vaunted Western lifestyle—its stark and soaring beauty—is undervalued or even ignored. As a Salmon, Idaho, rancher recently said of the spectacular Bitterroot Range, "To me these are all just damned mountains."

These regional mythologies powerfully affect the political system as well. The South's ruling classes, in Cash's view, successfully thwarted periodic waves of populist discontent, and any threat to the established order, by appealing to well-worn Southern myths, and the fears that underlay and reinforced those myths: equality between the races and Yankee meddling. A close parallel can be seen in modern Western politics, where Western extractive industries seek to veil their interests in the Myth of the Marlboro Man. For instance, the ranching industry calls down the Myth in full force to thwart federal grazing reform, while in fact the largest beneficiaries of grazing subsidies include corporate giants like J.R. Simplot Company, the Metropolitan Life Insurance Company, and the Zenchiku Corporation of Japan. Hardly rugged individualists in the Marlboro Man image. And hardly good candidates for welfare.

Similarly, the mining industry thwarts reform of the 1872 mining law by dressing itself in the buckskin of the solitary pick-and-shovel prospector, when in fact it is overwhelmingly the product of pin-striped multinational conglomerates based in Toronto, Brussels, or New York. Thus, the Clinton Administration's efforts to cut back on subsidies and giveaways that benefit entrenched western industries are not welcomed as a delivery to the promised land of bare-knuckles, individualist free enterprise, as one would expect if Western mythology matched with reality, but are decried as a "War on the West" by the region's politicians.

The regional mindset can have profound effects on the economic system as well. The South was so committed to its self-image as an agrarian power that for much of the Reconstruction era, it staked its future ever more heavily on cotton even as the price of cotton dropped steadily. The result was devastating. The South was drained of much of its capital. Tenant farmers and sharecroppers, always on the economic margin, were driven deeper into poverty. As marginal lands were pushed into cotton production, the independent farmers, who had once made a subsistence living with a little left over for market from these lands, were thrust into a steadily decaying market system. Soils were depleted by the voracious demands of the cotton for soil nutrients, so that by the beginning of the Depression, over 75 million acres of Southern farmland had been degraded by erosion. The decline of King Cotton in the South echoed even to the opposition to the civil rights movement, much of which arose from the resentments of displaced white cotton mill workers and the politicians who capitalized on that resentment.

The parallel with recent Western history is again striking. Despite a sustained decline in the prices for raw materials over at least two decades, many Western politicians seem committed to the view of the West as a raw materials colony to be exploited for the benefit of the rest of the nation. Similarly, many Westerners, even in the face of a steadily declining demand for beef and an industry that, even in the best of times, generally operates on the narrowest of margins, seem to believe that the Myth of the Marlboro Man provides an exemption from the laws of ecological sustainability and economic viability. Single-minded reliance on these industries could well produce in the twenty-first century the kind of economic disaster that the South's single-minded reliance on cotton produced in the late nineteenth and early twentieth centuries. Perhaps the ultimate tragedy is that continued economic reliance on these traditional extractive industries could actually undercut the West's economic future by damaging its environment, thereby making it a less attractive destination for tourism, now the largest industry in the world, and for entrepreneurs who, freed from the necessity of living in cities by the information superhighway, will increasingly seek out Western locations that offer a clean environment and a high quality of life.

The dominant mythology also produces infertile ground

for intellectuals. For much of its history, the South's brainpower flowed steadily toward the great Yankee universities of the Northeast, and even overseas. In Cash's view, this was the result of the "patriotic will to hold rigidly to the ancient pattern [of the frontier], to repudiate innovation and novelty in thought and behavior, whatever came from outside and was felt as belonging to Yankeedom or alien parts." Intellectual pursuits were discouraged not only by a frontier tradition that valued the production of tangible assets—cotton, tobacco, timber—over the intangible products of most intellectual pursuits, but also by extreme intolerance of any idea that could be viewed as challenging the South's mythologized view of itself. Thus, as Cash recounts, Enoch M. Banks, a native Georgian, was dismissed from the University of Florida faculty in 1911 merely for saying that in the Civil War "the North was relatively in the right, while the South was relatively in the wrong."

Again, the parallel to the West is striking. For much of its history, the West's greatest intellectuals have sought refuge in the distant universities of the East. For instance, Bernard DeVoto produced much of the most important work in Western history from his post at Harvard, thousands of miles and an intellectual world away from his Utah home, while Wallace Stegner led a revolution in Western Literature from Stanford, which, as any Westerner will tell you, is located in California and ipso facto is not part of the True West. Even today, the West does not welcome ideas that challenge the Myth of the Marlboro Man. This is brought home by the almost hysterical reaction in much of the West to Frank and Deborah Popper's *The Buffalo Commons*. This book produced extreme hostility not because it contained flawed ideas. Indeed, many of its arguments are compelling. Rather, the Poppers made the mistake of being from Princeton, which is in New Jersey, the state which epitomizes the industrialized, urbanized, decadent East. To the Western mind, this automatically disqualified them from speaking on things Western, especially when what they say suggests that the High Plains ecologically cannot sustain the culture of the Marlboro Man.

A few hopeful signs suggest that the West may finally be beginning to loosen its intellectual strait jacket and to lay the foundation of, in Stegner's words, "A society to match the scenery." This is most evident in the recent blossoming of Western literature, which, like the Southern literature of the 1930s, has recently produced more work of measurable significance than any other region by ignoring the traditional regional mythology, or even openly challenging that mythology. It has almost reached the point in some parts of the West that, like Cash's South of 1940, "anybody who fired off a gun in the region was practically certain to kill an author."

A few weeks after *The Mind of the South* was published in 1941, W.J. Cash hanged himself in a Mexico City hotel room. Let us hope that a similar frank self-examination by Westerners does not produce similar results. 📖

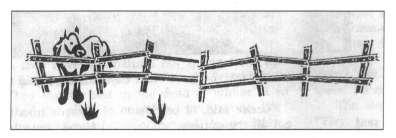

Fences, Pen & Ink Drawing by Scott Martin

Duckabush River

Peter Ludwin

On an empty bluff
above the river

we sprawl
naked,

the weak spring sun
never really warming

our tired bodies,
white as the undersides of fish

or the tines
of the scarred and heavy

elk antler that fell
across the trail

during the autumn rut.
Now, months later,

I remove it
and rope it to my pack.

Up ahead
snow still blocks the trail,

below the river seethes and boils,
driving through the gorge

on a white song of rage.
We cook and eat

to its accompaniment,
leaning

against our packs
while the sun fades

like the colors
from a dying trout.

Across the gorge
three coyotes

pad silently
down a faint track

and disappear
into the trees:

they are the mantra
of untamed things,

the secret longing
buried in stone.

Tails extended,
they begin

to chase the feral moon
rising beyond the forest,

the owl in the canyon,
the great black thighs of night.

Rattlesnake Ridge, 2017, b/w image of color painting,
by Judith Skillman

The Accident

Nancy Redwine

This is no emergency. This is an ordinary thing. My crushed hips are as daily as trees fallen. The forest floor is littered with smashed legs like mine. My collapsed lungs flutter like wilted poppies, fallen like blooms all over this hillside.

It was too hot to sleep in my house. The narrow river valley that creases the Gabilan mountains and holds my house in its cleavage was filled with summer. The land I live on is high enough up the coastal slope that the fog melts before it reaches me. Everything was turning from green to brown. Though I was fifteen minutes from the ocean, the air didn't smell like the sea, but like dirt and dry-bellied reptiles.

I took my pillow and a quilt and walked carefully across the meadow. I searched the sky for any sign of the moon. I entered the dark grove. I was always afraid there. I stood for a moment, paralyzed by the memory of how my own bed held me. My feet sank into the deep floor of needles where slugs, black widows, and scorpions slept. The grove was thick with redwoods and the dark smell of decay. I broke through spider webs and trampled chest high saplings in my haste to reach the clearing where the dirt was swept clear. I laid my quilt down and lowered myself onto it. I stuffed my pillow under my head and resisted the urge to look around. I closed my eyes and thought briefly about scorpions and how their backs curved as if they were always trying to wrap themselves around something. I thought about how when I'd imagined living in the woods I'd imagined myself to be a different person than who I was: someone braver and more at peace. I thought about May and about whether or not I loved her.

I've worked May like I worked her farm and we've never called it love. I sometimes look up from my flock and catch May watching me steadily like I'm a sign. I know her feelings for me are setting firm, like dirt around newly placed roots.

The night was so full of sound, I might not have heard the creak if it hadn't been for the fireworks of all the snapping branches. I woke, tangled in my quilt, stretched out on my back and full of the sound of the grove coming undone. I felt roots slithering through the ground beneath me. The air was thick with sap and my eyes stung. I felt everything around me breaking and then my own body breaking and then there was silence.

I woke with my arms pinned by branches and my tongue pierced by twigs. I laughed and then I fainted. I woke and the sky was light and there was a spider dangling in front of my face. I thought, I could be stung by scorpions, colonized by red ants, pumped full of death by black widows and it didn't matter to me. I was so glad to be so unexpectedly fearless, that I now wanted these things. I was no longer myself.

I couldn't breathe very well, but where I could breathe was deep and narrow and descended below me like a well. Bright particles floated in long banners of light and birds filled the gap where the tree had stood like flickering tongues in the groove of a missing tooth. I wished May was there.

I woke again and knew I would never get out from under the tree. I knew that enough of my blood and perhaps even long stretches of bone were sinking into the ground. Even if there came a kind family on a morning stroll across the barbed wire fences and past the no trespassing signs. And even if they were carrying jacks and rope and axes and they carefully lifted my broken skin, my torn nerves and my dangling veins out of this sunken hole shaped like my body—I would remain in the forest. The tree pressed so deeply into my body we had become each other.

I woke again and there was a bird, a common jay standing on the end of a broken branch, calling. Its voice was as dense as the shadows that swelled inside of me. Each time I started to fall back into the blinding mosaic shifting in my brain, it would call again. Call again. So that its call became the only whole part of me.

I woke again, remembering something about May. Something about May. Something I was supposed to say to her. Something I was supposed to do with her that I'd never done with her before. Something I mean to give her that I'd been holding on to. Something I mean to show her, and then I saw her face.

She filled my mouth with whiskey and left to get her jack and Bob, the cow man, to help her. When they returned, they worked quietly, lifting the tree from my body. I heard Bob tell May that the tree must have been 80 to 100 years old. As soon as it was lifted from me I wanted it back.

I felt no pain until I arrived at the hospital and the nurse gave me a shot of morphine. The morphine burned in my veins. When it hit my brain, I cried because it was like taking a ride on a fast train away from the tree. My body was curved around a missing trunk. My blood was somewhere else feeding saplings and fungus. Pieces of my bone were being woven into nests. My fear of the forest, the spiders and the scorpions, was something precious I would never again experience as long as I was carried further and further down the white hallways of health.

This is the emergency. These shots and IVs, these gurneys and doctors, these x-ray machines and these metal trays are the accident. This is the tragedy, not what happened in the grove. I now feel as if the hospital has fallen on me. This is what's killing me. The tree falling on me was the beginning of my life. This hospital will be the end.

I remember the moment the infection entered me. The light came across everything, illuminating cracks and edges. I no longer felt the weight of the tree on my body. It fit perfectly into the bowl of my pelvis. I saw everything through the branches of the tree. Everything was broken and framed in its own raggedness. The light lifted up the edges of my vision so that what grew up from under the severed places was illuminated. I had lost so much blood I had the awareness of a very small being, a vole or mouse. My vision was very bright and clear. I saw how being broken was the most important thing that could happen to anyone.

That first day, the orderly sat down next to my bed. I turned my head slowly to look at him. He was small and his black shiny hair was all I could register with my sap-burnt eyes. He asked if he could get me something. At first I thought he was speaking another language and then I understood what he'd said. "Help," I whispered, not sure he could hear me over the shush of oxygen blasting into my nostrils. He looked away and when he looked back his eyes were full of tears. "Girl, I don't know if you're asking me to press pillows into your face or to hoist you over my shoulder and carry you home, but you are asking the wrong fellow. Do I look like your salvation? Do I look like I have any sway in this place?" He sighed and brought his gaze back to mine. Then he stood up and left. I like him. He knows I am dying.

His name is Mac and he came back tonight. He didn't say anything until he finished emptying my catheter bag, took my temperature, and adjusted my oxygen. Then he sat down and he talked. He had gone to school in Manila to be a doctor. A navy recruiter came to his school in his last year of pre-med and told him that if he signed up the navy would give him medical training, free. Instead, the Navy taught him to cook inedible food. When the ship he was cooking on was bombed at Pearl Harbor, he left his kitchen and went to work removing shrapnel, performing amputations, and administering shots of morphine. When he got out of the Navy he couldn't find work, so he became a preacher.

Mac preached at the Filipino First Assembly of God in Modesto for fifteen years. He was asked to leave by his board of elders shortly after he preached that god was in fruit flies. He said god was in everything and that the cross and the garden and revelations were just a few small over-exalted examples of the presence of god. As it was clear that his time behind the pulpit was coming to an end, he felt compelled to be more and more ridiculous, though in the end that got him kicked out of his wife's house as well. He said god was in pigeons. God was in toothpaste. God was in single-ply toilet paper. He said you could hear the voice of god in car alarms and the music of Lawrence

Welk. He said you could find god's truth in the instructions on the bottle of mop and glow and in the rules on the inside of the lids of board games. When he told me this story he laughed deep in his belly. He wiped his eyes and then he looked around. He checked to make sure my morphine was still running and left.

Mac knew May's husband, Richard, who died last year after a cow kicked him in the head. When he came back at midnight to check my temperature, he took my hand and said, "May's a lucky woman to have found somebody like you." Mac's the only person who will squeeze my hand hard. I don't know why people think they can break me so easily. I sometimes want to say, hey it was a really big tree.

* * * *

From the window, I can see my hills in the distance. In the evening when the fog comes in, the hills are obscured and I watch the streets. I watch people park their cars and walk the long grey walk to the hospital entrance. I watch the lights of ambulances reflecting off the low clouds of evening. I watch the gardener trim the bushes into shapes reminiscent of bandages and boxes and dinner trays and beds.

May comes everyday and sits by my bed. Some days I can hardly wait for her to leave. I know she has things to do. Cherries to pick. Sheep to shear. Cows to milk. I am not accustomed to her worry. I want to tell her that I forgive her for taking me out of my grave and bringing me to this funeral, but I don't know if she's even sorry. I know she will not try to stop me from dying this time. She will stare steady as stone into the stories of my bones and my blood and know their meaning. I will not have to pretend at tragedy or horror or even gratitude towards those who are keeping me alive.

I am bleeding internally. The only organ that is not damaged is my heart. My lungs were both pierced by sticks. My liver is crushed. My stomach exploded with the impact of the tree. Most of my bones from my knees to my ribs are shattered. Somewhere in the basement of the hospital are big red plastic bags containing my gall bladder, my spleen, most of my intestines, my uterus, and both of my ovaries. What's left inside of me is infected. On my right is a bag of blood. On my left, a bag of antibiotics. Tucked into the sheets by my shoulder is a small machine that pumps morphine under my skin.

At night, I burn with fever. I am laid on slabs of ice. I am wrapped in wet sheets. At night, the delirium carries me down the slick roads of my nerves to collide with all the pain in the world. At night, the places where I am broken become the places where everything touches me. There is now no longer any curve to me anywhere. There is nowhere that I end smoothly. There is nowhere that I do not match all the ragged and the broken edges of the world. I lie melting their ice and envying those who believe that it is not pain that unites us, that it is not pain that teaches us to love.

The hospital chaplain came today to tell me his story. He knows why the tree fell on me. He came in the other night as May was saying goodnight. He already knows that May and I are more than farm owner and hired hand. It's a small town. He believes that the tree fell on me because I am mistaken about love.

* * * *

I don't know what my face looks like anymore. I don't know what makes him think this needs explaining. He believes that every event is explainable in terms of god's will and that his job is to part the swirling sea of experience based on blessing and vengeance. He offers me god's forgiveness for whatever created the vacuum in my being that sucked that tree over on top of me. He thinks of nature as god's ready arsenal.

I listen to him because he is wrong. His wrongness is like a florescent street light in a bright meadow, obliterating shadows. The only thing that was squeezed out of me when the tree fell was ignorance. The only sin I am guilty of is not being willing to be crushed to pieces before now.

The doctor comes. He is a different doctor every day. He says that they are getting the infection under control. He says that it's only a matter of time. He talks to me in a tone of voice that is comforting to him. He sits by my bed and tells himself stories. I don't mind. I need a break from the stories I tell myself.

The story I am telling myself today is that I am walking back to the grove. May carries a saw and a bottle of whiskey. She lays me down on the soft ground and walks around looking at each tree. Finally she picks a tall old redwood, licks her finger and feels for the air's direction. Then she saws and I lay and stare up at the broken sky. As the branches above me begin to break and the roots beneath me begin to slip against my back, I open my arms and I catch the tree in the curve of my body. 📖

III

Volume 7, Number 3,
Winter 1997-98
South Sound Edition

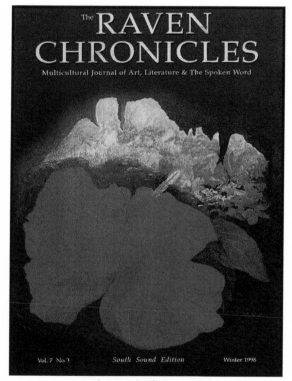

Attabeira en Cacibajagua, 1997,
oil/canvas painting, by Glenda J. Guilmet

Tracking Indian Creek

David Lloyd Whited

a bloodless man in a bloodied field, still, cold from the
hunt. finding Indian Creek: sure it had been there
year after regular year before. strewn with coyote scat
and bear paws fishing with the wind. the golden eagle
trailing the heron. his blues or his fish the object.
& of all concern. the flooded creek packed & moved in
near the cliffs & deep water of their shadows. each
of us growing quietly desperate. startled dismay may
strain awareness. a heart beating still within this pallid
bleeding thing. death & deathless peace at each end of the
string. stars like a carpet of prayers. stars like
this one time beach of sand.

no human hand might have touched his misted rock &
water fall. unbrellaed by the rock strewn trees. canyon
wind like an oven through the mist. the creek gone cinematic
& water fall dramatic. serenity crosses the river to escape.
May that buds and blossoms is gone, the summer leaving too.
September when the sweet plums fall will even soon be through.
& the trees will be bare as a coed's legs. though there's
nothing better this side of the grave & no one leaves alive.
life is a web of shining days & the butterflies catching the
slight updraft were not a dream.

Days

Gail E. Tremblay

There are days when grace is as simple
as the whisper of narrow leaves moving
in the breeze; the fragrance of sweetgrass
soothes the mind; then smell becomes
a passageway opening into all that is
wholly beautiful and wakes memory
of ceremony dancing with as much spirit
as bright feathered birds leaping into wind.

There are days when grace is as melancholy
as owls singing a soul away; then dark
magic blooms in the fire releasing flesh
from all the pain and limitation of being
human. The rind sloughs off and fertilizes
Earth, that fast moving woman who takes
what rots into herself to make new life;
spirit escapes; tingles naked in the shocking air.

There are days when grace refused to wake,
and longing fills the tunnels of rich blood
pulsing from dark chambers sequestered
in the ribcage out of sight, pumping
bright waves that feed the lonely cells
'til they remember how to invoke the sacred
names that call forth song. Then we sing
and grace comes around to touch our tongues.

The Peeler

Glenna Elizabeth Cook

I stand impatiently, watching
you peel peaches. You slash and gouge,
taking off the too-green skin
in thick and wasteful slices.
You tremble in your haste
and grunt with the effort.

I am reminded of being wakened
from childhood summer dreams
to join you in your steamy kitchen,
where I helped you can the golden fruit,
picked the day before at its peak
of sweetness.
No waste then. Emerging from their bath
of scalding water, their peels slipped off clean
in our fingers, and my small hands
fit them, halved, into their jars like flower petals
upside down. Just so,
or you made me do them over.

How I hate the way you are
peeling now, perhaps because I'm afraid
I shall be someday where you are.
I shall wake my daughter at six a.m.
to tell her in my stroke-broken speech
that I dreamed of peaches last night,
and I fear the season might pass
before I taste one.

When she brings them
(too green, for the season's just started,)
I shall make her stay to eat them with me,
though I can tell she wants to leave,
and that she's standing there hating
the way I grunt as I peel
and take the skins off in thick slices.

Northwest Woodcarver

Jeanne Ruth Lohmann

The accident on the icy road cannot be undone,
the thieving black bird will not give up your daughter.
Careful with the sun he carries in his beak, he

tells his plans to no one. Who can say where he goes
with that incandescence, the light of your days?
In the dark that is quiet around me, the fire

makes shadows, fragrance curling off the cedar,
dust and chips at my feet. There is good conversation
between the gouge and the adze, the mallet.

From the block on my knees, the bird
will not be hurried. In the sorrow of my hands
the details: wing feathers and eyes,

the clawed feet, my work rough as a cry
from the raven, grief talking the limits
of life and memory, how far love goes.

Dying Wish

Connie Walle

—Dedicated to Tom Heidlebaugh

Box me not in satin and pine
But gift me of fir and flowers
Or sea and shells   or
                    a little of both

Mix a little sand and sage
With my bones
Let the wind call my name
                    for the last time

Don't dampen the soil with your tears
But let a wish or a prayer
Be consumed in the flames
                    of my passing

Rejoice with my spirit
And if you need me
Call to me in your dreams

Then watch billboards
                    for my answer

Transit, Tape Transfer Collage, 2020, by Mark Sullo

The Heart of Displace

Kevin Miller

In downtown Seattle (1996), Jason Sprinkle (Subculture Joe) parked his pickup truck in front of Nordstrom's department store. The truck's bed held a huge, sculpted metal heart.

He let the air out of the tires. Seattle police responded, and since the word BOMB was spray painted on the front of the truck, called out the bomb squad and closed off the core of the city. They took Sprinkle to jail where he was held for weeks with bail set in six figures.

If Subculture Joe had anointed the truck with JESUS,
instead of BOMB, Seattle's metal heart
might have beaten instead of ticked.
Steve Largent might have understood
the black of the flat tires was *not* four pairs
of Mappelthorpe pants but Goodyears that hauled tin
rent and wrapped to pulse its way into the head
of a city held hostage by a store selling suits to judges
and charging ninety-five dollars for a button down shirt.

What price for art, who controls the heart
of a city whose walking streets end with shoe
salesmen calling the shots? If Westlake had fish,
there would be no bottom feeders, nothing to suck
away from a style. The mayor lures the businesses,
places named Town and Planet in a universe where laws
keep people from sleeping on steam vents.
Money moves, only the correct people should stop.
These people buy art and artists. They say,

No trucks stop here. No steel heart will slow our pace.
This store is no hammering man. This store is jobs.
We frame license plates—our name in gold.
How dare you sprinkle your rust on our street.
Restart the truck. We decide. We choose who stops.
Keep running. Get off our sidewalk. Drive by
until you pile the bed of the truck with enough envy,
then we will serve you like no one has ever served
you—on a silver platter with your heart in your mouth.

Repatriation

Deborah A. Miranda

One night I miss you so much my bones fall
right out of my body, land on the ground
and crawl thousands of miles to your banks.
My fingers all skinny and bleached rap
on your gate in the dark. You peer out, say,
"Must be cats, or coyotes,"
softly pull the latch closed

but I rattle and grate and thump
on the earth—probably scare the daylights
out of you! Look down, see
a lonesome pile of bones with no name,
no tribal ID, no stories but the one
in my teeth that led me here.
Will you know me? Without my long hair,
my brown flesh, no tongue in my skull
to speak? These bones,

they're all I have to offer.
Reassemble my skeleton here in the dust.
Do you remember me?
Do I look like anyone you know?
My long legs—a tendency to over-extend,
or to colonize? My worn jaw—
a trait found in storytellers,
or liars? Cradle my pelvic bones.
Do they tell you, "babies had to be cut
from her," do they whisper, "—mixedblood—"?

My bones confess everything.
My bones have been in the mouth of history.

My bones ache with bruises
from the echo of that turbulence.
Look me over, test me, tumble me.
Place your own wrinkled palm into the web
of my hand, that spiral of construction:
can you hear it? The rush of belonging
in my marrow?

Something in your waters
knows the river in me,
the fluid resistance of a tribe
that doesn't look back.

IV

Volume 8, Number 1,
Summer/Fall 1998
Migrations

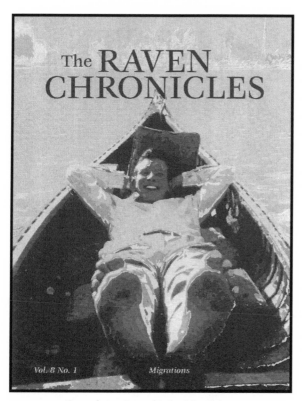

Cover design & graphics by Matt Briggs

Raven Notes

Lisa Purdy

My family has a history of migrating. In the 1800s, my great-great-grandparents came to Trinidad from China to work as indentured servants for a French family. My great-grandfather was born during the voyage, in the middle of the Atlantic. Eighty-five years later, my 18-year-old mother left Trinidad for the Rushgreen College of Nursing, in London. She met my father there, and in 1978, when I was eight years old, my father, in a fit of boredom, picked up our whole family and moved us to America. Once we got there, we met up with my mother's parents who, after she had moved to England, had taken her remaining nine brothers and sisters to live in Washington, D.C. Six weeks later, my parents, my brother, and I piled in our new Plymouth station wagon, drove around America for eight weeks (mainlining root beer and pecan pie along the way) until we landed in the furthest corner of the country: Washington State. I like to think we stopped here because it was the best place in America, that our careening around the country had been an audition of possible places to live. But I suspect my parents were just tired of driving.

What gives people the drive to be *anywhere but here*, and the courage to leave the familiar behind? Are people that migrate running away from their old lives or running toward a new life? What happens to the people who are left behind? Most of the stories, essays, poetry, and letters in this issue of *The Raven Chronicles* address these questions in one way or another. Some more obviously fit the theme of "Migrations," than others. In "Birthplace," Jacque Larrainzar, the first person the United States has ever granted political asylum to on the basis of sexuality, writes about how her immigration to America changed her from a person who thought, "life was something that happened to you, like being raped, abandoned, or gay," to someone who has "learned that freedom and love go together, that [she] can transform the world, if [she] dares kiss [her] partner . . . without fear." Anna Mockler's "Painting Wallpaper," follows one woman's decision to leave a city she loves, for an unknown city that holds the man that she loves.

Both "Girl in the Lake," by Phyllis Berman and "Breath," by Rebecca Brown look at the ultimate migration: death, both pieces examining the moment when life leaves, and what is left behind afterwards. In Brown's story, it is "the sound of something gone." In Berman's poem, it is a drowned girl's hair ". . . fanned out from her head / laced with seaweed, lush / and shining." Gordon Janow's "Skirting the Hindu Kush," opens with the line "The Ayatollah died"; Veronique Le Guen, the protagonist of Trisha Ready's "Circadian Rhythms," "lived life at a hundred miles an hour," but dies, "with the help of barbiturates," by the end of the story. In total, fourteen pieces in this magazine deal with or mention death. (And we thought we'd be publishing a bunch of travel pieces!)

We *were* lucky, this time, to have our own foreign correspondent; Phoebe Bosché, Managing Editor of *The Raven Chronicles*, has spent the last two months traveling in Europe, stopping in Poland, Russia, Italy, Finland, Sweden, Denmark, Switzerland, France and England. Everywhere she went, she found an Internet Cafe (battling foreign keyboards, stale pastries, and bad coffee as she went) and her emails are reprinted in our *Mailbox* section. Goofy (due to keyboard constraints) upper-lower casing of letters and random umlauts are included verbatim.

A section of stories and poems toward the end of this issue focus on the West. It is an area this magazine has focused on before (most recently in our *Images and Ideas of the West, Summer/Fall 1997*) and will focus on again. The centerpiece of this section includes excerpts from the wonderful book, *Death Valley Crossing*, a selection of poems adapted by Paul Hunter of Wood Works Press from the journals, *Death Valley in '49*, by William Lewis Manly. The poetry follows the adventures of "a lone young man, with the first wagon train to cross Death Valley in the 1849 gold rush," and fits perfectly with this issue's theme.

Migration is fundamentally about change, a move to one thing and away from something else. But migration is also the space between then and now; it is the moment or process of changing. As Gordon Janow writes in "Skirting the Hindu Kush," "Most events never really matter, only where you are when they occur." 📖

Song for the Sugar Cane

Virgil Suárez

Today at the Publix with my daughters
I spotted the stalks of sugar cane,

there under the boxed Holland tomatoes,
98 cents a stalk. I grabbed three

stalks left & brought them home.
My daughters, born in the U.S.,

unlike me, stand in the kitchen
in awe as I take a serrated knife

and peel away the hard green
of the stalks for the fibrous white

pure slices. "Here," I say,
"nothing is ever as sweet as this."

We stand in the kitchen & chew
on pieces of sugar cane,

I tell them this was my candy
when I was a kid growing up

in Havana, this was the only
constant sweetness in my childhood.

This delicious stalk. You chew
on a piece & remember how to love

what you can't have all the time.

The Bed, Scratch board drawing, 1992, by Gloria White Calico

Breath

Rebecca Brown

Earlier this year, my lover and my sister and I sat in my mother's house and listened to her breathe. It had been several months since she had walked. It had been a couple of weeks since she had eaten anything solid and days since she had been able to drink anything or take her pills through her mouth. The water we gave her we gave on a sponge. We put it in her mouth and she closed her mouth around it and sucked. I couldn't tell if it was willed or conscious or involuntary, the way a baby would suck. She didn't look at us. That is, sometimes her eyes would turn in what we thought was our direction but we couldn't tell if she was seeing us or something else, something beyond or past us. We couldn't see if she was seeing anymore.

Sometimes her body sweats. The sweat would pour from her and we would change and change again the sheets around her. Sometimes her body was very hot, her skin would flush with what the nurses called the terminal fever. At other times her skin felt cold. That happens when, the nurses said, what regulates the body's temperature breaks down. There are upper brain functions and lower brain functions and you can see the body shutting down in order.

It had been a while since anyone had tried to put something in her porta-cath or tried to find a vein to give her something new. She was beyond what anyone could do.

The last thing that she did alive was breathe. For days and nights we'd sit in her room with her, or in the rooms where we tried to sleep, and listen. We listened as her breath got short and ragged, as she seemed to gasp or gurgle, seemed to hold her breath. The periods of this got long. You'd count to 10 or 20 and you would think she wouldn't breathe again but then she would. The nurses called this apnea. They said that it began before the end.

We listened and waited. We listened after hope.

This was in the winter and we had the heat turned on.

When the furnace clicked on it hummed and clanked and you couldn't hear. If you were watching TV or a video, you turned the volume up. Then when the temperature got where you'd set the thermostat the furnace would click off and you could hear again.

My sister sat in our mother's room and listened to her breathe. The heat clicked on. It stayed on several minutes and then when it clicked off the room was quiet. My sister counted to 10, then 20, then more. Then she came into the room where Chris and I slept and we woke and went to our mother's room.

There was no more sound of breath. There was the sound of something gone. 📖

Painting Wallpaper

Anna Mockler

It came to me when I found myself crouched inside the linen closet of a one-story tract house in Hakomi, Oregon, peeling the last few wallpaper shreds from the shelves with a silver fruit knife. How the hell did I get here?

Here's the mathematics: In twenty years since I left my parents' house, seventeen and friendly, I'd lived in five major cities and thirty-one apartments, a number inflated by the years I crashed around on many beds and sofas, with and without: sensitive black Irish carpenters, handsome piano-tuning poets, tall scholars who could really dance, men of no profession who were good to climb trees with by moonlight, comics who turned out to be drug dealers, cabdrivers who turned out to be drug addicts, former newsmen who tap danced as they pushed cable cars around the lazy Susan terminal. When romance died out or grew difficult, I packed my things and stuck my thumb into the traffic until it snagged a passing lift. After I began to groan under the weight of bourgeois possessions, I'd heft my duffle bag, cord my trunk, and flag a cab to the nearest train station.

The thirty-one apartments run together in my mind now. They were all scruffy with lots of glass and wood floors. At least one sash cord was broken, and every kitchen had been left in a state. The first two days in a new place smelled of ammonia and chlorine bleach; the third day was latex paint. I painted every one sage green, a comfortable color that shows neither mold nor fungal bloom. Thirty-one late afternoons, the Stones on the tape player, roller-painting scrubbed walls. I painted right over wallpaper, stucco, whatever was on them. By the time the under surface broke through my two coats, I'd be long gone.

While the paint dried, a sortie to the Goodwill for a chair or two, and then home to tack art to the walls: postcards, prints, posters, magazine cut-outs, and one framed Braque print entitled "Patience," which I always felt in need of. A few scarves draped over blotchy surfaces, my pillows and my sleeping bag on its foam pad, four concrete blocks and two long shelves, and furnishing was complete.

At last I made it in New York, where my grandparents lived and died as tailors. After four years of studios and sublets, I found a one-bedroom on West 85th Street, half a block from the Hudson River. I never thought that I would leave the city. I loved it fiercely, the way its owners love their biting dog, a mother dotes on her junkie child. The clothes! The conversation! Rich, witty, diverse, informed, brash, inventive, unique, irreplaceable city. Every day I tucked the Times under my left arm as I ran down the 86th Street stairs to catch the downtown IRT, digging in my right-hand coat pocket for a token. After work, my small apartment wrapped itself around me, better than a lover.

"I've had it with love," I told my girlfriends. "Not looking for it any more. If it comes along, okay. But I'll interrogate it through the door chain pretty closely before I let it in."

Do you suppose the mischief-making gods overheard me? One month later, a platonic friend from two cities and seven years ago paid me a holiday visit. Owen came to town for one night only, to take the taste of Thanksgiving out of our mouths. We fell headlong.

Even now, I have to close my eyes and let a reminiscent smile push up the corners of my mouth. I was working swing shift at a print shop on West 23rd, but in the pre-dawn hours of the town we wailed some.

One night, dressed in black, we climbed a fire escape on 31st Street, right to the roof. Inside the water tower's shadow, we made love standing under cold cold winter stars. Owen picked a bathroom lock and we re-engaged, up against the porcelain sink, his face and my shoulders reflected in the mirror where secretaries checked their lipstick in the unreal daylight world. We believed, positively, that everyone around us was deaf and blind, that city parks were empty, our neighbors out of town. In this way, by constant exercise, considerable money was saved, since we did not need to purchase overcoats, or even sweaters.

We rode around in taxicabs, danced on tour ship prows, walked by night and day my beautiful city. We drank in Deco Soho bistros, chintz West Chelsea booths, slanted floor-lit bars that faced on Tompkins Square, eco-bars off Washington Square that tithed your drink price to the rain forest. "It's so civilized," said Owen. We rode in forward subway cars so he could watch the tracks. He leaned against the metal pole, held me from behind, sang in my ear: "You are my wife / Goodbye, city life" as we hurtled uptown to our warm bed.

I'm trying to explain the kind of man he was, yes, and trying to remember it, too, because now that we're home owners in a small Northwestern town, it's easy to forget. And I suppose I'm trying to find the first cause an inexpensive public-school education has led me to infer, for why I'm peeling little flowered shreds of paper from a closet shelf no one else will ever see. How I came to leave my beautiful solitary life of low-water checking, standing room at the opera, free jazz in plazas, for this four-by-two village on the world's wet western edge.

Owen and I fell into a sort of settled gladness. Shafts of evil monetary light bounced off the new growth we constantly added to our forest canopy. One day all that luxuriant green caught fire, revealing a broke and stony landscape.

Though millions do it, you cannot live poor in New York City. You live rich or you die. These are the simple options. Resumes fell from Owen's boughs until his limbs were bare.

One day when I came through the door he said, "I have this offer." Three thousand, one hundred twenty-two miles away. But the money! Six months of it would have settled all my problems with the agency that dunned me monthly for my student loan. "I'll have to take it," he said. "Come west, you'll love it."

"Will I?" I asked.

"Absolutely," he answered, and took me in his arms. Things proceeded as they do. On the inside of my eyelids rocky tide pools, cedars looming over giant sword ferns, waterfalls spilling on mossy rocks.

In the morning, when I looked out the window at a dozen

small street dramas, vacillation. "Why don't you go on out there," I suggested, "I'll follow when I can."

"What are you, crazy?" my girlfriends demanded. "Nice guy, good-looking, has a job, and he's hot for you. What are you waiting for?" I couldn't explain it to them, what mandragora the city was to me, how I couldn't put it from my lips. Who talks about God in public, or the kind of sex you're getting, or the way you feel about a place? Louts, that's who. Some conversations you only have with the interested other party.

A month went by, two months, three. Owen couldn't eat or sleep, no more could I: otherwise we hardly missed each other. What, after all, is human love? A tic, a trance, a passing thing, compared to a faceful of soft gritty Manhattan air.

My neighborhood was full of bookstores open until midnight, cheap Chinese noodle shops, kosher dairy deli, tyrants of paper-thin lox, European coffee houses, Euro-trash emporia, street sellers, flea markets, shops of every kind—you know the upper West Side. You can't save a dime there. My rent went up the statutory year-end ten percent. Tokens went up, the Times went up, a 20-story condo went up, right across the street. But I kept step with all these increases, what with not spending much on food. What little sleep I needed fitted nicely between my full-time and my part-time job. My scruffy apartment, full of makeshift comforts and too many books, drew me in and wrapped me every evening.

Until one night the shop's power failed and they sent the whole shift home at ten. I stepped off the IRT at 72nd Street, weary, excited, full of vinegar, the way you get when you work two jobs and an extra, unaccountable hour comes along. I climbed the stairs into dark city night air so crystalline the stars shone through it.

The weather had changed while I was in the subway. Light from the streetlamps clung to the bulbs, leaving the wet streets in darkness. Dry wind rasped the sidewalks, swirling crumpled trash into a rough and ready bundle which it swept uptown in half-block gusts. It swept the beggars into the deepest doorways, from which they emerged, brushing bits of leafmold from their whiskers, to peer at you with beady eyes, to cry 'Toll' in your ear. Dry dust, soot, cinders, phlegm, droppings, feathers, fewmets, the wind gathered up and blew uptown in clouds, in sheets, in genii shapes. An equinoctial evening!

I dug my hands deep in my coat pockets, settled a black beret more firmly on my head, and walked uptown along the line precise, steering between the curbside where the wind was fierce and the buildings with their deep doorways.

To walk the night city, you have to follow force lines, which don't necessarily lie along the streets you get advised to walk. Bright and well-lit doesn't mean safe; Sixth Avenue in midtown, for instance, will send a well-deserved cold chill down your back if you walk it after dark. Gang tags, windows solid-metal locked, nine-year-old lookouts posted at the corner, these are not the force lines. Once you've lived in a neighborhood a while you know what streets are good, full of stoop-sitters, maybe, or a firehouse.

Cold dry windy nights sweep people from their stoops into warm back kitchens; they send firemen upstairs to poker games. Shutters clang down, cracks are chinked against the dust. The rats are very bold, these nights.

Broadway from 72nd to the 86th Street Transverse is the upper West Side's spine, so full of movement always that the rats seldom tempt their fate here. This stretch is a real garbage flower that blooms on the heaps of too much money in too many people's pockets, still a little raffish the way the West Side used to be. The beggars are relics of those times, kept in the crevices of the neighborhood like historical plaques, preserving its former seediness in aspic.

72nd, where Broadway slices east through Amsterdam, is Needle Park. The park's a pride of well-fed, syphilitic lions. Healthy prey pass by unscathed, but how they spring on whatever stumbles. Nothing to worry about, so long as the spirochaetes corkscrewing through their brains don't mistake you.

The change starts at the stone and iron fortress bank that is the block between Amsterdam and Broadway from 73rd to 74th. It throws a confident consumer shadow uptown: Go on and spend, it says, plenty more where that came from. At 74th, the cold dry wind blew the market's smell across the street, composed of fruit, hot bread, pumpkin tortellini, radicchio, fennel, chanterelles, summer sausage, oil-cured olives, goat cheese. Latex women bounced silently behind second-story plate glass at 75th, above the cream and indigo Japanese restaurant. Here the zone of shops began, shops a person did well to pass after closing. Linen sheets with cutwork hems, glove-leather shoes, peplum jackets over pencil skirts, face creams in cut-glass jars, blue bowls heaped with prisms, lamps that came on when you whistled middle C; all the furnishings for the life genteel in studios and flats you couldn't swing a cat in.

At 81st Street, out of the blue, terror pushed the breath from my body. The corner bookstore had closed early for inventory. Display lights didn't penetrate the window glass. People in cafe windows could not see me through the condensation their hot breath and steamed drinks had made. Blue light flickered through drawn curtains at every apartment window.

Were the beggars skinnier, more determined than usual? Did the wind blow colder? Was there always this much litter, or had the night decanted foreign trash on our sidewalks?

Perhaps terror was the mere natural result of weeks spent not-sleeping not-eating. Perhaps. My heart was beating away like the whole front window of a hardware store at work. Mouth dry, face set, hands in pockets clenched around a spray of keys, I walked four blocks uptown. If only I had a knife, I could mark them when they sprang. Not knowing what they'd look like but certain they would come.

I walked past my street to the all-night Korean grocer's stand to throw them off the track, to spy them following after. No good: terror came right inside with me. Terror was in the salad bar, mixed with the snow peas, pasted to the soup cans. I wanted to leave without a purchase, but the family that owned it would stare so. A thing like that could tip my luck. Whatever I bought was small enough to fly out of a coat pocket along with a handkerchief.

I walked west from Broadway swallowing and swallowing again around the dry dust lodged in my throat, as the desiccated city flew up away from me.

The city abandoned me right there and then. That was what dried out my mouth. It had no more use for me and left me, hot choking pillar of salt, on the plains. That's it, a snap of the fingers, see you. It rose up on easy wing strokes to see what was doing by the river or on the roofs.

That's the truth of it. The stars shook slightly in their courses, as distinguishes them from planets. I walked backwards up my building steps, looking east and west and all around me. Nothing. Even the air was still, the wind only wanted to roar on Broadway. I bounded up two flights; no one in the hall. I slipped one key and then the other into my metal door; no one. No one in the closets, no one hiding in the shower curtain shadow. No one underneath the sink, no one crouched peering from the fire escape into my bedroom window.

I double-locked the door and chained it. I knelt at the window. Every building on the block dislimned, drifted up and out of sight. Coffee wouldn't bring it back, or beer. No more than you can call back the word misspoken would it return.

"Owen," I said, over three thousand miles of high-strung wire, "that's it. Circumstances are too strong for me. The party's over, the flock is gone, all my pretty ducklings and their dam. I have to fly to you, my dear, so that the city can settle down again on its strong granite foundations."

"Whatever," he said, "I don't understand a thing you're talking about, but make a reservation soon. Make it tomorrow. It's hell out here without you."

Is that nice? Is that what a girl likes to hear? Still, I was by the window all night until dawn. To no avail. The more I looked at them the more the landmarks disappeared.

There's never any point in asking, "Why?" when a love affair is over. So. Daylight found me chaffering with ghosts for packing boxes. I dragged the boxes home down streets which once existed. Everything I owned went in them, except what turned to dust and slipped between my fingers at my touch.

A nomadic life teaches you to make your good-byes short and sweet. Ten days later I was in a window seat above La Guardia. In the west, the city solidified as I rose.

Inside our small house, a new-found land that stays put. Where Owen wraps his long arms around me, and keeps my back from cold. I scrape clinging shreds of wallpaper down to bare wood. White enamel paint annuls the cracks and lines of use.

Behind the house, the stream of time issues from primeval coniferous shade, chatters over mossy rocks under twenty-story cedars. I sit by its banks until the cold's too strong for mammals. I can't stop marveling—nothing I've ever learned is useful here. This is how the world looks, naked. A peplum suit, a well-turned phrase, turn to dust and rise up, shimmering, above the dancing turquoise water. Upright among sword ferns, I cry to ravens over-head: "I don't know a thing!" Not a pinion flutters: it's just what they expect from humans.

I run indoors, pushing my ignorance down in my coat pockets for safekeeping. Owen comes through the door as the kettle boils. I'm living with someone! For the long haul! My heart's fireworks in that narrow kitchen. Such exaltation! An entire world I don't know a thing about.

The painted shelves are in the closet, stacked with sheets and towels. I close the door on them and walk out of the shadowed hallway into the windy cedar-scented shining afternoon. Not a drop of wine spills. 📖

Lula

Deborah Parks-Satterfield

The Beginning of the End. What they did not know about Lula could fill oceans. No sweet words for Lula. She'd take ya man, take ya woman, take ya food off the table. She could steal the sweetness out of a cookie and not break it. What they said about Lula. I say, what they said about Lula was the girl always had to have something in her mouth . . . cigarette, piece of chocolate or dick. . . . She could not pass up nothing. What they know about Lula was nothing. What they said about Lula could fill pages and those pages laid end to end would stretch around the earth. Lula had a venereal disease, Lula did it with dogs, and Lula once killed a man cuz he did not do the nasty to her satisfaction.

That's what they said.

Lula did not walk. Lula sailed. Lula was not born. One day there was not a Lula and the next day there was. Folks did not know what to make of it. It was not natural. Who her people? Where her husband? Why she do like she do?

Lula looked good. Lula was voracious. She could out eat, out drink, and out fuck anybody. But Lula was not doing half the stuff they thought she was doing. Oh, she was doing stuff that's for sure. But to do all the things people thought she was doing, she would have to be in three or four places at the same time. They talked about the girl so much, Lula's ears burned constantly.

All we knew was that Lula was not from 'round these parts.

Lula One

Everyone thought they knew Lula. They had to talk about Lula all the time. Lula's life was like a traffic accident. You did not wanna look, you did not wanna know, but you slowed down anyway and gawked just like everybody else. After the dishes dried and the young ones went to bed, Lula was the MAIN topic

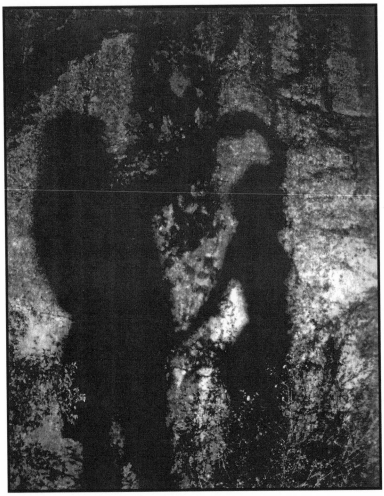

Shadow Dance #111, photograph, 2004, by Glenda J. Guilmet

of conversation. Lula this and Lula that. Shoot, if it was not for Lula woulda not had anything entertaining at all. They called Lula birthday cake cuz everybody got a piece. Remember that old, tired, white boy down at the gas station? They say he had one night with Lula and when she would not give him a second roll, he up and pitched his self in front of a semi on Highway 99. I believe it! Cuz Lula had the Devil in her. Jezebel! Oh, yes. Had a body that could make a Christian man break all Ten Commandments right on the spot. Yes, she did! They say she had a bit of a liking for women too. Lula's door swung both ways. And do not be standing there looking all blank as if you do not know what I'm talking about. Somebody said they saw her and one of Pastor Raymond's big ol' gals down there swimming in the quarry. They was hopping around, splashing, hugging up on each other . . . just having a good ol' time. And they both was naked as the day they was born. That somebody who saw them ran told Pastor Raymond. He marched down to that swimming hole and snatched his girl out by her hair. He would not even let her cover herself. He mad that big ol' gal kneel down in the mud and pray to the high Heavens to "wipe this filthy blemish from her immortal soul!" Then he tore his self a whipping switch and commenced to beating the poor girl in front of God and everybody. He beat the black-eyed peas and ham hocks outta that gal. He beat the girl so bad, his wife had to come down there yelling and screaming and flailing about. She covered all three of them from crown to foot.

By this time, the crowd had swelled to about a hundred folks. (Now mind you I am telling you what I heard, not what I saw.) Lula just sat in the water and stared, motionless like an evil crocodile. All of a sudden, she stood straight up, her dark brown body all slick and glistening. The sun bouncing off her like she was twenty-four carat gold. All the folks watching froze with their mouths hanging open like beached fish. Lula stretched, yawned, and slithered out of the water and past the crowd. She put on her clothes and without so much as a "Lord have mercy," undulated her ample behind back into town.

Lula Two

Mr. Jacobs's funeral was scheduled to start at 1 pm. But he was on colored people time, so of course it started at 3. I watched Lula check her red can-can slip for the umpteenth time. She was making sure that the proper amount of lace peeked out from below her nasty, little black satin skirt. She tried to look bored. But you see, Lula was not bored. I will tell you what kind of bored Lula was. You know how it is when you watching National Geographic and they show a panther crouched low in the bushes? And that panther is all coiled muscle, fangs and fur waiting to have some serious breakfast on a herd of gazelles? That cat is charging up its batteries, right? That's the kind of bored Lula was. I was surprised she had the nerve to show her face. She was trying to look all nonchalant, standing back there chewing her gum like some heifer in a pasture. But she did not fool me. Not for one minute. When Lula was in a room, you could be assured that something bad was gonna happen. Do not ask me how I know. I just know.

You would think she would lay low at a time like this. But sin don't NEVER take a holiday, amen. They say that Mr. Jacobs died on top of her. Can you believe that? How she had the audacity to strut herself into Pitt's Funeral Parlor and Gospel Music Emporium was beyond me. But there she was. And there was Mr. Jacobs, looking pretty good for a dead man. Mr. Pitt attended to the body personally. That's because when Mrs. Jacobs got wind of how her husband's body was discovered, she hot-footed it down to Pitt's and took a butcher knife to the corpse's face. Loretta, the girl who usually did the deceased's hair and make-up, had to use a spackling knife to fill in the gouges. I told Mr. Pitt that he did a good job on that face. Mr. Jacobs was nice enough, but he did his fair share of tipping out when his wife was out of town. He was slick as snot on a doorknob when it came to covering his tracks. But not this time. Don't be acting like it's such a big loss. After all he was just a man.

I watched Mrs. Jacobs playing the grieving widow as she greeted the mourners. She was acting so-o-o overcome, the woman could have won an Oscar. At one point, she fell out and had to be revived with smelling salts just like Scarlett O'Hara. Child, puhleeze! We all knew she'd mutilated her husband's body. Also, we know that when she was slicing and dicing, she was calling him everything but a child of God!

Lula sauntered up to the front row and plopped herself down right in front of the casket. She made a big to-do, spreading her skirt over the chairs on either side of her. I had myself a ringside seat near the buffet table. Mrs. Jacobs was working real hard not to notice Lula. The more Lula fluffed and flounced her skirt, the more agitated Mrs. Jacobs became. Then she couldn't ignore her any longer. After all, the little hellion had practically draped herself over the coffin. The air in the room got hot and heavy like just before a tornado. Mrs. Jacobs did a slow hundred and eighty degree turn, let out a howl, then rushed at Lula screaming, "LORD JESUS STOP ME FROM KILLING THIS HO!" Five lady church ushers grabbed Mrs. Jacobs and held on tight. Not that it helped. The roughest thing those lady ushers ever dealt with was when some mother of the church got taken over by the Holy Spirit. Mrs. Jacobs was hollering and carrying on so bad, she just shook those five women off like they was flies. She called Lula the "Ho of Babylon," and several other things that I don't quite remember . . . but they was all bad. Mrs. Jacobs broke free and threw herself at Lula. They locked horns and danced around the casket. With one well-placed hand, Lula ripped Mrs. Jacobs' hair weave right off her head. They both paused for a moment. The unattached hair looked like a big ol' dead black cat. Lula held that thing up like a trophy. Then, she threw her head back and laughed one of the wickedest laughs I have ever heard in my life. She flung the curly mass to the floor, spit on it, then dug her four inch spiked heel right into the center. I thought Mrs. Jacobs's eyes were gonna pop right out of the sockets. She howled like she was having a he-baby. The two women smacked into each other and fell to the floor. I knew the guests could not wait to see Mrs. Jacobs kick Lula's ass. Mrs. Jacobs was all over Lula like a cheap suit. They rolled from one side of the room to the other. All you could see was the panties and slips, then slips and panties. The pair was 'bout to roll back to the other side of the room when, somewhere, they got all tangled up in the skirting that hung around the casket. Sho' nuff they tipped the whole business over . . . casket, stand, Mr. Jacobs, everything was ass over tea cup. The corpse skidded across the floor and landed under the picture of the smiling Black Jesus. That did it! Old man Pitt was not having any of his good work go sliding across the floor. He sprang up and motioned for his sons to help him get the body back into the casket where it belonged. Mrs. Jacobs was on the floor astride Lula. She had a fist full of that vixen's hair and was about to pound her. Suddenly, Mrs. Jacobs gasped, clutched her chest, and keeled over right on top of Lula. Mrs. Neuwirth, the high school nurse, rushed over and placed two fingers on Mrs. Jacobs's neck. No pulse. "She dead," proclaimed Mrs. Neuwirth. Lula extricated herself from under the dead woman's body. She stood up, fluffed her can-can slip, unwrapped a fresh stick of gum, put it in her mouth, and threw the foil on top of Mrs. Jacobs's body. Then, with deliberate slowness, glided out of the room.

Lula Three

As I said before, Lula always had to have something in her mouth. I'm not lying. If she wasn't eating or talking or smoking, you could bet she was piled up in bed with somebody going to town on their . . . well never mind. You got the picture. I saw her in the ice cream parlor the other day. Rather than go in, I stood outside and watched her. I could tell she was up to some monkey, funny, or fishy business. She was wearing a sly cat face. You know how sometimes a cat will rub up against you like it wants to be held or pet? Then you go to touch it, it bites. That's what Lula looked like in the ice cream shop. She was acting all coy and unassuming. But I bet my last nickel she was up to no good. She moved slowly from one end of the glass case to the other. Every once in a while she would point and the counter boy would give her a sample of a certain flavor. Why she was acting as if she did not know what she wanted was beyond me. The menu hanging on the wall was five years older than black pepper. Most folks in town knew it by heart. I knew she was just flexing that boy's last neve. He would hand her a sample and she would sniff it, then lick all around the edge, and then sniff it again. Then she would put the whole spoon in her mouth and draw it out real slow. This went on for at least twenty minutes. Mind you, I was in a big hurry to get home. This little scene was much more fun than watching TV. I do not think Lula knew that I was watching her. Or maybe she did know and just did not care. Finally, she settled on a flavor. The boy turned his back to reach for a cone and faster than you could say Holy Mother Mary, Lula skittered around the counter and dipped her hand into the Chocolate Serenade. Lula yanked her hand out and commenced to licking and sucking like she was a starved animal. It was hot that day, but it wasn't THAT damned hot. The counter boy flew out from behind the ice cream case and grabbed that little Hellspawn by the hair. He attempted to throw her wicked ass out the door. Lula slapped her chocolate-covered hand all up and down the boy's clean, white uniform. Even knocked his paper hat right off his head. He wrestled her out on the sidewalk and threw her off to the ground. The boy was about to give her a good swift kick to the hind parts, but Lula rolled over and gave him a look that woulda melted steel. He ran back into the ice cream parlor and hung the "Closed" sign on the door. Lula lay there in the dust and laughed. 📖

Urban Writing Cover, 1999, photograph by Joel Sackett

V

Volume 8, Number 2, Spring 1999 Urban Writing

Photographs by Joel Sackett and Irene H. Kuniyuki. New Writing by Stacey Levine, Rosalie M. Kearns, Jesse Minkert, Bobby Anderson, Jeffrey Utzinger, Steve Potter, Matt Briggs, Willie Smith, Dan Raphael, Noel Franklin, Anna Mockler, T. Clear, Michael Daley, Irene Drennan, Joey Garcia, Kelly Jones, Tina Kelley, Pat Pedersen, Dennis Saleh, Marlaina Tanny, Michael Gregory, Julianne Adams, Greta Nintzel, Murray Gordon, Sheila Bender & Koon Woon. An Interview with Victor Hernández Cruz

Urban Writing Cover, 1999, photograph by Joel Sackett

Frances Johnson

Excerpt from the novel *Frances Johnson*

Stacey Levine

"I haven't the faintest idea what it is," Palmer said. Frances Johnson lay back on the table in her doctor's office, looking to the ceiling, considering what the man said as he cheerfully tapped the scar's outer penumbra with a paper clip, then went to wash his hands.

"Well—" Palmer let a little giggle escape his throat— "Guess what—? I lied! I do know what it is—probably! But let's not think about the scar just yet." He wrinkled his long nose and his pale, oblong face seemed to shine. "What about the other?" He was referring to a condition which amounted to little more than extremely frequent urination.

Lying on the table, Frances turned her head away. That condition was not really why she had come to Palmer's office today.

When Frances first had seen the doctor, years before, he had worn smaller glasses and, beneath his lab coat, the very tight pants that denoted fashion somewhere outside of tiny Munson, the town where she lived. Palmer was new to the town then, lured in from a far-away state in exchange for a house with pure copper plumbing. He quickly had set up his practice in an old building far from the center of Munson. He suggested that she, her mother, and sister (they all shared the same condition) come to him every few weeks for the newfangled, quick procedure, and the family had consented. Sharply painful, but over so quickly that the pain amounted to something that was indescribable and even unrecollectable, the procedure seemed to help somewhat. And when Frances endured the procedure's discomfort, Palmer sometimes shook his head as if she were strange, and sometimes laughed softly, as if from nerves.

He finished the procedure before either of them really knew it; as he stood there, arms dangling, a quality of suspension seemed to possess the room. Then Palmer left, and Frances rested on the table, drawing in air, listening to him enter another exam room, saying reproachingly, "Now, Mrs. Best . . ."

Slowly, Frances rose from the table, considering that she might buy a chicken for dinner. She dressed carefully and after waiting some time, tiptoed from the room through the long hallway, passing Palmer's office, a plain room crowded with books and slithery magazines which seemed to be falling variously to the floor. The doctor was sitting at his desk, and as she walked by, raced into the hall, hands extended, calling her. "Frances, Frances—come have a seat! Come in!" His glasses were askew and in his hand he held a buttered cracker with which he gestured for her to sit down; he cleared space for a chair. Eating the cracker, sitting, he smiled boyishly and shrugged.

"So. How goes life?"

She was lost.

"Mmm? How's your fellow—Ray—isn't that his name?"

"Fine. He's fine."

There was silence. "Well, life's full of drama!" the doctor offered, looking rather useless, she thought, and he grinned uncomfortably, setting his cracker on a plate.

"You mean—?" she sought an explanation.

"Actually, I prefer comedy to drama," he went on, straightening some pens along his desk. "I don't like the weight of drama. It bothers me."

"Oh?" Frances answered, feeling rather muddled.

The doctor leaned forward. "Not that it's any of my business. But . . . I've been thinking! In all the time I've been in Munson I've never seen anyone leave, not even for a honeymoon! Why is that? Don't people here like to get out?"

She shrugged. "We like to, sure! But we don't. We work hard, I suppose, because we have many potent responsibilities." She realized with withering despair that these were the exact words that Enoch Ruth, the town's council head, had used with her many times since childhood, and that Palmer's question put Frances in the position of defending the town, which she did not like.

He nodded.

She shrugged. "We know we don't go out much," she acknowledged, and tried to relax in the chair. He watched her in kind, wiping his own hands of crumbs. His big desk, green metal with very short legs, was depressing to Frances, making her recall dour rain.

"I've always watched the way people move about, all my life I've watched that." Palmer said murmuringly. "The way they leave each other, I've watched that too."

Frances suppressed a sob. She was, she realized, merely thinking of her dog, Missie.

"I've noticed other things—all the different ways people suffer," said the doctor. "And I am so ignorant!"

"What do you mean?"

"Pain doesn't bother you people here in Munson much, does it? But why? I don't understand. You people don't want medicine. Pain is something you endure, or else it's not taxing to you! Pain in California is not like that."

Frances stared. It came to her now that the doctor was rather compassionate, and she wondered if he could be trusted. With his hopeful eyes and rough skin, he looked indelibly promising to her, like a veteran, or possibly a baker.

He spun in his chair and stood, looking to the small opaque window above his desk. "The sky is so dark!" he cried suddenly and wiped his eyes.

"Palmer, I want to get out of this town," she said.

"Um, why not?" he said offhandedly, taking hold of a hard rubber doorstop from his desk and squeezing it. "Just keep an eye on those scars. Check them."

"What are they, Palmer?"

He sighed. "Well, as I said, Frances, I wouldn't worry too much."

"Do you recognize the condition?"

Palmer frowned. "I've seen it before. They called it, simply, 'cauliflower,' in the coastal medical school where I was trained. It may come from water, nerves, or something else. Where there's one case, there's often many." He turned to the high window again, tossing a few jacks in the air and catching them. "Huge crop of berries this year on the trees. Oh they are good."

"But Palmer! Do you mean others in Munson have the same scar I do?"

He turned back to her soberly. "Frances—things happen, and we can't know why." His longish face seemed to grow sad. "Why don't people in Munson feel pain much? But they don't. Why does a scar appear? But it does." He stared past her to the wide doorway.

With spirit, she put in, "And towns . . . entire towns . . . maybe they have illnesses, too." She too glanced at the open door, with a sense that someone was standing nearby, listening. The small window above their heads seemed absurd.

The doctor's face rose sardonically and he gave a tiny, tight smile. "Ha-ha! Oh Frances, you're a delight. Yes, a town may have an illness in its way; I'm with you there."

Doctor and patient looked at each other for a moment with bright interest.

He stood and wiped his hands, as if ready to leave. "Keep quiet about the scar, Frances. Don't ask others in town about it . . . people will get uneasy. Besides, what are you going to do? Walk into the square and call out, 'Hey, has anybody got a big scar?'" Palmer laughed loudly, slapping the desk, rubbing further tears away. "Oh, me." Then he grew severe and stared ahead of him for some time.

Frances was curious about the scar, and about the possibility that others in the town might have it too.

"So you're going away on a little trip?" the doctor said. "Gee, that makes you different."

"Palmer, don't tell anyone," she begged, standing. "I might not be able to go, so please."

"All right," he said plainly with unconcern and swiveled in his chair and switched on a small transistor radio. "Frances, do you ever feel guilty?"

"I don't know." Suddenly she had the peculiar feeling that the doctor could see everything about her—see the vulnerable surface of her heart which rippled with images of flight and pursuance.

Yet his eyes were closed as he rocked with feeling to the thin, tuneless radio music. "I have to admit, I myself feel guilty," he said, eyes still shut. "For being lazy sometimes. And because doctors can take all sorts of liberties, and no one is ever the wiser. I hope I haven't done that." He brought his head down to his hands, hair falling forward. "We try searching—not amongst our patients, but beyond them! Do you know what I mean?" He began to cry.

She looked at him without expression. "Palmer, do you have a wife?"

"I don't know!"

"Palmer, I've got to go."

He coughed. "Don't neglect your health on your vacation, Frances. Take plenty of fresh air. Avoid heavy foods—these may cause corns. Drink water—never the poison that is orange juice. Use fatted soap." He smiled broadly.

As Frances left the room, she realized it was dark outside, and as she turned back to look at Palmer, he picked up a pale glass marble from his desk, examining it carefully as if for wens. 📖

Get To Know Your Jacket

Murray Gordon

Reach into the closet for your jacket
and grasp the collar which was sewn on by
Nan. She has a quota of twenty-eight
dozen per day. Thrust a hand into one
sleeve and twist the other hand into the
second one. They were set by Sideth and
immediately afterwards topstitched by
Chong. Their machines are adjacent but they
are not allowed to speak to each other
for forty hours a week, fifty-two
weeks a year. Smooth the jacket around your
torso. Larita bodyseamed it for
you. She's been doing that job for more than
fifteen years breathing in lint all that time.

That the left and right fronts of your jacket
should match, Khamdy personally took a
marking pencil and marked your zipper at
the neck, yoke and waistband. Last year, she set
61,405
front zippers. The pocket welts were cut by
Eulalia who stands on her feet for
eight hours a day at the Reece machine.
The pocket zippers were set by Honee
who is so good that you will never
see a pucker at the corners because
she must make repairs on her own time. When
you put your keys, comb and change into
the pockets, you can do so with confidence.
They won't fall through because Jojo is the
pocket bagger. She is so fast that it

isn't necessary for her to think
anymore. William cut out the pattern—
360 ply. There is
not a moment anymore when he does
not hear the buzz of the cutting machines.

Pauline supervised the sewing line. They
gave her a raise, put her on salary
and now they don't have to pay her over-
time when the plant works on Saturdays. George
is the owner. He comes in late and leaves
early, takes two hour lunches and he
does not know the names of any workers.

Your jacket comes as an experienced
traveler. Ordered in Seattle from
a catalogue company in Maine, the
fabric was shipped from a Massachusetts
mill to the contractor in Seattle,
reshipped to a subcontractor in North
Carolina, sewn there and reshipped back
to Seattle to be inspected, tagged
and bagged, reshipped to Maine and then shipped to
your home address in Seattle. When you
wear the jacket no one will be able
to see any of this. What they will see
on the left front is a small label with
the name of a dead man woven on it.

Untitled, 1999, photograph by Joel Sackett

Writing A Place In The City

Bobby Anderson

When I first read Richard Hugo, I was struck by the work in *What Thou Lovest Well, Remains American*. Rage, alienation and shame appear in poems about, of all places, White Center!—a hop skip and a jump from where I grew up feeling similar sentiments.

I was five in 1960, the year my mother's boyfriend moved us away from my father's Greenwood house to 3010 SW Raymond, my home for the next thirteen years. As a boy growing up in West Seattle's High Point Housing Projects in the sixties and early seventies, poetry and poets were the furthest things from my mind. Little did I know then the significance of this period, how it would play a major role in my sense of self and other selves, of politics and art. The power of place was under my feet as I played baseball, ran with friends and later from police down streets with names like Myrtle, Juneau, Snake Hill. Poetry and the work of Hugo came later when I was a student in Carol Hall's Creative Writing class at Seattle Central Community College, freshly clean and sober, trying to get literate, to make sense; and later with Nelson Bentley; and, especially, Colleen McElroy, who helped me realize my heart and mind were not in the flora and fauna of the Pacific Northwest but in the city where I'd lived all my life. Well, I was hooked, trying to get it down, my triggering town, as though writing could save my life.

The first thing I recall about the projects wasn't the uniformity of poverty as mirrored in street after street of identical units, but the large trees and endless green expanses of common lawns with dozens of kids raring to play. Paradise. At that time before the Space Needle, before Boeing's big bust and later desegregation, High Point was a fairly self-contained community. Built for the war effort, to house workers from local industries, it was the largest housing project west of the Mississippi, with two thousand plus units. After the war, High Point was used to house low-income people: the elderly, the disabled, but mostly single-parent families, with women usually heading the household. We went to primary and elementary school in High Point; mothers shopped at Safeway and Albertsons on 35th SW; kids bought penny candy at Johnson's Market—all within walking distance from the projects.

Things were fine at our place until the loud arguments between my mother and Bernie accelerated into fist-fights. Paradise bashed. School became my refuge. What to do with images of abuse and unconditional love: your red-haired mother doubles over one night after a fight; Bernie scurries away for good; and the police arrive, one of the cops, shining arrogance, calls her a whore. Of course she's crying, the prettiest woman in the world, and you, at 6, commit your first crime—kicking a police officer in the shins. Hello powerlessness, hello shame and defiance.

This was not the last time I'd witness individual or small groups of police officers acting badly, using poverty as a cloak to give voice to their classism, misogyny, and in other situations, some quite brutal—racism. My mother was 25, beautiful and clueless, raised in a nice middle-class home by an older couple who adopted her. Nothing in her background could have prepared her for this life of violence, welfare checks, and bureaucratic home visits. She danced herself out at night to bluegrass and country western music at the Glendale Tavern, like one of the "bad mothers" in Hugo's poem "White Center" who "we call out of the taverns and point them sobbing for home." Drink and a good time were antidotes to her sense of worthlessness. And I, a few years later still the momma's boy, found shelter for awhile in various combinations of alcohol and amphetamines, barbiturates and hallucinogens. I reveled in being the project boy with a bad attitude: fighting at the roller rink in White Center, stealing wine from little mom-and-pop stores, dining and dashing at Ed's in Burien, drinking and driving down Delridge where I wrecked my first car, or ripping off money and drugs from kids living west of 35th Ave SW—kids who I envied.

Hugo writes: "I watched my face play out dreams of going north with clouds. North surely was soft . . . No grating scream to meals or gratuitous beatings, no crying, raging fists against closed doors." I had similar dreams but my "north" was much closer. As one who lived east of 35th Ave SW, which served as a demarcation, east being the wrong side, I secretly wanted nothing more than to be a part of a nice middle-class, nuclear family in West Seattle proper; to be normal. Early on, I knew life was different there, having been integrated into Fairmount Elementary school where the text books were crisp and current (not the ones, decades old, used at High Point Elementary), and where the kids had mothers and fathers, and new shoes. I looked west, but ended up Downtown, in places like Pennyland, the Double Header, 2nd and Union.

When I cleaned up a few years later, after living in a shack on the hillside overlooking the old dump site off of Beach Drive, and after a year stint in White Center Projects, the poetry of Richard Hugo made sense to me in a personal way. Aside from the references to familiar places, his insistence on making art from what many would consider profane or at best commonplace material, and the emotional honesty of his work, continue to influence my aesthetics. Recently, feeling gratitude for the many teachers and mentors I've had over the years, I drove past 3010 SW Raymond and noticed the now pastel yellow of the place, remembering different, deeper shades. As I watched the house I hoped, as Hugo hoped in his poem "The House on 15th SW," that the "Light would be soft and full, not harsh and dim remembered. The children, if there are children inside, would be normal, clean, not at all the soiled freaks I had counted on." 📖

The Buffalo Shoe Factory

Mark Svenvold

They made a line of boots for lumbermen—
steel-toes homely things, hobnailed
& treble-stitched along the outer welt,
high-topped, a yard of lacing to the shin,
the rust-brown tongue a supple, second skin,
the rest as stiff as sheet iron. The tread grabbed—
you could walk up the side of a house, it seemed—
they were ugly boots you'd bet your life on, or in,
if that were your lot—but it isn't, of course.
Yours is a thrift-store scene, an antiquarian's
eye presiding over whatever's left
of the world these boots are stand-ins for.
And bowling shirts, their names slant-stitched,
are castoffs you try on, laughing, for a fit.

[Cloudy Bright]

Mark Svenvold

You lived there for a sense of scale,
the factory gutted—just you and its square footage,
like a giant companion, more like acreage,
you said, the light rolling over the *schola*
cantorum you built with your carpenter's hands—
a bay view, half-loft, a half-darkened stage,
or era. The town faced a continent's western edge
that the *Bill Shively Band* might yammer & wail,
it seemed, and poetry happen. Malarkey, too,
those twin drunks applauding in the corner,
joined, as always, by the hip: we were all
prop wash and sputter and cool remove,
while you wore the mirrors, and stared
us down, and ranted, and climbed the walls.

Keeping Alive the Sense of Ceremony

An Interview with Victor Hernández Cruz

Paul E. Nelson

Victor Hernández Cruz was born in Puerto Rico in 1949. His books include *Mainland, Tropicalization, By Lingual Wholes, Red Beans,* and *Panoramas*. He was featured on Bill Moyers' *Language of Life* series on PBS, and has received numerous awards, including a National Endowment for the Arts Fellowship and a Guggenheim. He was twice crowned the World Heavyweight Poetry Champion in Taos, New Mexico.

[What follows is an edited version of a forty-five minute, on-the-air interview (KJR-FM, KSRB-AM and other stations), conducted by Paul E. Nelson, on November 22, 1998, after a visit by the poet to the NW Spokenword LAB in Auburn, Washington.]

Paul Nelson: You said over the weekend that we have a seed in us, from a very early age, of creativity. Sometimes it is recognized, and sometimes it is not. It might be painting; it might be singing or music. In your case, obviously, it was writing. Do you have a sense when you first realized you were a writer or had some kind of special talent?

Victor Hernández Cruz: I think it was very early on that I realized I was drawn toward the spoken word and the written word, the word in print. I was an avid reader. My reading skills were way up ahead of my mathematic skills. I noticed this right away; my teachers noticed this right away. They put me to read up in front of the class because I was able to read high school texts in the sixth grade. So, I knew I had a knack for language. I also had the same sensation when I heard my Uncle Carlos recite or declaim specific poems on certain holidays in our living room. I would get emotional; I would actually cry, as a child. I knew that language was going to be my life.

PEN: You were born in Aquas Buenas, Puerto Rico, which is inland, and until age five-and-a-half you lived there, at which time you moved to New York City. You grew up hanging around the tobacco-making shops, and poetry, or the spoken word, was part of the activities there. Why don't you tell us about that.

VHC: The tobacconist had a great tradition both in Cuba, in Puerto Rico, in Santo Domingo, and perhaps some other tobacco-making regions in the Americas. They would have a reader come in and read to them from a book. It could have been Victor Hugo in Spanish; could have been the works of Cervantes—Don Quixote. A reader would come in and read perhaps twenty pages, or a chapter or two a day, while the cigar makers rolled and went about their business of creating their cigars. Also, literature was discussed. Other things were also read: the local newspaper. People often gossiped and left messages there. The cigar shop was a place of communication. They also played music, guitar, and sang songs. My grandfather Julio was part of that tradition. He was a notorious singer in Aquas Buenas, and he was always called upon to give serenades.

This was the neighborhood barrio I was born into. It was a tobacco neighborhood of small places where they made cigars, and there were about four or five of them in this neighborhood. One was right across the street from the place where I was born. So, pretty much, once I started walking, I knew that I was amongst those leaves, hearing the declaimers declaim from their memories. That was my first encounter with poetry, and I always knew that poetry was both in the books and in the air, in people's voices.

PEN: There are a couple of things in your work that come out of that. First of all, with the people making the cigars, you had a first-hand view of craftsmanship, which you've obviously been able to use in your work.

VHC: Oh yeah, there is definitely a craftsmanship [to that work]. They have to know the texture of the leaf; they have to know the fragrance, the aroma, the odor of the leaf. Sometimes there are two different kinds of tobacco that they use. The leaf is one kind of tobacco. And what they call *la trepa*, which is the gut, the inside of the tobacco. There are different ways of rolling tobacco, and they sometimes put the leaves in layers and roll away the layers; and at other times crumbled leaf was inside. And after that there is a whole other process, other people who work making sure that the cigars are all the same shapes. And *before* it gets to the tobacconist there's a job for women who remove the stem from the middle of the large tobacco leaf, take the stem out to make two halves. That is a job for women. And there are jobs for kids, jobs putting the little rings on the cigars. This whole region in Puerto Rico was involved in the tobacco trade when it was an important agricultural product. And one of the traditions at the cigar shop was the oral tradition.

PEN: Victor, that's a tradition in your family, and it goes back to the *areíto* (oral tradition).

VHC: For the native peoples of the Americas, and for the native peoples of the Caribbean, specifically, there was a form known as *areíto*. It was done in a singsong dance. The dance was done in a round circle, and they played drums, maracas, and sang the songs that they had sung for thousands of years which spoke/ sang of their cosmology, their wanderings. It is known that the indigenous peoples of Puerto Rico originally came from an area of the Amazon, so they sang of their journeys, and they would keep these songs intact generation after generation.

PEN: Yet with that oral tradition that was kept alive in your family, because of all the prose that you read, you don't have the ability to be able to declaim. You're more of a text poet.

VHC: I'm more of a text poet, but I can declaim and I can sing. That is something you have to say right away in Puerto Rico. Sometimes, if you say you're a poet, they still hand you a guitar right away because they think you're also a musician. And they think you can declaim all the poetry of that tradition. Sometimes it is very flowery poetry. Sometimes it's about mothers, sometimes it's about love—usually about love—but it is an interesting form. If you look around in that form you can find some very vibrant, fresh lines. And also a lot of cliches, like in Hallmark cards. But if you really listen to bolero lyrics some are interesting, about broken hearts, treachery, loneliness.

PEN: Victor, it's time for you to read a poem, the one about hurricanes that you read on Bill Moyers' show.

VHC: (Reads the poem:)

Problems with Hurricanes

A campesino looked at the air
And told me:
With hurricanes it's not the wind
or the noise or the water.
I'll tell you he said:
it's the mangoes, avocados
Green plantains and bananas
flying into town like projectiles.

How would your family
feel if they had to tell
The generations that you
got killed by a flying
Banana.

Death by drowning has honor
If the wind picked you up
and slammed you
Against a mountain boulder
This would not carry shame
But
to suffer a mango smashing
Your skull

or a plantain hitting your
Temple at 70 miles per hour
is the ultimate disgrace.

The campesino takes off his hat—
As a sign of respect
towards the fury of the wind
And says:
Don't worry about the noise
Don't worry about the water
Don't worry about the wind—
If you are going out
beware of mangoes
And all such beautiful
sweet things.

PEN: Let's talk about the poem. A bit of double entendre there, "beware of mangoes / and all such beautiful / sweet things." What you might be saying is that what you *desire* in life, that is going to take you down.

VHC: It's a metaphor, for sure, and it goes way beyond the actual fact of a hurricane, which can be very dangerous. The fact is sweet things can be very dangerous too, so we have to know how, as human beings, to deal with those things that make us feel good, that we are attracted to, that we have to discipline ourselves in front of. The honey, the good stuff that is all around, we have to use in proportion and use in moderation. We have to know what to do with the sweet things, because sweet things *can do you in* if you are not careful.

PEN: What was the inspiration for that poem? Do you remember sitting down to write it?

VHC: It was right before Hurricane Hugo, a strong hurricane, and people were putting up paneling and tying things down with ropes. A group had gathered on a certain corner and was trying to analyze where to put cars, in terms of which telephone poles we thought were going to fall and in what direction. They were saying that in the past one of the things that had happened was that all the vegetation on the mountainside came down into the town: green bananas, plantains, oranges, grapefruit, mangoes, passion fruits—everything that is hanging. Everything is going to start flying through the air. Fruit can be very sweet but also very hard-skinned, very heavy, when flying around at one hundred miles per hour, and that is what someone pointed out. He said, "you know, someone got killed by a flying coconut," and I said, "really, when," and he said, "such and such." It was one of the stories that become legend.

So, I started thinking about that, and I produced that short poem. A poem I produced in one sitting and in one writing. I usually write down my poetry with a pencil, that is the first wave, and then I pass it over into my word processor and make a hard copy, then I go over that hard copy and make changes, then I come back to the word processor and make the changes. So, it is three motions, three rewritings, before I say, "This poem is finished." "This poem is ready for publication."

PEN: When you are editing, in a sense, you are going back to the oral tradition that you had as a very young man, and you're using sound to edit the poem. If something is kind of clunky, you take it out and fix it up.

VHC: To me, all poetry is sound. A thought you hear within the confines of your own mind. I have to hear the poem first, and then it is a second motion to get it down on paper. Even there the original flurry of the words change because you are trying to capture that original instinct. I think that all poetic movements, all poetic apparitions, are instincts that are captured. Even a long poem is a series of different instincts or flashes that come through; then you capture them, and you can get back to them. The spirit of spontaneity is not lost because you are still dealing with the same material—you are just rewriting it and reworking it, but with a little bit more consciousness. When I write poetry, I always find that there is an element of surprise, an element I did not plan, and that is the important moment of poetry, no matter what the poem is about. That element of discovery is something I never want to lose.

PEN: You talk about that trance state which is something that goes back to your heritage, and mine as well. In the Caribbean there is the tradition of the medium, someone who, in this day and age, in this culture, channels, for lack of a better word. In a sense, when you are writing poetry, you say you are in a trance state. So, you become a vessel for something bigger to come through you and write the poem itself. Is that accurate?

VHC: It is very interesting that William Carlos Williams' mother would go into trances occasionally and she would light her candles. His mother was from Puerto Rico, so he was part Puerto Rican, part Latino, and consequently that's why the *Carlos*—he was named after his mother's physician brother. She would go into a trance, sometimes to the embarrassment of Williams. He has written about his mother being possessed and speaking in tongues and doing things that were very un-American. It fascinated him, her sense of language, the way she spoke broken English and never quite got it together. How she spoke in fragments, creating what he considered a cubist language. Consequently, his admiration for the great Spanish painter Juan Gris. Williams' writing captured speech upon the page.

PEN: . . . in the American vernacular.

VHC: In the American vernacular. He wanted to bring that poetry home here to America. He was very much an American poet. Not only through reaching out for that, but through his mother, who was from the Americas, from the first European Americans, the Caribbean Americans. He was rooted in this soil.

I've always thought that when we [as poets] come to the first moments of poetic inspiration, something happens that we are conscious of, something happens that (for me) is a letting loose of the mind—taking us through regions where the discussion we are having with language [in the mind] is not conscious. [In this region] language—which is stronger than us physically, which is something that was here before us and will be here after us and is what controls us—takes over and does its thing. That's [the region] where great poetic production throughout history has occurred.

It is important to keep this type of inspiration alive, in this technological, scientific modernity that we are living through. I think poetry and poets are still at the core of human life, of keeping alive the sense of ceremony that is in the spoken word. For me, poetry is still the center of life. We are not a margin. Everyone else has marginalized themselves away.

PEN: Amen! Amen to that. You're preaching to the choir here. So, Williams, to get back to him, being proud of America and wanting to make it as an American, in a truly American way. Shedding the shackles of colonialism, unlike contemporaries Ezra Pound, who picked the wrong horse in WWII, and T.S. Eliot, who was born in St. Louis but bolted the United States to do his best work overseas in England.

VHC: Williams thought that T.S. Eliot's publishing of *The Waste Land* had put back American poetry by using iambic pentameters, forms that were developed within a different geographic space and time. He thought poetry should evolve and poetry should be local. All writing is really contemporary, no matter if it is Socrates or Plato or Aztec priest-poets. All of them wrote within a Now, within a space that was present.

PEN: They had a sense of place that they were very deeply connected to, which gives the spoken word more power. Importing something from somewhere else it is not going to be as powerful.

VHC: Right. Williams thought it was like having antiquities around. He thought we needed something that was in tune with the American people, the working-class people. He was in tune with working-class people. He was a physician, a pediatrician, and he delivered something like 2,000, 3,000 babies. He did his internship in the French hospital in New York City at the turn of the century. It was a working-class neighborhood of Irish, Italian, and Poles, and he was involved with them and their personal lives. He was going inside of women and taking babies out, how intimate can a person get with other human beings. And his sense of touch . . . if you read his poetry, you are very aware of his sense of touch and his sense of sexuality, his erotica. If you look at, say, Wallace Stevens, he was an insurance executive, and T.S. Eliot worked in a bank. But Williams was a poet who was in touch with human beings at a very intimate level, a very penetrating level.

PEN: Sensual.

VHC: Sensual. Because he was a doctor, he was always reading character and always looking at features to see signs of disease or signs of ill health. He knew how to read people that way. He is an amazing poet, and if you look back at him to discover his Latino side, there is so much double entendre in his poetry but he never came out and said, "I am half Puerto Rican." "I am half Latino." He never would have said that.

PEN: He had to suppress that.

VHC. Yes. But it comes out in his poetry as double entendres. Williams was also one of the first poets to use what we know as Spanglish. Many Chicano poets and Puerto Rican and Cuban writers from the United States have been using Spanglish within the last 10, 15 years, but Williams was using this in 1917.

PEN: And yet it is only in the last year and a half or so that he has been anthologized with other Latin American writers.

VHC: The first anthology of US Latino writers to include his work came out about a year ago. And that was an important move, to recognize his hidden side, his relation to his mother, and to his mother's culture by extension.

PEN: The advice you gave in your high school lecture at Auburn Riverside High School was, if you want to get published, just do it yourself, don't wait for someone to see how good you are, just put it out. It was something you did at about age sixteen or seventeen with a book called *Papo Got His Gun*.

VHC: Sure. I published my own book. But that is the poetic tradition of all the Spanish poets I know. Even Borges, the Argentinean poet, self-published his first book.

PEN: And Williams.

VHC: His first three books were self-published. This is the tradition and the way to do it. You start where you are at, and you publish with what you've got going, and you distribute first among your local population. Then you know that that is the seed you are planting. I did my first book *Papo Got His Gun* on one of those mimeographs that were popular and available in the 60s. The civil rights people and the anti-war movement always had mimeograph machines around. You had to get a stencil, and you had to have inks, all those toxic inks.

PEN: No soy-based inks back then.

VHC: No. Just the thing itself, man. We put it out in New York City, in a hot apartment—had to have all the windows open. We made a woodblock for the cover, made 300 copies, and distributed them ourselves. Walked the streets, took them to the bookstores. I wrote the poetry, I helped produce the book with my own hands, and that's how I started.

PEN: And it went, for what? A buck-and-a-half back then?

VHC: It went for 75 cents.

PEN: Oh, man.

VHC: I put it in the 8th Street Bookstore, a famous bookstore in the Village. I put my work there, right after [Robert] Creeley. Pretty much where all my books are, even today, always after Creeley. He's a fine poet and friend of mine.

PEN: And that 75 cents investment, if you have a copy of that book today, that's worth, what 500 bucks?

VHC: Well, you can contact Serenity Books in Berkeley and I think they'll give you something for that edition.

PEN: You write in open verse, not a free verse, but an open verse. Tell us about that.

VHC: Verse is never free. Nothing is free in this universe because everything has the limitations of its own form. I write in a form that has lots of sound, lots of harmony, and a sense of a beginning, middle, and end—and none of that is done at random. Nothing is done within the context of chaos which I think freedom, or *everything goes*, might imply. Everything doesn't go; everything doesn't go in human life. We can't say everything that is on our mind, we have to edit our mind, you know. In the same way, I don't publish everything that I write. I have a drawer full of po-etry that I consider not to be worthy of publishing because it is not quite there. I call it open verse and other people have called it other things. The free verse of Whitman; the kind of poetry that Williams was writing, which was a combination of things. He was a strong Imagist, he made pictures with his words, the idea of objects or things.

PEN: "No ideas but in things."

VHC: "No ideas but in things." What that meant to me was that reality was in his poetry, and that his sense was to make a picture with a poem way before making a concept, or before an intellectual flight of mind. He wanted to make reality the raw object of poems. And eventually you saw concepts once you read the poems, but more important than ideas to him was the picture of something, the thing itself.

PEN: Things are symbols of themselves. There is one more important thing that we really need to get across, and that is something you discussed yesterday at The Institute for Community Leadership, which helped bring you to town, and that is the poet's role in the community. You said the role of the poet is to illuminate the connection between things. In a sense the poet is a bridge builder, helping us understand that we are all connected. And poetry equals awareness.

VHC: I think that a poet is an explorer. You are free to explore your own nature and the circumstances of your own history; free to develop your individual style, an individual content, an individual way of using language. The more individual you are, in a sense the more collective you are because you are always using language, and language is also a social contract that we have all agreed upon. For me, especially coming from a Caribbean society, for me [the job of] poetic art is to illuminate the fibers and the many different strings of our culture—forms within dance, music, religion, cuisine, architecture. To illuminate how all these forms come together in synthesis and in fusion, and to know this, and to explain this to myself. By talking to myself [through poetry] about this history and culture, by extension I am hoping that other people can see themselves also and that it would be of use beyond the Caribbean. And like all literature that was once local, this local moment could be understood as being universal.

PEN: Amen. 📖

Forum

Koon Woon

O.K., I am going to take a forum now:
The oncoming future is vast!

From sweatshop shyness to unfettered Beat poetry,
From the crashing waves of the Pacific coast to a thimble of wine,
From the furniture factory to a seat at the University,
From the newspapers the homeless man is cradling
        to a medical prescription,
The forum for the future is vast . . .

More than glacier ice, more than Indonesian rice,
More than a cold night in the woods,
Things are coming out now,
And rain is beginning to fall
On princess and pauper alike,
And contradictions tightly interlock . . .

I am going to take this forum,
a dandelion in the inner city,
a letter from the other side of the world,
a microchip and garlic dip,
blinking lights,
a signal from a heretofore presumed dead planet,
over the dead silences of the vastness of time and space,
intelligence is coming,
we stop the moment and seize the orange in the sky
and take this forum:
the oncoming future is vast!

Multicultural Journal of Art, Literature & The Spoken Word

ISSN 1061-1983

Collage, Digital Art/Design, by Judy Horn

VI

Volume 8, Number 3, Summer 1999 South Sound Edition

Collage, Digital Art/Design, by Judy Horn

A Force They Could Not Control

Lois J. Red Elk-Reed

The buildings are gone now.
Not a planned demolition, but
a matter of structures slowly
wasting away. Now, only the
brown and gray pictures remain,
left in boxes in the attics of
abandoned buildings and
in the minds of young children
now in bodies fully grown.

Set up by the war department,
a school for the children
of the beguiled and helpless.
Taught to sew, to mend shoes,
to be carpenters or farmers,
and to touch secretly,
so that no one would know.
It was after all a school; and
they learned their lessons well.

The witnesses: places
quiet and cold; the kitchen,
the pantry, the dark, dank
basement. Tear-stained faces,
one by one.
One who closed his eyes real tight;
One whose face would turn blue;
One who lost his speech;
One fearful of running water.

The descendants sort through
old photographs; each face a memory.
This one became a rancher,
—rode the hell out of his horses.
This one killed himself,
—before his eighteenth birthday.
This one drank until he passed out.
And that one, that one,
passed on the legacy of touch.

They were told not to tell, but
they have, and look for their
lives in pictures and see
the cunning that taught them
touch and how to win the
trust of children. They did not
know that the touch would
lead them to the time when they too
would look upon the children with

A force they could not control.

A Skin You Shed

Cat Ruiz

The body is a shell, a skin
you shed when
you die,

my uncle said,
as he lay dying on a hospice
bed. I knew he could see far beyond
drawn eyelids and hear
my poetry
darting outside the
windows
of his years.

Yes, he could feel the end coming,
that great sweep behind the next hill
that would lift him out of my
world and into another
of his. But we both knew his
body had nothing to do with it.
It just refused to
house a spirit any longer,
a spirit now anxious
to fly.

The onset of death, he said, was to
know the end wasn't really
the end. It was only a leave-taking,
a shed skin,
a molted fur
cast off the shoulders
while the spirit,

a wolf, trots
off to a brighter,
deeper
place
with
northern
stars.

Rodeo Clown

Cynthia Pratt

Woman, you nag about the two-week stays,
the broken ribs, late nights at the tavs.
It's always the same.

When I slam this door, go to the corral
pull some mean brahma
off that down and out buckaroo,
everyone wants a painted smile,
even the man's wife.
Even me.

I come home, for you. To your cigarettes,
whiskey and tight, bleached hair,
to that blue terry robe,
so used to your body
you could be my sidekick.
All you do is tell me I'm loco.
God. Don't you think I know it?
Hell, we all are.

But, I'm damn good.
Who else could dance in front of those horns,
laugh that sucker right in the eye;
could come that close
and still hold off the devil.
Lady, that's why you married me.

Warm Springs, Oregon

Cat Ruiz

Woke up to the smell of sage,
sun rising, dew clinging to each
blade of grass. Mind still groggy
from turning into, against
a cold night and
trying to snuggle for warmth. Then the sun, the sage,
swept me to this river where rocks hide
under forever-churning waters. Across the road
the pow wow slowly awakens to another
day of dancing and upholding
and for me,
remembering, indigenous roots.

Just a moment ago, a minute ago,
two people sat on the rocks down river.
I turned around and they were gone.

A little river otter tried to visit me.
He bucked the strong current
swam upstream, raised his head and
said, "I know you."
I watched him glide along, a strip
of brown sail under water as he let himself
be carried by the current toward the bank,
then disappeared.

This is a bright, friendly river,
but many spirits reside here.
There were those
two people. Who were they?
Dark shadows at morning of others
who'd been here before. Then river otter.

There's something about that rock with its
head above the water.
There's something sturdy and stalwart about it.
I bet that rock has been there for years
dreaming, thinking, meditating in the sun.
It can show me a few things,
that rock.

There's something that reminds me of Mexico
here. The smell of sage, sunshine,
blue sky, desert river flowing.
But it's mainly the feel of the
indigenous past and
present which is always a part of
Mexico and
very much a part of here.

What can one learn from these places?
How to be strong, how to follow one's own
path, buck the current.

But also
how to flow with it like the river otter
who, after having a look, sails back down
stream. How to be taken forward
with the water
into the sun, over the rocks that have
been here for years, past spirits of older ones,
newer ones,
listening and learning
like you.

Salmon Beach

Jo Nelson

Tucked between cliff frown and wave ripple, beach houses pile
air to sand like stiff ballerinas. Barnacles crest frozen tutus
salt bleaches toward the worn patina of shingle.
A world apart, this wood path, these boards tacked against the tide
of traffic shuffle, the hard cost of stone and steep steps sky rising.
Dogs scuffle their wind sock tails trail each stranger passing,
their noses sharp as cracks between shells.
Spells spin the runoff, the sand tumble root to rock
black slick hoses twist with spring water.
A brass bell trolls shell rock tide wind tease
comforting as wool in the arms of a stove.
These paned windows, these rough floors,
        the grooved ceiling stained
lap the water world worn down
before life's tentacles sucked up the marrow of bones.

VII

Volume 9, Number 1-2, 1999-2000
Future: Shelter/Sustenance

Harvest, photograph by Clare McLean

A Woman Called Concha

Kathleen Alcalá

I am interested in the big questions: Who are we, and what is our place in the universe? I am interested in writing that connects people to people, people to the land, and people to God. These are the things I value in language:

-conciseness

-simplicity

-transparency

The first two are self-explanatory. Transparent language is that which acts as a conduit between people and ideas, shuttling the reader as quickly as possible to the image or situation being described, while calling a minimum amount of attention to itself: *A woman lived in the desert.* The opposite of this, language that demands to be acknowledged, pondered, and penetrated, I call opaque language: *Somewhere was water, and somewhere, there wasn't water. Somewhere, there wasn't a woman, and somewhere, there was.*

The irony of this is that concise, simple, transparent language is not always the quickest or most insightful way to a set of ideas. Thus, metaphor and description take their place. The reader must be taken on a journey in order to understand the images presented. The reader must be provided with context. And that context must provide a link between the reader's world, and the world within the words created or presented by the writer: *Once, there was a woman who travelled a long, hard way to live in Tucson. We have a photograph of her, and we can imagine her life. Her name was Concha.*

This is best done with great specificity: the more exact the detail, the more complex the ideas the writer is able to convey in a meaningful way: *Concha heard her name and turned. It was her real name, her Indian name, Shark's Tooth from the Sea, and it gave back to her memories of a childhood that she thought she had lost forever.*

A good story works like a musical composition. An idea is

presented, elaborated, debated and perhaps defeated, and finally, presented to the reader in a modified, more mature form that embodies the path that was travelled in order to reach that idea. By taking the reader on a journey, we, to a certain extent, can recreate in their experience the thought processes and emotions of our characters. This should be done with compassion, humor, and generosity. But again like music, we can provide a pattern, a symmetry and closure that one seldom encounters in life. That is why reading good writing is pleasurable and fulfilling. That is why listening to good music can induce ecstasy.

The writer and her language should be the humble servant of the reader. To me, the act of writing is not fulfilled until it is read. The words need to be read, digested, and assembled within the context of the reader's mind and experiences in order to be complete. In other words, every reader is 'reading' a different story, because every reader brings a different set of experiences and sensibilities to the story. The word 'desert' might evoke the smell of sage. Concha might mean the touch of a work-worn hand. It also means 'shell'. If the reader fails to understand the writing, then we (the writer and her language) have failed to do our job, which is to engage, entertain, or provoke the reader in some way. This assumes that the reader is interested in these ideas to begin with, and motivated enough to read the text. Not all writing, of course, is meant for all readers. Not all seed falls on fertile ground.

Storytelling is a necessary part of the human condition. We must tell stories. It is what makes us who we are. Linguists and neurologists strongly suspect that the act of learning language physically shapes the organization of our brains. Without language, we are incapable of the full range of human interaction and reasoning. By telling stories to our children, we give them language, and so a passport into the condition of human mortality. But also, a window onto the immortal, for stories will outlive all of us.

I have chosen (or have been chosen by) a specific set of ideas on which to concentrate my writing, and will turn all of my creative efforts towards conveying these ideas in the most accessible and memorable ways possible. I want these ideas to go out and re-form and repeat and recreate themselves in as many ways as possible.

Their source might be forgotten, or misremembered. That is alright with me, because I think the ideas are more important than I am as an individual writer.

I want my writing to insinuate itself into the subconscious of the people of the Southwest, so that we might remember who we were and who we will be, since so little time is spent in the present. I feel as strongly about this as any fanatic. This is my job. *Once, there was a woman who lived in the desert. She travelled a long, hard way to tell me this story. I never met her, but even now, I can recall her face.* 📖

Her Instructions

Janet Sekijima

My mother heaps rice
steaming in snowy mounds
on the lacquer tray she uses
to make *sushi*.
The trick, she says, *is to coat each grain*
of rice with vinegar
to make it beautiful.

Then you must fan the rice
cool it quickly to bring out its shine.

Like this—she reaches for her round fan
painted with geese
flying over mountains.

I watch as peaks shimmer
in her hand—a blur
of *sumi* ink on paper sky.

Here, now you try.
I follow her motions
until each stroke of my hand
is a wing beating the air.

Yes, she nods, *like that.*

Turning the black tray around
and around, she parts
and folds the rice
over and over
—grains glistening white.

When my mother's *shamuji* paddle
comes to rest,
not one grain is left
unpolished.

Marie Antoinette's Last Supper

A pantoum

Judith Roche

I wanted to give them cake for a treat.
Now my jailers force it upon me.
It sticks in my throat.
Tomorrow they will cut off my head.

Now my jailers force it upon me,
making coarse jokes about foie gras.
Tomorrow they will cut off my head.
Once I played at being a simple goose girl.

Making coarse jokes about foie gras
they tell me how the masses didn't have bread.
Once I played at being a simple goose girl,
Tonight they pull my hair and force my mouth open.

Now they tell me the masses didn't have bread
but no one told me when I was Queen.
They pull my hair and force my mouth open.
I tried to make a simple beauty in the midst of opulence.

No one told me when I was Queen,
how the babies and grandmas became bone.
My simple beauty in the midst of opulence
did not include real hunger.

It sticks in my throat
how the babies and grandmas became bone.
I wanted to give them cake for a treat.
I did not know about real hunger.

Portrait of Jacob Lawrence, 1941, by Carl Van Vechten

Jacob Lawrence: Our Beauty is not Complete Without Your Hands ♦♦♦

Carletta Carrington Wilson

In 1990, Joe Keppler asked me to review the retrospective exhibition *Jacob Lawrence: American Painter* at Seattle Art Museum for his journal *Poets. Painters. Composers.* I was honored to be asked and overwhelmed by the charge of commenting on Lawrence's work. Beginning with the intent of writing a prose piece, I discovered, after several hours, that my best response could only be in the form of a poem. The result was "An Impressionistic Response to Jacob Lawrence: American Painter" in the form of a poem entitled "this light called darkness."

In the early 80s, when I used to live in the U District, I frequently encountered Jacob Lawrence while walking on the Ave. He was, as often has been described of him, warm and gracious as both of us acknowledged one another cordially and briefly.

There is one sterling moment, however, that rests in my mind. Toni Morrison had come to read at Elliott Bay. I don't recall the year. Of course, there was a spillover crowd. After the reading, milling around with some friends, Rick Simonson asked if I wanted to join them—him, his wife, Barbara Earl Thomas, and Toni Morrison, at the Sorrento Hotel.

When I arrived, they were already there. On the couch, Jacob Lawrence was sitting in the middle and Gwen Knight and Toni Morrison were sitting close on each side. Their heads leaned in (reminiscent of those lovers on the couch in one of his paintings), taking pleasure in the listening now that the moment of the surprise had passed, for Toni Morrison had no idea that the Lawrences would join them. They seemed, to me, to be basking in memory. Perhaps they were talking about New York. It never occurred to me, until that moment, that they even knew one another. I spent, in fact, a good bit of time trying to recall any connection that I may have come across that spoke of their friendship. Friends they were, though. Their voices were soft, the laughter gentle and easy. Their eyes embraced one another with unmistakable glee. I have no idea what they talked about that night. It was an act of remembrance, a joyous reunion, and I felt honored to witness their happiness.

Surprise encounters have been the tenure of my history with Jacob Lawrence. Finding him there, unexpectedly, at the Sorrento Hotel, turning a corner as our eyes meet, acknowledging him in the bookstore or standing before his work absorbing a world wrought by his hands. It comes to me that his paintings are paintings of destination, psychic and psychological destinations. With titles like *Going Home*, *Rooftops*, or the *Migration and Builders Series*, a sense of movement rides and runs through the paintings in an attempt to articulate the concept of home, of belonging, of every being's claim to a place in the world. His images describe the journey of a people, descendants of those whose blood, flesh and breath have engendered the birth of nations. I believe, in Lawrence's world, something always seems slightly askew. In his visual code, something always sits on an angle. Some object in the painting rests on a diagonal plane. In this transverse world, the men, women, and children Lawrence invokes migrate, build, live and love in a particular time yet they embody and evoke the timeless will and desire of all peoples in this world. To make a place in the world, to "take place" in this world. To call *somewhere* home, to live out their dreams, and to learn what it truly means to be a human being. 📖

this light called darkness

Carletta Carrington Wilson

painter
i remember the impact
visions swarming in
traveling the torrid narrowness
turning thin/thin/thinner
til translucent
      breath beckoned
spills its mighty weight
and the throng billowing
blows against seams of light
northern/ geometric/ and hungry
converging
     so-much rural
        so-very urban
           laboring on
               shadows climb
                   spit/ sound/ and pulse
            the intimate metropolis
          seasoning the struggle
        glowing the color canvas
     with a passion red   axial   and bone
rigidly brushed between four edges
stark faces   bold minds
thirsty strands of stars calling
thistledown thirty-down
comin' down the road and round
painted lady   strut your stuff
cryin' baby that's enuf
got my gal and headed for town now
bluuueeessssss
turning purple   turning thicker   and black
our certain kind our beauty   not complete

without your hands migrating into centuries
receding and advancing against the dark/ light
georgia night sky with beauty so black/so blue/so raw
                                        with contrast

   windowmaker   seer
talismans in torrents
knock the canvas
inverted keloids brush against bone
in rooms other than our own
kinky iridescence
disembarking there   dismembering there
flesh and flesh landing miles on   onto streets
throwing texture/ shadow/ color
light rises   rises to witness
our implements
our long haul labor's bloom
blooming   upon
            the
                    dark/ still canvas
onto which
                    lives
  thickly brushed
                have been left
naked to dry
            against   time

Homecomings

Paul Hunter

Writing refashions the world in miniature, making it at once lush and spare and immediate, accessible to our feelings. Unlike the real world, the one seen in language is filtered through history, touched by centuries of men and women trying to say what they have meant, how they have done, occasionally saying more and better than they've even known. So embedded into the words themselves that the most private utterance can turn instantly public. Though I have chosen them, these are not my words. I only borrow and in hopefully fertile recombinations pass them along.

So writing is an act of congruency, of association with the past, as well as an art of indirection, suggestion, innuendo. Like submarines rising to periscope depth, as readers we come to our senses to find out where and who we are. So this art is at its most fundamental a declaration of identity and purpose that renews and reaffirms our place in the world. There is at once the delight of novelty and the shock of recognition, a departure and a coming home.

For a long time I wrote plays and poetry for what appeared to be different audiences, attempting to achieve different ends. Then one day it occurred to me the separation might be artificial, that I could enjoy the compressed and figurative and muscular language that occasionally comes from the mouths of ordinary folks telling their own stories of confrontation and transformation, in effect the plots of what could be plays. We perk up our ears whenever we hear people who have been changed by their experiences, who have been moved to turn from a dead-end and do something else. There is a ring of truth in both the voice and the story that can be refreshing, that can empower us listeners to do likewise.

So I collect these stories, turning the situations over and around, searching for the viewpoint of the one who was changed most. What happens then are the poetic and storytelling effects—compressed and charged expression, rhythm and music in the lines, the occasional gleaming image or metaphor to impale the memory, the cunning of what follows what, where to begin and end. I am humbled by these stories, these lives that in the telling continue to reach up and flower. 📖

House Dressing

Paul Hunter

I quit therapy a while back.
Found out the guy wasn't making it
with me, never was, never would be.
Realized here was a guy not my type,
you know? Guy you would not search out
at parties, or hang around waiting for
pearls to come squeezing out.
I'm sorry this sounds like I'm critical
but the poor man didn't like me,
he didn't eat at my table so to speak.

I mean, why bother with anyone
you wouldn't eat around? This profound
revelation would no doubt bowl you over
until I say I came to it
one Friday after a movie
in the Burger Shack around one a.m.

There was my therapist right in front of me
ordering up a snack—
two cheeseburgers, large fries,
large coke and one of those apple turnovers
that looks like a sugar smile.
That's how I see 'em anyhow.

So there we are, and it all looked just right
so I said so, and ordered the same thing.

Now can you believe it, this offended him
in some vague way. He was probably
struck by my lack of originality
modeling my junkfood behavior
after his smooth act, but anyhow
it was one a.m. in the Burger Shack
and there was nobody else much in there,
a night owl or two maybe,
and the fluorescent lights made everything
look like the view from a dentist chair
or the bloodbank wallpaper,
and the burgers had been under
those heat lamps for quite a while
so the cheese glued itself to the foil
and tasted, you know, old—
so who was kidding who?
Anyhow, he wouldn't eat with me,
and sat there in a corner booth
deliberately chewing his food down
like there was something
written on every bite.
Now maybe I'm wrong but
the Burger Shack is not all that tough
to get your face around.
"Join me?" "No, think I'd rather not."
I'll go to my grave with that little mouth
of his puckering like an asshole,
and his mohair sweater looking
diseased in that bluish light.
I mean, he was not my type.
I mean, he knew all about me
if he bothered to listen
to what I coughed up
week after week, fifty-minute hours

at a buck a minute.
And me like a garbage truck
backed up to this empty hole
straining my guts out.

And now here it was economics.
I'd caught him dining out
for say two-ninety-eight
and he's gotta act like
he's got this big thing to study out,
some deep human problem,
some crap from the office
that wouldn't keep,
so he couldn't share
a little companionship
man to man, burger to burger.
And you know why? I think
because he sold his by the minute,
nodding his heavy head,
taking a little note
once in a while in a manila file
with a silver mechanical pencil.
I mean, who the hell would ever
use such an implement?
Whoever jots anything
they can't use a ballpoint
or number two yellow pencil for?
"No," he'd "rather not."

Reminds me of the first date
I ever had with my ex-wife.
I'm outa work but I want to impress her,
nothing's too good—fact of the matter is
I want to get in her pants tonight
but don't know it myself, I'm so innocent,
so anyhow I order all this expensive
crap with the French names,

I forget what-all at this late date,
and the guy says "What for ze salad?"
and I say the house dressing
is fine with me. Well, he leaves
and she launches right in
on how I gotta make some kind of "statement"
and not give in to the dumb fake frog,
not surrender my freedom of choice to him.
Well, I didn't mind really,
I don't get my rocks off
dressing down some head waiter
like my old man used to.
Shoulda been in the restaurant business,
had a chain so he'd have the excuse
to go around raising a stink night after night,
sending back the fillet or poached trout
quivering in its wine sauce
where his old man would have
slid his dinner across the bar
and said "put a head on it, willya."
I should have known she was not for me
right then when the food came
and she looked like my salad had leprosy
when it was just fine

like the Burger Shack there at one a.m.
and thank God I wasn't married to him.
I eat like it deserves to be eaten,
and how hungry I feel, which is to say
some things you savor
and some you wolf down,
and I bet to this day
in some nook in my stomach
there must be a cheeseburg
with the teethmarks still on it,
parked in its own little pharaoh's tomb
of a styrofoam box, for all I care.

I mean forget it right then and there,
here's your divorce and a soda straw
but the catsup's extra.
Sure, a session or two till
I knew enough to quit, then
another year till I figured why and all,
but I'm getting better about these things.
Now when they come to me
in the dark of night by some streetlamp
or even here
I'm more apt to go with 'em
and not spend the six years
patching it up dinner after dinner.
I like to cook about half the time,
simple food for the likes of me
and anyone nearby who could use a meal.
I can't say as I enjoy recipes or much follow 'em.
I just mess around
without thinking it to pieces
and taste a lot,
and the things I like slowly change
over time, like maybe a whale song—
you take something out, you start
putting something else in. Who knows?
Goodbye Paprika, hello Oregano.
You follow me? And it all tastes fine,
if you stir while you're talking
over a low heat and not leave it
sit around until one a.m. and get burnt black,
believe me, it tastes fine.

Trade Tastings

Doug Nufer

Watching me go through the samples at a party, some-body asked what I was doing. Plenty had already been opened, so there was no reason why anyone should have been methodically uncorking every bottle on the counter. It seemed wasteful, because we wouldn't need that much, or disso-lutely hopeful to expect that we would. He noticed I wasn't only opening the fancy ones, or trying one more after rejecting what had been served: I had to pop them all. Somehow, the explana-tion that this was how I normally drank wine didn't satisfy him.

"It's like this. You enter a room full of bottles set up on tables where people stand ready to pour. You swirl a bit in the glass, look at it, smell it for a while, take a sip and slosh it around in your mouth before spitting, making a note, and trying another. Sometimes, I swallow. And I always bring a corkscrew."

He nodded, but what he said confused me. I had been work-ing in a wine shop part time—what the post office want ads now call "casual labor." This gave me many opportunities to learn the trade at tastings put on by distributors. After months of practice, I knew how most wines in the market should taste and wondered how long it took to be able to predict how wines age. For better or worse, tasting was a minor part of what I did—more of the job was to describe flavors, make suggestions, give information, and take money. I was a shop clerk, but the way he put it sounded like a joke or an accusation: "You're a professional wine taster!"

Although the dubious distinction of being a professional wine taster may seem glamorous, qualifications for the job are loose. Anyone employed by a restaurant or store that sells wine may attend most trade tastings and act as a professional; importers, distributors, food and drink writers, and others in the business, such as the winemakers themselves, also qualify. In the 1980s, prom-scale extravaganzas were the rage, as competing wholesalers spent tens of thousands of dollars hosting events in hotel dining rooms, mansions, penthouse restaurants, and other snazzy locales, opening the pro ranks to all comers; these days, most trade tastings are aimed at an inner circle of buyers. While many buyers' interests touch on but don't revolve around the business of tasting wine (cocktail bartenders cruising for glass pours), there are a few of us whose jobs depend on the wines we pick. Now that I run a small wine shop, I'm one of the few in Seattle who's engaged in a direct mercantile relationship with this ancient, often mystifying, and ultimately fundamental product. "I sell what I buy."

The term "professional" loses its gloss when you realize that a gaggle of hedonistic millionaires can swim through more seas of fine wine than anyone in the business can dip into. Money buys experience and rearranges it vertically, treating members of deluxe tasting clubs to several different vintages at one sitting. Aside from this advantage based on experience, some people in and out of the business have a physical tasting advantage. Tongues endowed with extra taste buds lurk in about ten percent of the population, creating an elite of "super tasters." Being super-sensitive to sensations on the tongue helps a taster detect flaws and nuances, but there's something metaphysically absurd and commercially problematic about a taster who can describe flavors that ninety percent of the population can't detect. At the other extreme, a professional wine buyer could do a decent job without ever tasting anything. Reviews in the *Wine Spectator* and *Wine Advocate* magazines, newspaper tips, Internet chat lines, and last year's invoices versus this year's inventory can have more influence over buying decisions than anyone's personal taste. By catering to pet categories (Chilean reds), bagging trophy wines (Silver Oak, Leonetti, ad nauseam), paying attention to actual cost and perceived quality of wines at every price, and mastering the lingo of enological descriptors, an abject teetotaler could masquerade as a purchasing connoisseur.

Of course, there are probably more atheist priests than neo-Prohibitionist wine buyers. I don't know anyone in the business who doesn't enjoy tasting wine. There are, however, many pro tasters who come to despise the rigmarole of the trade tasting, tasters who taste only at certain times and in certain circumstances,

Doug Nufer with Kiwi, photo by Peggy Sullivan

who sensibly refuse to drive home from (and therefore to) tastings, who resent the cattle call ambiance of the old style full-catalog showcase and the effete pretensions of the high-end pre-sale roll-outs, who don't see the point of trying wines they have no immediate use for—unless that juice happens to cost more per bottle than a pedigreed dog. Personally, I can't stand seminars, where some shill takes hours to present a dozen wines while you sit in thrall to his genius, but there is, even in this type of hype, a certain irresistible sense of resolution I appreciate as an inner voice appealing to my Protestant work ethic: "Pal, this is your job."

In David Mamet's late Capitalism paean, *Glengarry Glen Ross,* a wheeler-dealer has his hopes for a sale lovingly dashed by a rival, who points out that the prospects he thinks he has found aren't really customers but wackos, who are infamous for their pastime of choice, "They *like* talking to salesmen!" Not just as a job, but also as theater (drinker theater?), trade tastings command a similar affection. I actually like the rigmarole, in all of its sales pitch guises. The beauty of the wine sales pitch, however, condenses to an elegant truth: nothing they say matters as much as what you taste. The pitch is the pour. And yet, wine trade shows aren't mere product displays. They educate and entertain, thanking you with a lavish display of temptations which, unlike the trade shows buyers in other lines of work enjoy, are supposedly and ironically for sampling rather than for getting you drunk. Sometimes it seems that these occasions exist primarily because they exist, to throw a party for everyone who passes the intelligence test coded into the time, date, and place printed on an invitation; that your business, their business and the whole infrastructure of commerce, law, and society exists to support these institutions of spit and glut.

Before consolidation beset the wholesale end of the business, October would pose a marathon for pro tasters: five a week, three a day, lunches and dinners with winemakers, sales reps dropping by the shop at all hours with bags full of new samples—work, work, work. "You can't taste them all," veterans haze rookies by saying the obvious, as if we weren't duty-bound to explore the realm of the senses. Even when you know that the human tongue can't taste more than twenty wines without scrambling the flavors or that the mouth absorbs enough alcohol to influence the most assiduous spitters or that gaudy zinfandels thrash delicate pinot noirs once you've bagged a hundred, you go on.

There were Burgundy tastings in good years where they wanted to sell theirs before anyone else got to you, Bordeaux tastings in bad years where they wanted to sell you anything they could and so poured the Latour, Mouton, Lafite, and Haut-Brion (but not the Petrus or Yquem), Spanish tastings staged by federal commissions and guarded by a force of secret police, Italian tastings where the idiot in charge forgot to provide food, tastings in Union Station where they thought the ceiling was high enough to accommodate a barbecue until the whole place filled with smoke, tastings on boats where you spat at Bill Gates' house, tastings at a warehouse on the bike trail where you spat at joggers, tastings where you spat in the water pitchers by mistake, tastings at a night club where the drunks roared at cabaret tables while a stand-up comic knocked off a routine, tastings where a sword-wagging aristocrat knocked open a bottle of Champagne, tastings at the top of the Columbia Tower where nobody knew the color of the sky, tastings at Boeing Field where nobody could hear anything but the sky, tastings where the good stuff was tucked under the table but you got to try it just by asking Jack, tastings in the middle of winter on a pier over the Sound where everyone wore Hawaiian shirts for no goddamn reason at all, tastings in a basement where the toilet was a hole in the floor and the CEO screamed about the fucking parasites who took an extra thirty percent for handling what he could sell for less and if you doubted him he made you **name one** wine that was anywhere near as good as what he'd just poured into your glass, tastings in the Space Needle where the tourist-packed elevators didn't stop for you at the lower level and you set off alarms when you hit the door, tastings where hired beauties poured, tastings where they knew you and so talked baseball instead of trying to bullshit you about the wine, tastings where they called you by the name stuck on your chest, tastings in the best restaurants in town with visiting wine celebrities, tastings in restaurants where $5 of Louisiana cayenne wiped out $5,000 of Côtes de Nuits grape, tastings of champion oyster wines where the oysters tasted better than the wines and the wines tasted awful unless you had them with oysters, tastings on loading docks where they grilled bratwurst that was marinated in Belgian ale, tastings where the winemaker himself stood before you like a freelance writer with a manuscript that wasn't just a wine you couldn't use but was awful in ways you recognized in things you had done that had been awful, tastings where every bottle was still in shock from being recently shipped and the wine tasted so bad it was funny, tastings where too much was too good, tastings on the floors of skyscrapers under construction, tastings when it started to snow, tastings in swank hotels that ended in saloon-style fist fights, and tastings in a warehouse where a band of delivery drivers played innocuous jazz that crept into "Stairway to Heaven."

Another time, there was a phone call inviting me to an address in Ballard the next day. I arrived late, but nobody else was there, except for the owner. He led me to a room containing samples of everything he carried: Barolo, Barbaresco, and Barbera, Chianti Classico and Rufina, Vino Nobile de Montepulciano and Brunello di Montalcino. "Open whatever you want," he said, and left without leaving a corkscrew. 📖

Alice Alone

Alice B. Toklas 1877-1967

Peter Pereira

Iced consommé, sweet breads,
a bottle of Beaujolais—
Any good cook knows the best recipes
are not found in books.
The feast is at the table.

But I never had much to say about art.
That was Gertrude's realm. The salon
was her baby, all of them
gathered around her great bosom
like a litter of pups.

Henri and Pablo with their pictures. Poor Leo
sulking in the corner. If I had a centime
for every time Marcel made eyes
at Sherwood, then sheepishly turned away.
Such nice young men.

Or to see my Gertrude again,
putting Ernest in his place.
(He was so full of bull.)

Afterwards, I'd shuttle between
them with plates of strudel, hot coffee,
orange and raspberry liqueur.

The palate was my canvas.
Each dish a poem.

Now, I have no one left
to cook for but myself, and an old woman
doesn't eat much.

Recipe for Great Aquante (Endurance)!

Suzanne A. Villegas

For generations, *Latina* women have taken great pains to pass down meals that feed and nurture their *familias*. It is with much regret, I take my turn and pass down the most vital of those recipes, the one that has a little something for everyone, it's called: *Aquante* (pronounced *Awante*: endurance)! You will need to make sure your home always says *"bienvenidos"* (welcome) and reflects the warmth and compassion of a good *Latino* home. Decorate your table with a *mantel* (tablecloth) made of Mama's *Chichi* (mother's breast), woven specifically for suckling throughout a lifetime of *Aquante*! Light a few votive *velitas* (candles) to add to the ambiance; remember, they might be the only warmth inside your *Casita de Sufrimiento* (house of suffering).

Appetizer: PINCHE TRABAJO (DAMN JOB)
SALSA Y CHIPS

In a large bowl, finely chop a series of nowhere *pinchi trabajos* (damn jobs), fill it to the rim with any number of *escusas* (excuses) for not paying the bills. Place the bowl in the center of an all occasion platter surrounded by *tortilla* chips for dipping (have no fear, you will never run out).

Main course: CABRON BIEN HECHO
(WELL MADE ASSHOLE) SOUFFLÉ

   Serves generations!
Ingredients:
   + 1part *pobre pinchi vieja* (poor damn Woman/wife/old lady)
   + 2 parts (or more) spicy *Sancha* (other woman—*Puta Picosa*, spicy whore) brand
   + 1 part duct tape and bailing wire
   + 2 big hairy *huevos/cojones* (balls)

In one large *hoya* (pot), gently stir in the spicy *Sancha* (other woman), making sure to keep her in full view and acceptance of all. Grate in a large helping of duct tape and bailing wire for all of those home improvement efforts ala *Mexican* engineering known as *babosadas* (stupidities). In a separate bowl beat and whip the *vieja* (woman/wife) until her head remains in a permanently bowed position. Add in the 2 big *huevos* (balls) to thicken things up.

Preheat oven to 700 degrees, to ensure it is overdone to perfection. Baste frequently with scalding insults to guarantee the toughness of the skin, but not enough so you can't keep sinking your teeth into it. Don't ever let the dish rest before serving. Garnish with a few decorative *hijos* (kids), legitimate and/or otherwise, to serve as symbols of power of that wonderful *macho verga* (manly penis).

Dessert: AYE QUE CHULO (OH, WHAT A CUTEMAN) CHEESE CAKE

Remember, when preparing this *Hitone* (stuckup) package, it doesn't have to taste good, it just has to look good, presentation is key. This dish is served best chilled.

Combine equal portions of:
+ Tupperware cowboy boots (the kind with the toes curled up)
+ *Taco* cowboy hat
+ *Grande* (big) belt buckle, *barriga* (gut) must be able to hang over
+ Jeans (must be tight enough to see which side Mr. Right or Mr. Left sit on)
+ Top with a starched dress shirt, opened to the waist, to reveal the *sudor* (sweat) and stylish gold chains.

Beverages: RAMFLITA CHINGONA (FUCKING CAR) COLADA

In a frosty mug, combine 1 gallon of prize Chevy (1957 was

a good year), 1 *botella de Tequila* (bottle of tequila), 1 *barril de cervesa* (barrel of beer), and whatever else you want on ice, *rocas* (rocks) or *molidas* (blended)! Shake, stir, then line them up for a lifetime of avoidance in a bottle.

Note: If this does not sound appealing, as a progressive Latina, your only two options are:

> A.) Keep quiet and keep serving.
> B.) Leave the fold and be labeled a *sin-verguensa* (without shame).

[*Aquante* (pronounced *Awante*), is a noun, meaning endurance, fortitude or resistance.] 📖

VIII

Volume 9, Number 3,
Fall 2000
South South Edition

Cover art & design by Joel A. Derefield

Cathexis

Margot F. Boyer

He reminds me of all I'm not getting in this life
and can't live without though his skin reeks
of machine oil, he wraps his cut finger
in black electrical tape, enters the tavern
at five with his hair full of grease
for pleasure he shoots the last ball in the pocket.

I was always a difficult woman to know
bursting into cryptic recitations
my eyelids wet and hard to color
hem ripped, backpack shredded
with the weight of references.
Too many evenings I walked domestic streets
as sunset water-colored housefronts copper and peach
climbed the hill by the spring amid roses
and rotting plums, ordered whiskey
for all the wrong reasons.

He won't be known until the fourth drink
is inside him. Then he says
his mother sold the books and let
the cat freeze on the stoop, his brother
killed the dog and sisters fled, it's no wonder
he'd rather sleep in a chair by the fire
than in a bed. Once in a dream
I caught him weeping in a hayloft, fenced in
by his collection of broken machines;
school bus, pipe-organ, reel-to-reel deck, and knew
it's me he can't receive
not the books unopened, jars of jam
abandoned on his dirty kitchen counter.

Still, I look for him
while the sirens are wailing
every last dog in town is howling
and the last abandoned warehouse on the dock
is going up in flames. The gibbous moon
rises late at the end of the summer and the scent
of stargazer lilies fills my house at night.
He's ripping out walls and smashing floors
hauling barrows of busted concrete up the alley
he's setting up colored balls for the break
squeezing the lemon and laying down
the money. When he let me rest my palm
for a moment on the smooth skin of his left cheek
it was like nothing else, what I can't live without

all I'm not getting in this life.

Miami

Mary Lou Sanelli

All I do is stare, mutely, at the girl
cowering by the beach-side grocery, at layers of torn clothing,
her feet with a missing toe like a gap between teeth, eyes
like moons in the midnight of her skin.

In one week I have learned to distinguish Cuban from Haitian,
the black tourist from Jersey from Caribbean born,
this young woman from ones who learned enough English
to clean hotel rooms and stand in loose-fitting shifts
waiting for the bus. Women who braved these fringey streets
until someone came, waving and shouting, prodding them
into a van, or whispering a few kind words
like a length of silk eased through their fear.

People hurry past to buy beer, creams
to protect their skin from the sun they seek,
inflatable hoops of plastic to keep children afloat.
Next to me, a short, quivering woman smirks,
reminds me of the mother on Jerry Seinfeld,
the whine in her voice, the stiff-dyed-upright hair,
a clear sheet of vinyl I imagine covers her couch.
I watch her spit at the girl whose head hangs down,
whose whole body acquiesces and I think, god, it's true,
the most oppressed oppress the most.

On hot asphalt in front of this store, a girl is adrift
on a makeshift raft in open sea, searching
for this high-rise reef that promises work, life.
I see cane fields across the Atlantic, a machete
slashing her toe. I see a glossy catalogue in her lap,
all the things she wants to have—

and because I do not live here,
have not trained myself to pass, obliviously, I see
myself in her.

The Endless Sentence, Monroe State Reformatory, 2003,
drawing by Jeff Niles Hacking

Prison

Bill Yake

Monks and inmates wear saffron.
You cannot jail a sleeping man.

Each of us is a voice
that cannot be raised,
so it is short and flat.

In the yard, men crawl
beneath voices and tongues
of barbed wire—crimped
until they sing tight,
little tunes. Bend the notes blue.

Never negotiate. Even justice is a loop.

Each of us is pressed into a dry brick.

These walls go for flesh.

Latecomers

Susan Landgraf

We walk over mollusks.
We walk over triceratops.
Some days we dig up a
Kennewick Man.
   We know how
to keep him safe in foam
and plastic. We have scopes,
temperature-controlled rooms,
gloves to tell his story,
trace his clan, pinpoint the epoch
in which he lived, maybe
the year he died.
   Clans argue ownership
and whether to bury him
again, even though we are all
of us latecomers, after Sun
and Saturn, after our old, old
mother. Five million years
back
   North America was a lake.
We still fish other waters,
and some nights the boats' holds
fill, fish scales gleaming
in the dark. Other nights,
fishermen are lost.
   Saturn's rings
are thin. Compared to the fire
that rages inside the earth,
fields, cliffs and sandy beaches
are like flesh.
   It's the bones
we're after, as if they tell the story
we're hungry for.

The Readings at the Richard Hugo House

Joan Swift

Alone in shades of gray, a bottle of Jack Daniels
on the bar for you, I listen through the Coke machine's
loud hum for words. Everyone—or almost everyone—

is in the auditorium but me, the room where
writers read aloud what they have written.
I lean to the loudspeaker's distant throat for syllables

like salmon in your River Sky whispering through
the current, glints of voices no more discernible
than fish scales seen through glacier water.

They're reading in your memory. You'd think,
because you asked me once to go fishing on Lake
Kapowsin with you, I'd rise like the trout we never caught

and pull the plug for the Coke machine out of the wall.
A girl in a red plaid skirt does that. The lake was still
at dawn, you said, and there'd be mist. It was April

in the house of the poet reading now. I didn't go.
Like that, chance passes like a meteor through space.
Now you're too big to catch in anyone's net,

out there on some migration all of us will make,
trailing the weeds of every lake you cast a fly in,
the universe taking its time so we don't forget.

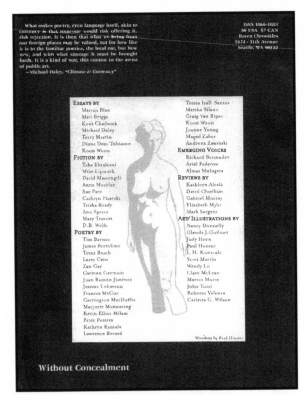

from *Naked Woman Chapbook*,
Wookcut, by Paul Hunter

IX

Volume 10, Number 1, 2001
Without Concealment

Shadow . . . Dreaming, original collage,
by Carletta Carrington Wilson

I Do Not Cry

Sue Pace

The sun hasn't come up yet but the telephone rings anyway. I drink my coffee and rattle the morning paper. I am reading the International Weather Report and turning Celsius into Fahrenheit. London 11 degrees. Paris 17. Madrid 28.

"Europe is having its worst winter in years," I say. "Ten people were found frozen in their beds."

My husband plunges his fork into the yellow eye of his egg. The telephone rings again as he dips a triangle of toast into the unblinking orb. He cannot—will not—be bothered by a telephone that nags before dawn. Feet pound down the hall and I realize who will stop the noise if I do not. I lay the paper across my empty plate and I do not cry. Not yet.

I lift the receiver and a mechanical voice, tinny and thin, speaks from an ocean away. "Will you accept a trans-Atlantic collect call from Spain from a...."

I know two people in Spain. One is my daughter. The other is a weasel that walks and talks like a man and who would never, under any circumstance, call me. "LeAnn!" I shout. "Yes! Yes!" Thousands of miles away, my oldest daughter waits. This is the way it has always been between us. I scramble for a connection while she stays just out of reach.

"*Hola!*" there is an echo that rings and fades. "I haven't been able to figure out the time difference but I thought I'd let you know I'm here and fine. Well not fine but as close as I'll ever be in a country that refuses to speak English."

So, I think. She's playing it tough. "I'm glad you called," I say. I am more than glad. Amazed. Astounded. Frightened. Suspicious. Pathetically grateful. They, she and the weasel, have been gone eight days. "I've been reading the world weather report," I offer. "It says Madrid is cold."

"Not bad. Of course, my luggage was stolen."

She's calling for money, I think. Of course.

"But I still have my money and my passport and pictures of the girls."

The girls are her two younger half-sisters. Semi-siblings who were a nuisance when all three lived together in the same house. Now she dotes on them but they don't have time for her. She missed that crucial period of development when loyalties are established. They only remember the face with the angry smirk in family snapshots. The face of an adolescent at risk.

At risk. That is what they are called now, these bright young women who drink too much and dope too much and who are attracted to dangerous men. A decade ago they were drop-outs.

"Where are you?" I ask.

Her reply is laconic. "Still in Madrid."

"Still?" I thought you and Michael. . . ."

"That asshole," she slurs before pulling her act together. Her voice is curiously flat. "Has he called you?"

"Why would he call me?" I lean against the wall.

"Just a shot in the dark." The phone is blank for a moment. I can almost see her light the cigarette that dangles between pouty red lips. "We had a fight. He threw his camera at me and stomped out."

"When was that?"

"A week ago. We were still at the airport. Unloading." The slur is back along with a thickness.

"Where, exactly, are you calling from?" I know the answer but I ask it anyway. The cacophony of drunken revelry is the same in Spain as when she called from ten miles away.

"Don't worry, Mom." I hear her inhale and exhale. I can almost see the blue smoke. "The Spanish are really a *kind* people," she says. And they have the best, *the best*, bartenders in the world."

She talks to someone I can't even imagine. Then she's back to me. "I think I'll stick around here for a couple months."

I close my eyes. I'm being too emotional, I think. She feeds on emotion. "So," I force myself to speak lightly. "Will you be okay?"

"I'm fine!" she snaps. "I *know* how to take care of myself!"

In a year—maybe five—she'll be dead of liver failure. That's how well she knows to take care of herself. I do not point out the doctor's prediction. "Of course you'll be fine," I say, "but you're alone in Spain and how much fun is that?"

She laughs. Talks to someone. There is general rumbling laughter from a wooden-floored *taverna* with bright pictures painted on the walls and tasseled hats pinned above the cash register. It looks like the Mexican restaurant where I order enchiladas or chicken fajita or the lunch special for $6.95. It looks like the postcards my husband and I sent to LeAnn when we honeymooned in Mexico and she stayed with her father, my ex-husband. That is as close to Spain as I can imagine.

"I've got to go," she mutters.

I open my eyes and see that my husband has finished eating. His back is to me and I stifle the urge to touch his neck, his collar, his still damp hair. "You can always come back home," I say. "You know you're always welcome here."

"I'll call Michael's sister. Maybe she's heard from him. I'll get things nailed down. He was mad, that's all."

Michael's sister is a junkie. Or a nun. I know nothing about Michael-the-weasel as I've only seen him once and that was under the worst of circumstances. He and LeAnn were leaving for Europe but first needed to cadge some money and say good-bye. LeAnn was going to have a final fling then die in Michael's arms. Her ashes would be scattered over the Aegean Sea. It was the plot of a very bad movie.

"So," I say, "You'll call me next week?"

"Yeah. Sure." She coughs wetly. "Sunday," she says. "I'll get the time change figured out by then. It's almost two here. Everybody's ready for a siesta."

"I love you," I say. Her half-sisters stand before me. The youngest one's mouth is thin and white with anger; the middle one's face smooth—composed—like her father's. It is 6:30 in the morning. Not a bad time to tell an oldest daughter that she, too, is loved.

"I love you, too." The line falls silent.

It is true. She does love me. More than she knew back when we all co-existed in the same space. A diagnosis of hepatitis-induced liver cancer lifted the curtain she once hid those tender emotions behind. She spoke of love. She offered hugs to her sisters.

That was in the beginning. Before she sold everything she had and left on this mad—insane—trip across Europe with Michael. The same weasel who dumped her in Spain and has, actually, little reason to return to Madrid while she makes friends with every bartender in the city.

"I'm going to be late for band," whines my youngest.

"No, you won't," I say. "You can ride with your father."

"Then I'll be early."

"So, walk." I turn to the sink and stare at the light fixture. Dust has, somehow, accumulated on the inside of the opaque glass. We all know that my youngest will not walk. It is early and it is dark. I will drive her like always.

My middle daughter says nothing. She gathers her book bag and her letterman's jacket and her life and goes silently to the car to wait for her father to take her to the private high school in which she was enrolled to keep her from emulating an older sister. My husband bends to kiss my cheek. He never knows whether I will be stiff and bristly or weepy and without bones now that my daughter, not his, has re-entered our lives. He says nothing. He simply goes to work and comes home and holds me or not as circumstances decree. I could not endure this without him. Still, sometimes I can't stand his touch.

"I hate her," my youngest says. She is twelve and in control of her life. She has friends and a father of her own and a place—first clarinet—in band. She is not at risk. Neither of my two youngest daughters are. I stare at the light fixture and am profoundly grateful for this.

"Eat your breakfast," I finally say. My voice hardly wobbles at all.

"When are you going to get back to normal?" she asks. She is still angry.

"I don't know."

I turn and draw her into the circle of my arms. Her hair is clean. It smells of apple shampoo, lemon conditioner and gel of some other fruit. "What's normal?" I ask.

"When are you going to sing and dance and be silly?"

"I thought that embarrassed you."

"It does." She snuggles closer.

I think about this. I've embarrassed each of my children. One daughter by a first husband. Two daughters by a second. I am forty-five years old with two families and it's true, I've been silly and embarrassed them equally. I've been fair in that at least.

"I don't know when I'll get back to normal," I finally say. "Soon, I hope."

"Me, too." She pulls away to look at me carefully, judging the impact of her next words. Finally she asks, "Will you French braid my hair?"

After I take her to school I run errands. I stop at the cleaners and the grocery store. I stop at the pharmacy and the video store. I pick up two videos: an animated Disney and a comedy. I engage the answering machine and pull down the blinds and check again to see that the doors are locked before I push the ON switch to the VCR.

I let the world of laughter fill my house. My right hand is clenched so tightly that my arm has begun to shake so I hold it between my knees—pressing until the jiggling stops—and keep watching. I watch all the way through both of the videos and ponder whether to watch the Disney animation again but decide I can, later, when everyone has gone to bed.

This is the way it is when a daughter is dying. It doesn't matter that she is twenty-six and has been on her own for ten years. Age does not erase the love. It doesn't matter if she is in the next room or spilling beer in Madrid. Distance does not dilute the pain.

She calls a week later. It is late afternoon.

"*Hola!*" she says. "I'm in Valencia. You wouldn't fucking believe the train system here." The music and laughter are loud.

"How are you?" I press *pause* on my printer. The monthly spreadsheets can wait. "When are you coming home?"

"Have you heard from Michael?" she slurs. The laughter is loud. A male voice rumbles something repeatedly in Spanish.

"What time is it there?" I ask.

"Almost midnight." The line crackles and she says, "I had this feeling he'd called you."

"No."

"I think I'll stay for awhile. I got a good deal on a hostel and it's almost warm. It has sheets, anyway."

The line goes dead.

She calls again, collect, within five minutes.

"I'll phone a couple times a week," she says, "on the off chance that Michael might want you to relay a message, okay?" Anyway, it seems prudent for me to keep in touch."

She has never been prudent before. Never wanted to keep in touch. Now I spend weeks answering the telephone and listening to my oldest daughter read poetry she writes in her journal. Poetry because she is dying. Poetry because it doesn't take up as much space as prose. Poetry that she composes in her mind while walking the streets of Valencia, drinking vodka mixed with orange juice and watching dark-eyed, lisping Spaniards go about their lives.

She reads to me because there is no one in the bar who understands English. She explains the poetic references. She laughs at personal jokes. I am the audience and I listen and murmur she should call again. Anytime. Sadness wells up inside me. I will never tell her the truth. I will never reveal that her poetry is not at the cutting edge of a new wave or even a ragged counter-culture.

She has lost the language skills and diamond hard wordplay. She has lost the breathtaking insights based on the turn of a phrase. She has lost the rhythm and blues and thrust of her poetry from ten years ago. This poetry stinks. It's the rambling of an alcoholic who gave too many brain cells to drink and disease.

"I love you," she says before she hangs up. The line fizzles in metallic splendor then sinks into thick, heavy silence.

"I love you, too," I say to the air.

It has been six weeks since LeAnn first called from Spain and my clothes no longer fit. Cashiers in all manner of stores compliment me on the lost weight. They want to know how I did it—what tricks of willpower and diet I used. I do not know how to answer so I tell them I work at home—which is true—and I'm expecting an important phone call. This is also true.

LeAnn calls, collect, three times a week from Valencia and Madrid and Barcelona. I come home from shopping or meetings with accountants to aborted calls on the answering machine; calls with no message. I know they are from her. Even when logic and experience recognize that at least some of them must be from clients and friends and fundraisers and brigades of commissioned telemarketers, my heart knows they are all from her, my oldest daughter.

I push away images of European hospitals and jails. I do not think of dark alleys and women who have lost their way. I plan dinner. I mix a batch of cookies and put the bowl of dough into the refrigerator to chill for an hour or two. The cookies are not for me. They are for my husband and youngest daughters who deserve a wife and mother who notices them, too.

I stand in the shower until the hot water drains from the tank then I walk, dripping, to my bedroom and curl beneath the comforter and wait until the clock says it's almost time for school to be out. I dress again. I comb my hair and wet down the parts that stick out. I turn on my computer and the light above my desk. I pre-heat the oven and shape cookies into balls or crescents or flattened moons with crisscrossed fork marks. I breathe lightly and listen for the front door to open. I strain to hear one daughter or another cry, "Mo-om, I'm home."

She, the one who will not stay on the same continent with me, no longer phones but sends postcards from Seville. From Segovia. From Cadiz. The postcards are bright with Flamenco dancers and olive orchards and the turrets of white castles set against a blue sky like sharp semi-precious stones. I read her looping scrawl and cannot make out her words. Give the girls my love. I'm almost positive that's what the circles and dips mean. They do not want her love. Only I crave it like a drug.

I have my picture taken and drive to the post office to stand in the line marked *Passports*. Angry voices echo down the long hallway as I wait for my interview. Vacationers have come with papers and money but the woman in the glass-enclosed office shakes her head. Six weeks, she says firmly to each supplicant. You should have come in sooner.

I hear the wails and I know it is true. I should have stood in this line when LeAnn was twelve or thirteen. Back when I first saw that for her there was no good solution to being brilliant and female. There was only awkwardness on one side and the attraction of the flame on the other.

When it is my turn I hand documents and certificates and neatly completed forms to the woman behind the desk. "What country?" she asks.

I stare at her.

"What country?" she repeats impatiently. "What are your travel plans?"

"I don't know. Not exactly. Maybe Greece. Or Spain."

She folds her arms and looks at the clock on the wall. She hates her job. Even I can see that.

I begin again. "My daughter is sick. She's in Spain right now but she wants to go to Greece. My husband thinks I should let her die where she wants to but she's twenty-six. She can't possibly know where she wants to die. Not really. Who will bury her? And where? This trip was a stupid idea." I'm rambling but the words keep coming; rivulets joining to become a stream, a river, a flood. "She should have stayed here. With me. But her idiot boyfriend wanted one grand tour of Europe and he couldn't take the pressure—couldn't take her constant drinking—so he left her there! *The bastard left her!*"

I am shouting and the woman across the desk has put her palms flat on the cluttered surface and pushes away as if trying to escape this awful torrent. We are like drowning shipmates. "I'm her mother," I whisper. "I have to be ready but I don't know when and I don't know where."

The woman stares at me, unblinking.

"I have to be ready," I repeat, dry-eyed. "What if she changes her mind? What if she doesn't really want to die alone?"

I leave the Post Office and drive to the park across town. I creep down the boat ramp and over the barrier of driftwood. The tide is coming in but a strip of soft gray sand remains. I sit on my folded coat, feet pointed toward the water, and knead the cold grit with frozen fingers. When the water reaches the soles of my shoes, hissing then falling away, I walk back to the car and drive home.

Two weeks later my passport arrives in the mail.

"What's this?" my husband asks. It is Saturday morning and soon we will leave for my middle daughter's basketball game.

"I'm going to Spain," I say. "Or Greece." My voice is high, like the top string on a violin.

"When?" asks my youngest. "Will you miss my concert?"

"No," I say. "I would never miss your concert."

"I have a solo," she says. "I've been working on it all year."

"You don't even know where she is," says my middle daughter. Her voice is flat and her face is smooth. Not like my husband's after all but like mine. "Nobody knows."

"I do," I say with a confidence I don't feel.

"No," my husband says firmly. "You don't know."

I see the three of them on one side and my oldest daughter on the other. I am in the middle. If any of us changes position this boat called family will capsize. I fear this more than anything. More than famine or pestilence or germ warfare.

"But I want to know." My voice is the groan of someone having an amputation without anesthesia.

"I hate her," says my youngest. "She makes you cry."

I stare at this child in wonder. I haven't cried in years. I swear it. I see that my love for LeAnn does not neutralize their hate but makes it stronger like some alchemy of water turning into fire. Love and hate gush from the same vessel. I feel a shifting tide hiss and fall away as it pulls an oldest daughter into an uncharted ocean. Her course isn't set by the compass of love and the sextant of home. It is set by the bottle. Only the bottle.

"I hate her, too," I say. "I wish I didn't but sometimes—often— I do."

The envelope with my passport lies unopened on the table. My throat is tight and my face, once stiff, dissolves into the shape of pain—the sound of weeping. It is as if ancient, rusted hinges are finally forced to yield and I don't realize what is happening until my middle daughter's face crumples to mirror my own. This is when I cry. When all hope is gone and there is no way to bring a lost love home. 📖

Corvid, Seattle, Washington, photograph by Alfredo Arreguín

Intersections

Maged Zaher

All the women I loved lived in studio apartments.
It was not the proper time to start counting
the number of Cyclops in the Greek mythology.
It was the hood, and I was whiter than necessary
which, temporarily, fucked up my minority status.

I admit: I needed intersections where God exists,
and guards the stop signs; intersections where cars
might stop indefinitely. She was in China; in her
apartment the bed could either stay a bed or turn
into a couch: That limited our supply of sexual
positions.

You have to start without memories, then, slowly,
learn to accumulate the knowledge of the
alphabet.
I dreamt of a world where the Greeks
stop loving their mothers. I admit: I am the only
hope you have.

A picture is not worth a single word. Death is
an accident. Death in an accident is accidental.
Keep your tattoo to yourself. You dream in circles
I dream in paragraphs. In her apartment she
keeps an album of each of her lovers.

In Detroit's Greyhound station the punks were
angry. I agreed to pay the ransom and the tips.
He pointed the gun to his head so I screamed:
Remember China, remember China. We were not
really there. They had to pass the pizza under
the door so we don't kill them.

In her apartment I could not look in the mirror.
The light was not enough. I had to remember him
occasionally. In the morning we turned the bed
into a couch and left forever.

Bus Tunnel, Seattle, Washington, 2013, photograph, by Toni Lee Bennett

Seattle is a Vortex

Matt Briggs

I often stumble into a new part of Seattle. The smell of freshly poured concrete and sprayed paint creates a sensation like vertigo, like standing on top of the Aurora Bridge, staring down into the ship canal, and realizing I'm standing on a shell of asphalt and concrete and steel wrapping the wind and current and muck. I might stand on a Seattle street with crowds milling around me next to a ten-story structure. Only three months ago that high-rise didn't exist. Only twenty-years ago, the previous building didn't even exist as a blueprint. A hundred and fifty years ago (a catnap in the life of most cities) Seattle didn't exist at all. The shock of Seattle's instant architecture makes me keenly aware that all this asphalt, concrete, steel is just a by-product of something else. I've run into this sensation enough now since the building spree started when I was fifteen (and maybe it was like this before?) that the sensation no longer really causes a shock but merely a sense of movement, like stepping onto a bus. On a Seattle street, I expect to hear the keen of seagulls, smell Elliott Bay brine, and have this sense of architectural vertigo. I've stumbled into new skyscrapers. I've walked along the waterfront and realized I had somehow entered a new convention center. I've spilled out of a movie theater crowd onto an oddly familiar street corner and realized I came out of a mall that stands where something else stood that I thought still existed even though I couldn't quite recall what was there before.

Seattle isn't a city like Rome or Baltimore. It's a new kind of city. It's a whirlpool, sucking old buildings down the drain. In Seattle, to lament disappearance is to lament the vital energy of the city; Seattle is an energy and not a geography.

A city's architectural geography represents, in literally concrete terms, culture. How much space do we turn over to preserving the past and keeping old idioms alive? What kind of structures do we build? How does the city manage its growth and preserve its past? I'm talking about Seattle, which I know reveals my Seattle-centricity that can drive people in Redmond crazy and really, really pisses off people in Yakima, Tacoma, Centralia, Portland, Everett, and Yelm—but I think most cities on the western side of the Cascades have similar forces moving things forward. But I can't help but seeing things through Seattle-goggles. I was born in Seattle and so Seattle is my point of reference. Compared to Baltimore, where I lived for a year, these West Coast place names aren't even recognizable as cities. Everett, Tacoma, Olympia, Portland, Seattle, and even Spokane are basically company camps with histories of rapid growth followed by economic stagnation. The business of these places is business; culture for these cities is the same as the terra-cotta ornamentation on bank buildings. The real cultural documentation of these places finds itself in corporate charters.

To locate Seattle in a sort of mass-history of disappearance, I'd like to say the nature of disappearance concerns the mass destruction and dwindling down of culture and language that has occurred since the advent of agriculture. Our milestones then would start with the 16th century, after Columbus stumbled into America and Gutenberg began using moveable type, and the Industrial Revolution, the ensuing conquest of the planet by European powers, the harnessing of electrical power and invention of the telegraph, invention of the radio, World War II, The Green Revolution, and our present post-hyphenated status where all of these big events are no longer seen as positive developments. In the 1950s, progress was good and change was good because change meant things get better and that a person didn't have to iron their clothes with a block of steel heated on their wood-burning Franklin and that they didn't have to haul water up from the crick. Now, progress isn't what it used to be. Progress is often a synonym for destruction. Change means a loss of things and often a loss we can't fathom until the thing is gone.

Seattle fits into this history as a tiny little case study of a new city in a new state-of-being on the new ocean. Maybe looking at the specifics of what has happened and is happening here can give some clues about changing culture and what is meant by cultural disappearance and loss?

The cultural shift currently underway measures along the order of the move from an oral culture to a print culture (if we look at the change as starting in the 17th century and maybe realizing itself in another hundred or two hundred years, provided we survive)—so we're talking a shift as big as pre-agriculture to post-agriculture—and in this case not back to an oral culture but a culture fused with accelerated technology and business, where literate people use both the public domain language like English and the alphabet and also patented languages like Extensible Mark-Up Language (XML); actually XML is an open-source language as is Hypertext Mark-Up Language (HTML) but both of these languages require patented technologies to use. For those of you who don't know what XML is, it is a convention to describe a mark-up language; that is, it is purely a language (as such as things are languages) to describe the code (HTML) that converts your vanilla alphabet into the stuff you see on the World Wide Web. In this sense XML is a good language for Seattle; it is a language to anticipate change in the language *and* one that requires a corporation to use.

In calculus, you have a grid system showing the map of your equation; essentially the equation is invisible. The equation describes this structure. If you go to any single point in the structure, things may seem stable and good, but then a little time passes, and things have changed a great deal. If you are aware of everything being in a state of flux, that really what you see around you is an illusion being controlled by the external properties of change, you won't be so surprised when things disappear and new things come along, when Ben Paris on Westlake is gone one day and Westlake mall is there the next. You might think I really liked the way things were back when x=19 and y=75. That was a nice time. And it is still there whenever x=19 and y=75.

Anyway, to get to the very specific items I want to look at in Seattle as a sort of way of triangulating the moving target of Seattle, I have found the following three things: banana slugs, Ben Paris, and feeder stumps.

1) Banana slugs illustrating the theme of displacement.

100 years ago, the only large native slug in the Pacific Northwest was the Banana Slug (*Ariolimax columbianus*). Since then, many species of foreign slugs have been introduced on imported European garden plants. These foreign invaders are extremely fierce. They attack weaker individuals of their own and other species, driving them out of shelters and away from food. Combat begins when the aggressor slug touches its victim with its tentacles. Then it lifts the forepart of its body off the ground and slashes down at its victim with its toothy radula.

My father lives at the base of Mount Si in a valley separated from the Snoqualmie valley floor by the North Fork of the Snoqualmie. Banana slugs thrive there. He has another house just two miles away and you can't really find them there. They've been driven into the hills like the Picts in Wales.

2) Ben Paris illustrating the theme of submergence.

A combination restaurant, lounge, pool hall, pull-tab parlor, barber shop, and sporting goods establishment, it was located on Fourth, facing the Bon Marché. A kind of "guy mall" kind of place, a bastion for fishermen (and I do mean fishermen) and other local sportsmen, it had a definite subterranean, almost speakeasy, feel to it (partly from its being down a flight of stairs, below street level). It had a large glass tank with live bass swimming in it (not a live trout pool, as I read in one account). For an account, see "America's Oldest Bass Club," an article about the Western Bass Club, which began meeting in the Ben Paris in 1938. The founder, Ben Paris, supposedly started the very first fishing derby here, back in 1931. Ben Paris also published a comprehensive Northwest fishing guide. (From *A Seattle Lexicon*, by Steve Callihan.)

Ben Paris represents something that has sort of seeped away in the Northwest, what I'd like to call the Cult of the Outdoorsmen. Somewhere in the 1980s, the Outdoorsmen disappeared and was replaced by Mountain Climbers, Bow Hunters, trail joggers, and Preservationists. REI used to supply gear to the Outdoorsmen and was more like Warshall's and Ben Paris. But REI made the decision sometime in the 1990s not to carry fishing gear. The hunters that are left are sort of ridiculous figures; the image of them are beer-swilling, meat-eating lumps looking for a place to piss in the woods. Outdoorsmen, on the other hand, put on intellectual airs ala Hemingway, researched hunting routes, and viewed the wilderness as a public resource to be managed. One of their organizations, The Trail Blazers, bombed mountain lakes with trout species, transforming formally sterile Alpine Lakes into habitats for game fish, like cutthroat, rainbow, and golden trout. The Trail Blazers were an organization of über-Outdoorsmen. Here is evidence, I think, of the disappearance of this entire subculture. A contemporary reaction to the activity of The Trail Blazers is: "Say what? You dropped a *ton* of foreign biomass into a pristine lake, forever obliterating its fragile ecological balance?" A Trail Blazer believes he has made something that wasn't there before. A Preservationist believes the Trail Blazer has destroyed something that was already there.

3) Feeder Stumps illustrating the theme of superimposition.

Throughout the forest where I grew up, huge feeder stumps rose almost to the height of the house I lived in. They were covered with moss, and huckleberries grew like hair from their scalps. Many of them were hollow and I would climb up on them and lower myself into their cavernous insides, smelling the ancient root wood of cedar and wait for my father or my brother to pass. I could hear them walking through the woods for a long way off. Sticks cracked. Bushes rattled like ghost chains. The forest wasn't quiet. The tall trees always made noise as they rubbed against the other trees and their whole length shifted back and forth in the wind. Birds called to each other. Woodpeckers tapped at rotting trees. But it was still quiet enough to hear people walking. And these stumps were there because they grew there. They weren't planted. They weren't landscape designed. They fell into a bed of shady moss and slowly grew up, in a crush of competing seedlings, and one of them won out centuries ago, this tree that is now a decaying stump that'll be in somebody's backyard if a good landscape engineer gets his hands on this suburb, or otherwise it'll be chipped and sent off to cushion the fall of children from swings. I grew up with a sense that there had been something here before that was a forest of gigantic, silent trees. I also had a repeated daydream nightmare of walking under the cedar trees and then coming out into a street with old sidewalks and walking into a used TV store with a big, sign hanging out over the sidewalk that said ZENITH, right next door to a 7-11, knowing that one day the second growth in Fall City would look just like Capitol Hill. 📖

Into the Hills

An homage to the film, Life and Nothing More

Taha Ebrahimi

"Yes sir, this road goes to Poshteh. The bridge was covered with boulders after the earthquake. But now they are gone.

The bridge has been clear since this morning. This road will go to Poshteh. Follow it up. Up, into those hills. And as you get to the top of that hill . . . that one . . . you see? The one where the two women wearing pink *chadors* are? As you get to the top of that hill you will see Poshteh. But the road is rough, sir. This car you are driving won't make it. It is steep and there is no gravel and your car is not strong enough."

"This car has come 400 kilometers from Tehran. It will have to make it up those hills."

"Sir, this road is steep and there is no gravel and your car is not strong enough." The man let the heavy tube of carpet fall to the ground, dusty-wet, unrolling worn-woven colors.

"Yesterday, I drove this car up to Manjeel. Then the guards told me to turn around because the road was only for emergency earthquake vehicles. The road was blocked for miles. I drove all the way back to Tehran. Today, I took the paved road as far as Manjeel, then I took a dirt road that went through a valley, and then up a hill, and then through Koker. And now this car will take me up those hills, to Poshteh."

"Sir, the road is rough. . . ."

"Do not waste your breath, sir. Do you need a lift? Your carpet is heavy and if you are going to Poshteh too, it will be hard. Here . . . put this carpet on top of my car. I have wires in the back. We will fasten it and it will not fall off. I will take you to Poshteh."

"Thank you. I like walking."

"Please, come. Your carpet is heavy and it is wet."

"No. Truly. I like to walk. I survived the earthquake. Surely I will survive a walk."

"*Inshallah.* How long will it take to reach Poshteh from here?"

He wiped the sweat away from his eyes, off his tanned, stubbly face. "Maybe an hour and forty minutes with car. Four hours by foot."

"Thank you." And the yellow Renault rolled ahead.

It was hot, and the road rippled in the windshield, and his glasses kept sliding down his nose, and all the windows in the car were rolled down, but only thick, hot air came in. The sweat-sun sat high and bright and swelled sorely like a tired beast who's forgotten how to breathe. The fact that all these years she had been happy, sending him scrawled notes, living in these filthy hills, shook him.

And the road was rough.

There were pebbles and rocks and the Renault was light and almost tipped over. Sometimes, the dirt road drowned in mountain brush as the car raked through thick grass, and desert weed, and prickly purple thistle. All this made the trip longer, and he wished the radio worked. Heavy-pregnant trees revealed the silver under-sides of their leaves in the warm road-gusts. The car was layered in road-dust and there were smashed insects all over the headlights. But the good car kept going.

His sister's family did not own a phone and the only way to find out if they were still alive was to drive there. He wondered how he had lived in Poshteh all those years without a telephone. All those years, and he could not even remember the road or the land now. They had to be alive, or else all these years spent in the city, where he'd been ridiculed for being from the country, were for nothing. They had to be alive, or else being a doctor wasn't worth it. Certainly, they were alive. But if he had been sure, he would not have been driving now, the road stretched out ahead, like a dirty memory pulling him back.

The road bent up the side of the hill, then it turned into a switch-back trail, back and forth, up the side of the hill; back and forth up the side of the hill; back and forth up the side of the hill.

He passed a woman with cloth wrapped around her head, a dirty face, and holding a child. He passed a man with his wife, holding a toilet ceramic (a precious stone of cool cold blue). He passed an old man with no shoes, leading a black cow with a few gray spots.

Below the hill was the paved highway that he had left over an hour ago—snakes of trucks stuck for miles. Carrying army-issue green-nylon tents and crates of tomatoes that would not be enough, even though half a million were dead. One truck carried an antenna: an antenna so that the living could watch the soccer match (Brazil vs. Scotland). It would be a small TV with gray fuzz, but it would be a good TV and the whole village could see the game. In his home, in Tehran, he owned a large color television that he never had time to watch.

The road turned away from the highway. He stopped the car at a bank. He peeled himself out, and stumbled down the stony ravine. There were trees. Skinny trees with shallow roots. Larger trees grew by the stream. He looked at the stream. Then he looked up at the top of the bank, at his yellow car, and then walked towards the stream. Down by the trees, the air was cooler and moist and easier to breathe. He stepped out on the soft rocks to the center of the stream and he hunched over and cupped his hands in the cool-running water. He splashed his face and blew his nose and washed his glasses. He shook his face and wiped it off with his wet hands and when he opened his eyes, he saw a boy.

"Sir, you shouldn't drink that water. The earthquake split the cow pasture and the cows have been coming here now. They piss in that water. You shouldn't drink it," the boy blinked.

"I didn't drink the water. I was washing my face. That is my car . . . the yellow Renault up there. I am on my way to Poshteh. Do you know how much further"?

"No. I'm from Koker."

"You don't know how much to Poshteh?"

"It is up this hill."

"This I know. Do you know how much time left to get to Poshteh?

"No."

The man dried his glasses on his shirt and put them on his face. "What are you doing here?"

"Me and my parents live over there for now, where that plastic is, by the red tree."

"Plastic?"

"Yes, my father had some plastic. The earthquake destroyed our house and we use sticks to hold the plastic up."

"Tell me . . . how did you come to live?"

"I was sleeping in the house with my brother, and my parents were sleeping outside. But I couldn't fall asleep. There were too many mosquitoes. They were biting me and buzzing in my ears. I kept turning and trying to ignore them, but I couldn't, so I went outside, to sleep with my parents and . . ."

"That is when the earthquake happened?"

"Yes. The roof of our house came down."

"And your brother was caught?"

"We tried to get him out, but he was dead. The roof was too heavy. But we saved a tea kettle and some bags of rice."

"So I suppose we can say that the mosquitoes saved your life?"

"That is what my father says, but my mother gets angry. She says 'Then why didn't they like the taste of Reza? Why did they let Reza sleep?'"

"At least you and your parents are okay. You are sure this road goes to Poshteh?"

"I am sure."

When the man returned to his car and tried to start it, it chugged and groaned and coughed and his heart sank: scared. He got out and went back down to the stream and filled an empty Coca-Cola bottle with water and climbed back up and opened the hood of the Renault and poured water onto the engine. He waited while his car sizzled and steamed. But when he turned the ignition this time the engine caught and he breathed again.

And the yellow Renault rolled ahead.

The land was more barren now. Fewer trees. The road stopped switching back and forth, and instead, went down a rise, then straight ahead, and then up again, between purple grass.

The car moved down the road easily and rolled on the level part well. The road was bumpy and it was getting late. The road was straight for a long time and there were no landmarks, and this too made him uneasy, and it seemed he would never get to the top of the hill. The car went slowly, each turn of the thin rubber tires a strain. He worried about the engine and about the car stopping again. He passed many who looked like they might need rides. The seats in his car were empty, but he could not stop or the engine might die. In his solitude, he cursed his stupid sister for staying in Poshteh, for not coming with him when he came back to take them all away from this ignorant-backwardness and poverty.

The road became steeper. It climbed straight up an incline, to a landing where there was a rock wall. At the landing, the road turned 90 degrees and turned up another steep incline, then switched back and rode above the rock wall that would lead over the cleft where the women wearing pink *chadors* had been. Cicadas screamed and the green-fever bushes seemed to shake like nervous onlookers. Dust-colored birds hopped from shrub to shrub and disappeared in the background.

The car moved slowly up the first incline. Then it slowed and the engine cut halfway up the first steep pass. The car begin rolling down the hill. He turned the key, but it did not catch. He turned the key again and cursed, and this time the engine caught and it sputtered and the car blew dust out its rear and the yellow Renault kept plodding up the hill. Up the hill, past the point where the engine had given out before, and further, until it reached the landing where the rock wall stood and where the road turned 90 degrees.

The car wheezed and gasped for air on the landing and they were so close to Poshteh that they would have to make it up the next incline, above the rock wall, and over the cleft. The Renault laboriously lugged up the way. Rocks and pebbles pelted down and the man was sweating even though the sun was going down and it was much cooler.

Six feet from the next landing, the car coughed again. Not enough power. Not enough traction. The car was not used to this. And the engine stopped and the car slid. Slid back. He turned the ignition and it did not catch and the car kept rolling back. He turned the ignition again and this time the engine yawned awake, spit rocks behind its wheels and climbed, almost to the point it had reached before it had slipped the first time. Then the engine stopped and the Renault rolled back again.

He turned the ignition, but it did not catch. It did not catch. It did not catch. And the car rolled backwards. And it did not catch. And his heart pounded through his shirt and the steering wheel was slimy under his hands. And the car rolled back faster, until it slowed down at the bottom of the incline and finally stopped at the landing.

He got out of the car. He was wet with perspiration, and he was panting. It was getting dark and the heat was slipping away. His car was silent and tired. He reached inside for his jacket and he put it on and put his hands in his pockets. He looked around. He looked at the dusty incline, still billowing with his car's attempts at climbing and raising dirt. He dug his hands deeper into his pockets. The mosquitoes were coming out and hanging in busy-black clouds. He looked at the bushes. The cicadas were getting quieter. Grasshoppers were rubbing wings now. He watched the dusty-colored birds hop from bush to bush. He looked up at the rock wall that was growing shadow dusk-dark. He was remembering that once this was how it had always been—hard and real.

He shook his head, no. Yes, he would drive home now and maybe make it back to Tehran before his wife put the dinner food away. He would tell his wife and his parents the truth, "The car couldn't make it. The hills were too steep." Yes, the country is backwards and he had no idea why she stayed on.

He got into the car and turned the ignition. It would not catch. He tried a few more times, cursed, then prayed; lonely. Then, up the incline a man came, hunched with the weight of what he was carrying: a heavy metal oil can for a gas stove. He was sweating, but seeing the trouble that the car was having, he slung it off his back and went to the back of the yellow Renault. The man with the oil can pushed and leaned against the bumper, while the other man sat in the car and kept forcing the ignition, until the car started rolling, and the engine caught. The small car went down the incline, away over the lip, giving up back towards the city, and was gone.

The man with the oil can watched the car go, then he wiped his hands on his pants and went to his oil can and slung it on his back again. He bent over with the weight and hiked up the incline. Sometimes his feet slipped under him, but his knee would brace the fall and he'd get back up and continue. He breathed hard and the oil can was round and awkward, but he made it up the incline and began the trek over the rock wall. His back ached and his arms were tired.

Then he heard dirt being ground and crunched behind him, and he looked and he saw the yellow Renault coming back up the incline: it had come back and it labored past the man with the oil can and stopped a few feet ahead.

"Do you need a ride? Hurry in, or the engine may stop."

The man slung the heavy oil can on the rack above the car and climbed in.

"Are you on your way to the Poshteh hills?" The man in the yellow Renault asked.

"Yes, sir."

"Is it much longer to get there?"

"No. No, not much longer at all." He paused and then awhile later, "It did not look like your car could make it up these steep hills."

"I decided to try one more time and this time the car changed its mind."

"Then it is lucky for me that you tried," the man laughed.

The Renault gripped the rocky ledge and slowly crept on.

"How are you, if I may ask, sir?"

"I have lost my house and my family, but this oil can is not too heavy."

And they continued on, up and away, into the hills. 📖

This is Not the Last
Poem about Pears

Martha Silano

and certainly not the first,
but I'm not talking
about D'Anjous, Comices,
Boscs, the ones you find
at a Safeway or a Food Lion
while under Muzak's spell,
pears which are sometimes sweet
like a kiss on the lips after many kisses
on the cheek, but more often not—
are like gnawing on the branch of a willow.
No. I'm talking about a pear from a tree
in your own yard, where rain, sun, and wind,
the occasional, inadvertent stumble
of a spider or an ant are all that has touched it.
And, at the very beginning, the petals,
on a rainy, or sunny, or windy day
which fall all at once like laundry
fresh from the spinning wash.
When they fall they leave behind
hundreds of parasols not unlike
the ones you saw as you gazed into pond water
under a microscope. Over the summer,
whether you notice or not,
they swell to miniature blowfish
but your father, each time you ask,
not yet, so while rodents, bees, birds, worms . . .

you wait till he pulls in the drive and,
instead of heading straight for a nap,
joins you, picks one up—his tired body holding
the scent of machinery overworked—
looks it over, points to the one place not
worm-riddled, squirrel-gnawed,
hornet-bored, grackle-pecked:
Here, try that. It could've been mealy.
You could have swallowed
thorax, stinger, rotting flesh.
Instead your mouth is honored,
in a single bite, by a tiny planet
sweetened by a father's
immeasurable sacrifice.

Decade, Tape Transfer Collage, 2020, by Mark Sullo

Climate & Currency

An excerpt

Michael Daley

I was working in Boston as a laborer most of the summer, but I lost that job by admitting my lifelong fear of heights while atop a four-story ladder unable to let go long enough to move a paint brush over brownstone window trim. I got another job soon, working in the hottest days for a young contractor overburdened with clients. When I arrived Friday of the third week, no one was there. All week the crew had bet against Karl making payroll. On Tuesday they told me to look out the window onto the docks of Boston Harbor: a big guy with long hair was hooking my precious little Saab beater to his tow truck. By the time he climbed into his cab, I had the chain off my front bumper and shot away. That was the car I'd rebuilt from tattered Xeroxed manuals intending to drive it back to Washington. So that was a bad day; I should have recognized the signs. On Wednesday, he laid off the secretary, by Thursday the crew was tense.

But on Friday, faithful as ever, I was mixing paint, cleaning rollers, putting on overalls. By noon still alone, I sat eating lunch as a man in a black business suit entered the room. "Wet Paint," I said through a mouthful of peanut butter. He set his sparkling leather briefcase on the plastic tarp over the kitchen counter and asked for Karl. His Boston accent, the rich and flagrant "a" of "Kahl," of all my youthful vowels the most sincere, reminded me how I'd replaced it with that harsh Western "ar," our ubiquitous standard. He began telling me, and I couldn't gather why, that Karl was deeply in debt, had backed out of contracts, was being sued for everything he and his family owned.

I continued eating till the man left, closed the paint cans tightly, and went home.

When I arrived at Karl's house that night, the neighbor across the street stepped onto his porch, holding paycheck envelopes Karl, who'd gone into hiding, paid him to distribute. Mine was attached to a note, "Mike, this is all I have now, the rest next week. I sorry." I sorry? Fifty dollars, and he owed me three hundred. I staked out his house for a week, leaving conciliatory notes and my mother's phone number. One night, voice muffled like a man in a dark closet, he said he'd hire me for this really big job.

Long story short, I worked for Karl that winter and spring remodeling an old brick building in downtown Boston. He hired one or two friends he hadn't screwed yet, from the old neighborhood. He paid what he owed me in installments as we gutted and framed; at lunch we watched dust float out the door and onto the shoulders of accountants and their secretaries. He said he called me, not the rest of the crew, because I left the note. A note would have never occurred to those boys who hadn't shown up Friday. I thought I knew them. Their accents and Karl's were from my own neighborhood, but I had moved away long ago, and self-conscious of being tagged by my voice, I emulated sharper, more unassuming enunciations. I knew too that because I was a stranger, and no longer native, I could suggest there was a right thing to do without making a threat. Natives of a place may expect more or give in to outrage when politicians or fellow citizens commit wrong. The outsider assumes through a universal principle that change should occur, but the native, affronted by negative behavior, accepts his losses, vows revenge, or throws up his hands and looks for work elsewhere.

The root of "native," and "nature," *natura* in Latin, comes up from the ground. Like native products we nailed together from Maine, Vermont, and Quebec forests, these boys came from a climate either the cause or the effect of granite hills, brittle sun, deciduously quilted sidewalks, clipped verbs, and blunt manners. They knew the language of payback. I never found out how they approached him, or how Karl paid them off, but some currency must have changed hands. They knew his parents after all, they'd recognize his car. One phone call and they'd have shown up on our downtown site to haul away tools or break windows. Come to think of it, he might have given them his car. Why else was I called into service as driver every morning? Sometimes his girl-friend squeezed in, the recently laid-off secretary spilling coffee and smoking through the crawl of traffic to an office near a tunnel.

Once, after I had gotten Karl to hire my good friends, Tim McNulty and Chuck Easton, the Saab broke down on the Southeast Expressway. Tim and I were pulled over, the hood up, staring down at the engine, when a steaming old Chrysler rattled in behind us. The driver and passenger, burly guys in shabby parkas, stared under the hood with us for a minute, commiserating but not ready to offer a lift. Then, after they'd already said goodbye and good luck, they were sorry, but they were almost out of gas, and could they hit us up for a couple bucks?

Currency is why we have jobs. Yet so much of it goes toward getting there, not to mention investments in consumables to contain the restless spirit. Currency is the roll we pull out, the rock that translates the weather, renders it into milled planks, and labors toward local prizes. In an interdependent world the fair exchange is an offline elite of supply, demand, and trust. When Europeans discovered interdependent native communities among inhabitants of the New World, they created dentalia factories to subvert the economy. Dentalia shells, already in use in trade between tribes, became inflated and were superseded by the coin of the realm.

Some transactions require the buyer to decide a thing's worth, a gamble if he was outside of the "current," so to speak; the seller must choose among strangers' offerings—which stone, or tree bark, pelt, shell, fish is worth which commodity. Europeans witnessed this. The white trader who dealt in blankets and alcohol, guns and gingham, even the humiliation of hats and uniforms after the buffalo was removed, had to value and determine barter, and had to know his customer. He had to know he supplied only what natives needed to live with whites who wanted them gone, to supply commodities and teach consumerism; supply and demand led to replacement currencies in the pacification of the West.

When Karl found out I wrote poetry, he mocked me for such a low-paying art form as I waited for him to buy Lotto tickets. He forgot the remark, avidly scraping metallic dust with a dirty fingernail to reveal a three-dollar winning number. I watched him slip the card into his wallet and smile about his lucky streak. "I won ten dollars yesterday." He didn't redeem Lotto winnings and had a stash of silver cards. Maybe little cards saved in wallets, or glove compartments, cupboards or libraries as tacky bookmarks, will be valuable not for their redemptive qualities, but for their colors, or numbers, or as symbols of exchange in some *Mad Max* post-apocalypse or *Lord of the Flies* island.

Karl was too cagey to have gone to war. Had the draft been instituted when he turned eighteen, he'd have managed to keep from seeing service. He was a young man who wanted to make money, and war would have been too distracting. Those young men of his first crew, though, would have been cannon fodder. Too young for Vietnam and too old when the Gulf War came along, what they did when not in Karl's fruitless employ involved petty theft and brawling. They would have lived their entire lives outside Boston in Dorchester or Southie. Through family pressures and lack of foresight, they would breed. There would be one currency, and they would slave to amass as much as their wives, or the courts demanded.

When Karl mocked notoriously ill-paid poets, he spoke for them too. He spoke from his neighborhood, two little antagonistic communities, Dorchester and Southie, where my parents were born, where I was native, where I learned what they had learned: poetry is not for men. Having left their birthplaces, to the extent anyone is capable, some poets find in striving to perfect their native dialects a currency to spend perhaps in bars and on certain streets in rain and wind where those who pass would themselves give up all their wealth for a chance to declaim. Maybe it was the same with migrating people who performed stories and songs to keep alive what they were leaving. But Karl's crew, no. Whatever they were leaving was the same as where they were going. Currency didn't change because risk didn't. What makes poetry and language akin to currency is that someone risks offering it, risks rejection. What we bring from our native places may be valued, not for how like it is to the familiar poetics and the local ear, but how new, and with what courage it must be brought forth. It is a kind of war, this contest in the arena of public art. We become self-conscious, but we affirm that consciousness is not delusion, and we are not mad. We compete with ourselves and others to be different or alike. Currency as language gives away our influences, origins, and predecessors. For stamps of approval from peers and strangers, we knock off formal poems keeping in notes our more dangerous opinions of the world.

When North American tribes interacted, they created currency. When they left native soil, following a herd, crop depletion, or a change of weather, the means of exchange may have been gifts. Yet the Northwest potlatch, for instance, wasn't always enjoyable gift-giving. The competition at potlatches defined the greatest personal and tribal wealth by the most abundant giving. The belief that one could gather more from the surroundings than anyone else led to sometimes deadly contests. Native peoples, after the creation of the New World, failed initially as economic entities because they did not anticipate how through cupidity, one could take what was already free by calling it property. The potlatch exemplified wealth consciousness before wealth eroded. The replacement value of goods offered by white societies created an untenable materialism when a resource like buffalo still flourished and the hunt gave communities strength. Other currencies arose as Native Americans were pushed farther away from lands they were used to. Just as Europeans brought more than they needed to survive, and could bestow what they considered trinkets, so tribes pushing into new territories brought products of their native climates, prized far away because they fit in the palm of a hand and enlarged the world. Much as Odysseus, bearing an object on his shoulder, walked inland till someone asked, "is that a tool for winnowing?" "An oar," he said and began work on the altar and the slaughter of bulls far from an ocean that had until then been unimagined.

Born of plenty, currency represents precious, rare, and distant climates. Yet Incas valued gold for aesthetic reasons and abundance and had no need to trade until Hernán Cortés recognized it as the foundation of wealth and established the currency of New Spain. Gold from Incan gift exchange and ornaments in blood sacrifice enabled the establishment of a European division of wealth and labor and was worth the destruction of a race. The entire history of the subversion of native economies in the New World took place before what Albert Camus calls the advent of modern times, 1789. The French Revolution began the "history of nations," and ended the history of Divine Right. The will of God, through the infallible conduits of the rulers of Europe, commanded that native races on this continent be subjugated or eliminated, and the societal structure of Europe emulated. The plan to subvert native economies wasn't difficult to implement; Cortez could have used it had bloodshed not been his mission. Prior to his arrival, the Incas may have traveled and used gold as currency, but such occasions would have been rare.

Crossing The Sea of Cortés

The Sea of Cortés lifts and rolls,
the body of a whale rides thousands
of swells. Moon touches the horizon,
and we, on the M. M. Puerto V.,
we ride these wastes.
Lovers on deck walk like us.
They steal into shadow.
We stand at the rail.
A star is on the Sea of Cortés.
We watch it race,
the sudden prey of sharks upon the waves,
until we see it is a hand, palm up,
lying on a swell. It drifts
into the foam, until we see it is a face.
We turn so quickly from the rail
the lovers lift their eyes.
We turn back, and watch it float,
eyes shut, folded in moon.
We make ourselves leave the rail.
The lovers walk before us
to find a place to lie.
Cortés, long ago, was a god returning,
his hair prophecy's last detail.

Moctezuma sent a legion of his best.
Hernán Cortés returned each man's right hand.
Now only moon shatters the swells.
The heart of a young man is a thin reed pipe.
In two years he destroyed the Aztecs.
Tonight families lie on blankets
on the floor of the salon.
Why have I come here?
To see a man and woman
roll and fall into one another,
his hand on her hip?
The morning sun
counts dimes
on their spines.
In waves the light
is a bird, great Condor,
splashing where the lost
map floats.

My mother on the beach stoops to fill one plastic bag after another with beach glass of all colors and holds up each to the sun. She keeps them in a special place on a high windowsill. She can never use them. She can't go anywhere and hand them over for a loaf of bread or a carton of milk. She keeps them for their beauty and abundance, these discards of the sea. California's black market on abalone shells became so inflated that heaps of the shells were hauled away from front yards in coastal towns. A man named Charlie told me he filled his truck at the dump. Traveling east, he spent them on the Hopi reservation for breakfast, groceries, and gasoline. They loved it and took all he had; he got everything he needed to keep going. The eagle feather fastened to a tipi pole stuck out flat and broad as a shelf. I sat there late one night, smoke flying up the smoke hole. One swallow flew in and alighted quietly beside another; they stayed that way all night. In our tenuous ecological balance, to gather wealth from the land is against the law; national parks and beaches prohibit taking rocks, moss, plants, or disturbing wilderness habitat. Yet climate creates currency. Stones, shells, eagle feathers, woodpecker scalps the Sioux used, are nurtured by ageless climate, the current of air, fire, wind. I approach a man and woman on stools in a Seattle bar. Near closing time, I'm drunk, almost broke, my unemployment check used up. I know the man, a famous poet, but not the woman. He will not mention her to his wife tomorrow. Taking both in with a sweeping gesture in my oil-stained Army field jacket, I say, "What I really want to know," clumsily yanking my hand out of the jacket pocket, "is why I can't spend this stuff." In that dark city the three of us stare down sadly, resigned to the way things are, at the curled and hollow shapes, a handful of broken shells, shining twisted glass, a smear of white sand along my fingers. 📖

From the streets at dawn

Koon Woon

street corners look-see boys
telescope the streets and alleys
and the exhausted, spent cooks emerge
from the Great Celestial Club
with another necessary hope
echoes of mahjong tiles still banging
their brains

Guangzhou is so far away
a place without winter
three crops of rice a year
the muddy rivers
the Pearl River,
a grown son waiting,
and on the banks of rice paddies
lychee trees burdened with ripe,
unpicked fruit

A phone call at 49 cents a minute
connects the South China monsoons
with the Seattle Chinatown's
Maynard Street,
if you should be praised in Beijing
or romanced in Guilin,
still you want to eat the freshest seafood
of Guangzhou

Connected to these streets
a couple of blocks away
me in my room begin my day
with Pepsi or jasmine tea
and mourn the Kingdome's coming
doom

the red cranes out in the bay
grain elevators filling up hulls of ships
and summers without malice
the noise seems to surround the city
without a shot being fired

When 6 a.m. promises a sun
and Maxan's deli preparing charsiu buns
crane by crane
north of Safeco Field
portray an immense baseball game
but if you look at the edge of Chinatown
at Dearborn,
the immigration and naturalization compound
betrays the former architecture and use—
a federal prison, this, at the edge
of Chinatown.

X

Volume 10, Number 2, 2002
Law, Justice, Freedom

Acquisition, original collage by Mark Sullo

Double Take

Larry Laurence

Let's say you were a painter, an impressionest, and woke up one day to find Cubism invented, was in fact the leading edge, was where the juice was (apparently you slept through Fauvism). Yes, you'd been growing weary of Impressionism and had wondered privately how so many artists could see the world the same way. Had even for the last few years changed your palette and intensity of color. Chosen subjects others shied away from. You'd been painting twenty years, had never painted better, were even getting some small recognition. And you wake up to a changed world. And though you'd like to argue that the picture plane remains the picture plane and the vanishing point remains the vanishing point and always will, you have such a strong intuition that the change is not only inevitable but needed, you don't say anything. You are suddenly a beginner again. And despite the insecurity inherent in beginnings, you feel a great deal of energy. You pick up your brushes. . . .

Although I'm poking fun at myself a bit, the above is not far from my situation. If I had been asked even twelve months ago to contribute to this column I'd have been more sure of myself—I knew what a poem was and how to write one. Now, I don't know. I grew up (poetically) in Fresno, California under the mentorship of Philip Levine and Peter Everwine. We wrote first person lyric/narratives, testimonials, stories in linear time (I'm thinking of two book titles—neither from Fresno poets—*The Adventures Of The Letter i* by Louis Simpson, and *Letters To An Imaginary Friend* by Tom McGrath, which might well describe our writing). There were excesses of course: the poet as hero, victim, doomed seer; bathos at turning thirty or being dumped. But there were successes as well. Many fine poems and many fine poets. The best work was accessible, passionately democratic, musical, energetic, and well constructed and well seen. "No ideas but in things"—we were far from academic. I don't believe any Fresno poet could be accused of being scholarly. I don't believe any of us would hole up a year in a university's special collections (even if such were available in Fresno) researching some iconic personage to eventually emerge with a book-length biography in verse. Clearly the most dazzling poet was Larry Levis. His last (sadly, posthumous) book, *Elegies*, has everything I ever wanted in poems. Perhaps the book is an elegy for the first person lyric/ narrative. Or at least the way the form (mode is probably a better word as it has been used in many different streams of poetry) has been used for so many years in America.

Levine or Everwine (I don't remember) was fond of saying we, each of us, only write one poem throughout our life. It was said a bit facetiously of course. I think we may, if we're lucky, write two or three or even several poems in a lifetime. We may be able to write more than one way as well. So for now I'm junking the way I used to write. I'm reading widely (even an old enemy, John Ashbury) and looking at what others are doing. Ideas still come to me in first person, but I'm translating, in a way, these ideas into something else. It's too early for me to tell where I'll end up.

I thought, dear reader, I'd test your patience and present two versions of an idea, a germ of a poem, to show you what I'm doing. I call them "Take One" and "Take Two." They both have working titles. They are drafts; "Take One" was done before I woke up to changes happening in poetry now. "Take Two" is an attempt to remove myself as a character in the poem. Neither I consider finished or satisfying to me yet. I don't consider "Take Two" in any way revolutionary, but it is different for me and, curiously, seemed to demand a different sort of music.

Take One (One Theory On What Happens After Death)

What are you doing here? I hear myself asking myself
though the voice is my mother's, may she rest in peace,
no, the voice is my sister's. I'm on the gym's second floor
on my way up from the weight room to the aerobics room,
I'm standing at the window, my weight on my right foot,
my forehead against glass looking out at the canal—

How wonderful to live where canals are—
and my body loves me, so easily fooled: a few stretches,
a hamstring curl and then *Yes! I knew it! I knew
you loved me. I knew last night didn't mean a thing.*

The canal is deep green but there's yellow in it and black
where the poplars' shadows fall on its smooth surface,
poplars from the early 1900s when the canal
was dug by immigrants helped by mules
till a spur was finished at last to the rail yard,
saving the mules much grief—Two laborers die
and poplars are set down into holes as a gesture
to a governor's wife. Records do not mention if she was pleased.
How could she not be—They're nearly bare now
and it's nearly dusk. Cormorants are roosting in them
and more are coming, arriving at treetop, choosing
one tree (How do cormorants choose), dropping 20 or 30 feet
then climbing abruptly to a stall and, wings flapping
rapidly, settling on branches so slim a branch will bend
almost in two before springing up. If another bird's
too close, more wing-flapping, and the newcomer
rises, banks, and begins the approach
again. The other adjusts itself, the branch gradually stills.
The interaction is not friendly (Had the one been dreaming),
it is rough and ill-tempered and unfriendly
but it is not hostile. Please it is not hostile.

Take Two (I Am Afraid To Die And Will Miss My Life Terribly)

How wonderful to live where canals are

    deep green though there's yellow in it & slate
    black where the poplars' shadows fall on the smooth surfaces

    production of immigrants helped by mules
    until at last a spur to the rail yard saving the mules
    much grief—two laborers die & poplars are set down

into holes as a gesture to a governor's wife

How wonderful to live where poplars are

nearly bare now & nearly dusk

roosts for cormorants with more coming
arriving at treetop to choose one tree (How do cormorants
choose) dropping then climbing abruptly to a stall
to land on branches so slim a branch will bend almost in two
before springing up

How wonderful to live where cormorants are

dead still at dusk Dead still unless another settles
too close then more wing-flapping & the newcomer
rises banks begins again the approach

unfriendly at the beginning of evening (Had the one
been dreaming) rough & ill-tempered & not friendly
but not hostile Please not hostile

How wonderful to live where canals are 📖

Stone Gardens

Diane Westergaard

Bouquets of peonies swell against granite,
wine stains in this vineyard of memory.
The flagpole exerts a centripetal strength.
It is dedicated to a man whose death
was so close to the end,
it was not announced until the war was over.
A man, who grew up across the street,
tells me he has never come here to walk among
the unsettled whispers of his ancestors.

Three brothers, whose parents locked them
out of the house, line up like the three figures
who cannot see, hear, or speak evil.
One died in an accident, one of diabetes,
and the third hung himself after burning
a barn where prize horses screamed
until silenced by heat and smoke.

I thought I had forgotten
who drank too much,
who bled to death after an illegal abortion,
who gave me candy when visiting their houses.
The flat stones of the Indians
rest darkly at the edge of the laurel.

In a dream I travel to a friend's house,
look out the window to the cemetery next door.
Headstones rise, shadows in the gray light
of a cloudy day, transform into statues,
statues of saints I don't recognize.

Something moves, comes into focus
so clear I want to speak with them:
the three Magi. They laugh,
the closest wears a red silk robe
embroidered in gold.

P/V

Danny Romero

One

I live in a barrio
in my head never very
far from a taco truck
on the corner of Florence
and Holmes Avenues

It makes no difference
if I stroll down Rodeo
Drive the surrounding
opulence worlds away
from el remate on Saturday
afternoon where families
with five or six or seven
children each sweat for
the ninety-nine cent
bargains and afterwards
una raspada de limón

Still I live
in a barrio in my
head never very far
from my mother's
tortillas hot off the
fire and the little
ones she made especially
for me when I was
just a boy

Most every meal in my
house now comes wrapped
en harina o maíz warm
as memories and as good
as life can get (it seems
just about at times)

I will never forget
houses too small for
families too large
enchiladas de queso
on Fridays during Lent
comida made with love
and kindness in my
grandfather's kitchen
nor the smell of crude
oil in the Wilmington air

Two

I left Los Angeles in a
flurry of rifle shots
from a passing car
18 years old and high
on Angel Dust I followed
those railroad tracks
into the world ready
for life or death

I will never forget
Sunday morning drunks
Mexican men on horseback

galloping through the
back alleys of our
lives I can still hear
KGFJ radio from the
heart of Watts Angeles
pinche chota chase me
home at night stop
me search me "to
protect and serve"

So I live in a barrio
in my head always just
an arm's length from
jail it makes no
difference if I walk
across Independence Mall
these stolen streets still
stained with blood of
slave and Indian before
me I hear the air still
filled with their screams

Murals of La Virgen swirl
'round this barrio in my
head not Capitol Hill
those seats of power so
far from my reach standing
at this end of a long and
unyielding American night

Voting for the First Time

James R. Lee

The line snakes
then loops for miles—
Old men walking with canes,
women wearing rags tied around their heads,
some carrying babies on their backs.
Young men dressed in short pants,
feet bare like the red earth.

They all wait in silence
while democracy comes step by step.
It walks slowly from Robben Island,
rides the train from Soweto,
from Cape Town.

Three Greek Women, Matala, Greece, 2001, drawing by Nancy D. Donnelly

Geoglossa, Listening to Greece

Mark Sargent

The earth speaks many tongues, most of which are indecipherable, but there is a sound in *this* land on the planet where the meeting of sky and earth is clean and sharp. We recognize the sound, it is deeply familiar. We know the cadences in our blood, but more than that, there is an identification at the level of consciousness, where you forge your tools in the fires of culture. And the reason for this is: *The Greek landscape speaks a human language.*

There are several factors at work here. Dimension: there is an accessibility to the land, you can touch it with the eye's hand and feel its texture. It's not just size, for here *can* be big. I am sitting in a village some 1400 feet above sea level. Directly above the village is the Taygetos range that varies from 6,000 to 8,000 feet in elevation. When I say above I mean it is a very steep ascent; perhaps a mile away is an elevation of 7,000 feet. Across the valley is the Parnonas mountain range which is nearly as high as the Taygetos. I can see all of this from the house as well as the Byzantine castle of Mystras which lies a couple of miles south; some claim that on certain clear days you can see the sea twenty-five miles to the south, but at that distance, who can tell from the sea and sky. And so, although you never get the sense of immense size that the American West can give you, you can still get big, panoramic; as opposed to a place such as England, for instance, which is heavily peopled and difficult to get a big view of.

But back to the eye's hand and how it (and what it) touches. It is difficult to speak with an originality about this country—it has been described so many thousands of times: when you see Greece you are indeed dipping into a collective memory, yet how it speaks can be startlingly fresh because it runs so deep. For some, the shock of recognition leaves them speechless and contemplating dramatic life changes: *finally, I am where I belong.*

This had happened to many. Although I haven't been there, I get the impression from written accounts that Palestine can have the same effect. But here's one of the most interesting questions: would someone without a European heritage have this reaction? Would someone from Beijing or Tahiti or Madagascar be able to tap into the Greco-Judeo-Christian memory stream when they stepped upon this land? Or, conversely, what would the Arabian desert, what would Mecca say to us? And I don't mean a spiritual presence, really. Certainly many people, such as myself, have the pretension to believe that we are attuned to the spirit of holy haunted places such as Ankor Wat or Mycenae, but this isn't what I mean.

Let me reiterate my thesis: *The Greek landscape speaks a human language.* The land has a tongue: Geoglossa, if you will. Is it the human history talking? But where doesn't this history exist? Even the top of Mount Everest now has a human tradition. And yet, this is where it springs from. Man is naked on this earth and nowhere more so than Greece. Mountains, rock and sea. And against this stark backdrop the echoes of man, be they written in stone or on the wind, stand in stark relief. Olives and wine. The ethereal light and the scent of thyme. When you look at the hills, when you walk them, when you listen, you hear the human years stretching back: a gush of tears and suffering broken by brief spasms of clarity and consciousness. Of poetry. Homer and Pindar still walk this earth and speak. Read Hesiod and then walk into the olive orchards shimmering in the light, the cicadas ascream, goat bells tinkling in the hard mountain air, and you will *know* his gods. The Peloponnesian War happened yesterday and Thucydides is holding forth beneath the plane tree in the platea. A human language you can comprehend.

As always, you have to be ready to hear. And that brings me back to who can hear. Is a saturation from birth in European culture required? This is a mysterious thing. Maybe it's the olive trees whispering? They live for hundreds of years, even a thousand. They have heard everything and look to have suffered because of it: twisted, gnarled and writhing they cover the hills in every direction, their silver green leaves flickering the light. A shimmer through the afternoon haze . . . And what does the land say? It says: *This is it.* All of your sufferings and joys will be played out *here* on this hard tired earth in this sharp clear light. *And then I will suck the flesh from your bones and that will be that.* The only life after death is the song that throbs in your children. And when we are hypnotized by the Greek landscape it is that distant song passing through us that we are hearing.

I was born and raised in Olympia, Washington, and have spent many days on the waters of Puget Sound and in the mountains that surround it. In high school we would often hike into the Olympics for days with a minimum of gear: no tents or sleeping pads, just matches, coffee, fishing tackle, a couple of cans of beans and a chunk of bacon. I have sailed everywhere on the Sound. And since leaving my hometown at nineteen I have been all over the American West. It is a vast and fantastic place. I love it and will always come back for another taste. I can feel its spirit and power; I can revel in its beauty and destructive force, but it does not speak to me in a language I can decipher. Perhaps it is too big? Or I am too small. One impression I do get is a sense of the vast interdependence of things and the impossibility of truly understanding the infinite nature of time, but it is all very vague and difficult to grasp.

I am willing to believe that it speaks to the native peoples in a language they understand. Many years ago, I spent some time at Crow Dog's Paradise in the Black Hills, and many of the Lakota Sioux and members of other tribes I met gave me the impression that they were attuned to a language I could only guess at. And this language was spoken not only by the land itself but by the creatures who lived upon that land. Interspecies communication on a spiritual level was an integral part of their tradition. When deciding whether to accept a Federal Government offer (this was during the Wounded Knee occupation), an elaborate ceremony was held, puppy stew being the main bill-o-fare, wherein different creatures spoke through Chief Foolscrow. When they spoke they made the sounds they make in the wild, though channeled by the Chief, and it was up to the elders to interpret what particular animals spoke. In this instance an owl, a seemingly universal symbol of wisdom, spoke last and this was taken to mean that whatever decision the Chief made would be righteous indeed. The Wounded Knee confrontation had also awoken many young urban Indians and they had come to South Dakota to attempt to find their culture. They were having a very difficult time. The native path was as foreign to them as it was to me. They had had no preparation, and couldn't tell a crow from eagle. For them to begin they had to listen to their blood. So perhaps it is a matter of the language of the land you are on, and whether you have been trained to hear it?

Here, in Greece, the history of the land, the last three thousand years anyway, has been written out for us. The language-obsessed West has given us a record that is easily accessible. In the canyon below our house the Spartan soldiers used to march double-time while hurrying over the mountains to Messina to put down revolts. Across the canyon is the village of Tripi (which means hole in Ancient Greek and still has the same meaning in Modern Greek—imagine, Sophocles used the same word, they are using many words that are at least 2,500 years old and have retained their meaning). In Tripi is a cleft in the rock where the Spartans used to leave unwanted infants. And on; everywhere you look the human drama has been played out, over and over. In this terrain we see ourselves, it is part of us, and it sings. A cycle completed, a music remembered. And once you hear it, you can't ever truly turn it off. And why would you? It has always been there. 📖

Didn't It Rain

Paul r. Harding

Scripture escaped me last night
where the space is where we're
most alone in the rain, where
heart houses the mind
in a waiting wheelchair while
she walks with an ancient cane;
not incurable is this
lame
wanting that space where sympathy
the sound of prison rain be-
hind misty eye cloud-
lets, gray-rose lightning
flashed window pane.

doesn't it rain?

Always in prayer, I know she
knows I and others know, been
hoping for plantation years on her
fascist leg, wooden racist foot, bad
sexist hip, limping lies
as big as moon landings, sad
as Southeast Asian village
burnings.

how it rains . . .

Watched peaceful Falun Gong exercises
in the morning rain; de-
pression was the fog and my being
rice fields of napalm, London when
Nazis knew in bombs what

Americans had known in Mexico, what
the homesteaders knew in Kansas, what
Queen Elizabeth knew in the
Caribbean, what Forster
knew in India, what the
Portuguese knew in West Africa,
Langston Hughes knew in Cuba, Marcus
Garvey knew in a rank jail cell,
Lady Day knew between blessing
and a child, what
King knew on the terrace of a Memphis
motel . . .

oh, does it rain . . .

What Coltrane knows in ascension.
What Sydney knew on Cat Island.
What Lorraine Hansberry knew between
youth, gift and blackness.
What El Hazz Malik Shabazz
found out in Mecca . . .

how it pours and pours and pours.

That the world was paralyzed,
disoriented in her story,
barely able to stand
on bending crutches.

how it darkens the skies with monsoon tears.

We didn't know the promise was
on its last legs when we marched
and screamed, held hands and
sat at diner counters and took
over campus buildings and shut

down banks and city halls.
Didn't know what

Mahalia Jackson meant when she sang:

> "Oh, didn't it rain . . .
> Children, didn't it rain . . .
> Oh, Lord, didn't it rain . . ."

XI

Volume 10, Number 3
2002-2003
Dimensions of Time

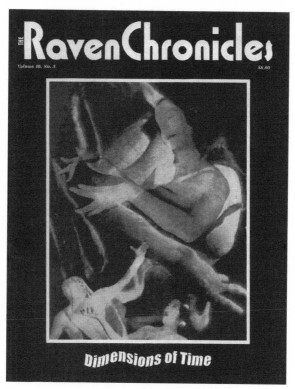

GooSayTen, Butoh Duo: Itto & Mika,
from Sapporo, Japan, photograph by I.H Kuniyuki

Hickory Dickory Dock

Polly Buckingham

Day

"Nice tie," one man said to another man in the elevator.

"Thanks," the other man said.

The tie was a giant cloth wristwatch.

"I have a salmon one," the first man said.

Jennifer stared at the unmoving hands on the face of the clock over the stretched shirt, the too-many-lunches-out stomach. She felt the man watching her—and she thought, but he's the one with the freaky tie. She rubbed the corner of her forehead just beyond the hairline; the pain would not go away. All day there had been a buzzing deep in her ear, an echo of the alarm that had forced her awake. When the elevator doors opened, she tripped across the gap. Recently she'd been prone to dizziness. Probably from the elevators. Ten times a day, twice coming and going, twice at each of three breaks. Add in the revolving glass doors, and a certain flightiness and loss of direction was sure to set it.

Even the numbers she entered on the computer moved in circles, patterns that could only be decoded by some sinister man hidden in the basement. 08 209 21 11 212 13 214 and so on. The sounds of fifteen keyboards striking patterned numbers fed into her aching brain like a punch hole card translatable only in sleep. Jennifer needed a vacation.

She left work early that day, the day the man on the elevator complimented another man on his clock tie, the day her head hurt so badly she turned down the brightness and contrast knobs on the computer and squinted at the dark screen. She left work with her eyes averted from the florescent lights; she dropped silently through the floors; outside the elevator a haggard woman leaning against the wall said, "They just can't do anything about it;" the marble floor and archaic columns, the wood paneled walls pressed in on her; the air was stale and cold. A mermaid fountain spit spheres of water into a marble basin. Jennifer was drowning.

The revolving doors spit her out onto the rainy street. She stood stunned as a bus pulled off the curb and blew exhaust into her face. People swooshed out of the spinning doors and parted around her. More stood by the curb waiting for the next bus. Something smelled like a rotting stomach. She looked down at a jellyfish blob of clear bile with bits of blood and mucus. It was the size of a dinner plate. She stepped away from the people. A man brushed by her and stopped. She watched, as if in slow motion, the black work boot hover over the bloody bile and finally drop into it. The man stood unmoving. Jennifer turned away. The courthouse was only five blocks. What she wanted most was to sit on the curb and cry. But she knew better, and so, with some cartoon jingle in her head, she put one foot in front of the other and kept on.

Months ago, she'd been pulled over because her left brake light had been out. She'd missed her first court date, and, owing enough money already, and paying enough insurance already, she could not afford to miss this one. *Put one foot in front of the other and soon you'll be walking 'cross the floor-or-or-or.*

To her surprise, the cop actually showed up at the hearing. She sat in the front row resting her elbows on the wood rail. The judge's bushy eyebrows met above his nose. His graying hair was streaked with red. She meant to prepare a song and dance which might prove her innocence, but she hardly had the energy to sing or to dance—though lying was not out of the question. Behind the judge a clock with a large white face ticked in the silence before she spoke.

"I always check all my car lights weekly," she said. "I'm certain the light had been working just the day before. I'm sure of it. I remember because it was Monday, and Monday is when I check my lights." Tick tick tick tick tick.

They let her off. The cop was leaning against the doorframe as she left the courtroom. He had small ears that stuck straight out of the sides of his big, blotchy face. He winked at her and formed a gun with his fingers. Jennifer paused and gave him one long stare. Her mouth opened then closed again. "Just keeping you on your toes," he said and made a little shooting sound. Pop pop. *Put one foot in front of the other, and soon you'll be walking out the door-or-or-or.*

Outside the dark of day was turning to the dark of night. The wind was picking up. Far off someone screamed. Jennifer pulled the hood of her thrift store rain jacket over her head as rain fell in slants across her face. The jacket had a belt that dangled behind her. She could hear it swishing against the jacket. She didn't like belts, and she didn't like shopping.

A woman on the bus said, "I like to put bats in my purse. It helps me fly at night." She said this to no one. "Especially when it's cold. You have to fly when it's cold. So you don't feel it. You know what I mean?"

"Jesus, shut up," a man three seats in front of the woman said. But he didn't say it to her, he just said it. Like one more word, and he'd fly off some imaginary plain too.

"About the not feeling, I mean. You know what that's like. Lovely. A nice sleep. Bats. That's the trick." Rain hit the window as the bus crossed the 12th Avenue Bridge. Below was not a river, but the concrete of three highways converging. The noise was not a waterfall, but traffic, constant, always, as if it were the very sound of silence itself. The new headlights of cars were blurry and bright. Jennifer closed her eyes as each one passed. The alarm in her inner ear buzzed away, and pain pushed against the inside of her head so that when she looked out through that gauzy pain and out through the window and out through the rain and the dark, she felt trapped and exhausted. The lights of the city, of the cars on the highway below, of the streetlamps and the far away windows of towers, were like lights caught in rain drops on the other side of a window. The sound of the traffic below made her feel as if she were standing on a runway, and jets were taking off, angling over the top of her head. When would this ever end?

Outside, hazy clouds moved across a full moon. She missed the daylight. Her toes through her black thrift store work shoes were cold. The shoes were busting along the inside seams. The rubber bottoms were bubbled and filled with air pockets. Rain water eased into her socks. Behind a construction fence, a dirty, long-haired kitten was wailing. Its hair was matted. Jennifer stopped and bent down. The kitten hissed and spat and backed away, its tiny teeth sharp against the red red mouth.

She didn't have the energy to go to the store for food. Even if she had felt safe driving at night with the brake light still out—for a month it'd been out—she only wanted to lay down. For an hour or more she lay sprawled on the carpet of her living room smelling the old tenants in the marbled shag, listening to the traffic outside, to the neighbors' music, to the kids in the hall of her apartment building. And finally to the groan of her stomach. It wasn't like she could sleep. But eating, she understood, however ill she felt, was like walking 'cross the floor. One foot in front of the other.

The cupboards looked empty except for the roaches that fell like rain across the cracked countertop. Still, she peered in. Back in the shadows was a box. She pulled it forward. Pancake mix. She didn't even remember buying this. Sometimes morning and night were hard to distinguish. Could she make pancakes with water?

Her chin in the cradle of her palms, she stared at the drawing on the pancake mix box. It was of a lodge built on the cliff of a huge waterfall. Dry Falls Lodge VitaLife Pancake and Waffle Mix. She imagined the sound of the waterfall blocking out all other sounds. She imagined the smell of the pine trees which were skillfully drawn right up to the cliff's edge. Gray granite mountains hovered in the background, and little white clouds were poised against a green sky.

Jennifer needed a vacation. The lodge was in the desert, just on the other side of the mountains. She needed the light. She searched the box for a phone number. She searched her wallet for her credit card. It was over the limit, but what the hell. She'd try.

First she called the lodge. "I need a vacation," she said.

"Is the darkness getting to you?" a man said from the other side of the state.

"Yes," she admitted.

"Too much rain?"

"Yes."

"Too many people?"

"Yes."

Dry Falls, 2002, drawing by Nancy D. Donnelly

"What's your favorite number?"

"32."

"Okay," the man said. "It's empty. We'll be seeing you as soon as you get here. Dry Falls is on the map. The lodge is right above it. Will you be driving?"

"I'll be flying," Jennifer said.

A small airline would take her to a small town on the other side of the state. The small airline accepted the bad credit card. She was beyond questioning. She would then take a bus from the small town to the lodge. She dialed for airport van service. She packed a bag and waited.

Dinner was served on the plane. Chicken cordon bleu. It was still frozen on the inside. The big moon remained out her window the entire flight. There was vomit in the vomit bag tucked into the seat in front of her. She'd become used to things.

Dusk

"Pretty place, Dry Falls," the bus driver said. He was actually a van driver, the driver of an old van with torn seats.

"I've heard," Jennifer said. Dark sky and stars filled the windows. She rested her forehead against the glass and watched the flat land covered with night whiz by.

The entire day, the man with the wristwatch tie, the cop with his finger like a gun, the old woman and her bats, roamed through her mind. It was as if she could see all those odd people out there in the dark, running in small crazy circles kicking up desert, exhausting themselves of their tired little lives.

With her eyes closed, Jennifer's mind eased into that place between dreaming and waking where your surroundings mutate into other vaguely familiar things. The rattling of a loose window, for example, became the sound of large metal wheels on a gravelly road. And the buzz of the heater, the clip clop of horses. The people she'd imagined outside the window were creatures with black wings flying frantic and furious circles. And the bus stop where another passenger got on, was where the mechanic, his bundle of large wrought iron tools wrapped in a black cloak, spoke conspiratorially with the stage coach driver. His face was white, and his lips bright red. He would not lift his eyes to meet hers.

Night

Jennifer woke. She stepped out of the van as a sleeper steps out of bed. The tails of the mechanic's jacket flapped as he leaned into a gust of wind. The little silver toolbox swung half way round in his hand, lifted its lid and winked. Three bats with moon faces flew out of a triangle window in a dormer at the top of the lodge. The bats flew past her and out over the edge of a vast canyon. The canyon had one marked cliff from which white moonlight was cascading into the valley. The cold, dry wind screamed around her.

The driver handed Jennifer her luggage, a white laundry bag. The mechanic stepped down into the darkness of a basement stairwell. A big wooden door with a diamond-shaped stained glass window covered with an iron grid creaked open. A man in a tuxedo with small, red ears and a big face beckoned her with a crooked finger.

"Take your bag?" he said.

"I can carry it myself," she said.

"You need a vacation," he said.

"I can carry it myself," she repeated.

"There will be a show later. We'd love you to join us. If you could just prepare a song. We'll be waiting for you in the ballroom."

The sound of pipes banging into one another erupted from beneath the lodge. Green light twinkled from the cracks between the floorboards.

"Music, we'll need music now," the man in the tuxedo said and rushed down a corridor from which, instantly, wild piano music began. Musical notes flew out into the living room, bumping not so gracefully into the chandelier which shook and tinkled.

She carried her bag up a mahogany staircase winding around three quarters of the living room and forming a long upstairs balcony lined with doors. A red velvet runner slipped beneath her feet, and the steps tilted side to side. Each time she took a crooked step, another step would appear at the top. So she took two steps at a time, and in this manner, she reached the landing.

Some doors had digits, others had none, and yet others had only half their digits. Little nails poked out of the doors where the numbers should have been. 2 3 5 8 0 11 4 1 16 and so on. Her door was 3 and a little nail, but the door didn't open. She turned back down the hallway and followed the red runner. Ragtime piano music faded behind her.

A door on the left was slightly ajar. She pushed it open. Moonlight fell through the windows into an empty room with wooden floors. Thick, black curtains lined with white lace gauze hung from the windows. She stood in the folds of the curtain and looked out across the desert. The bats, tiny specks, hovered uneasily above the cliff where no water poured into the valley.

A heavy wind rattled the window. The small black clasp holding the two sides of the window together gave way and the doors swung open. Jennifer, still holding the laundry bag, buried herself deeper into the curtain as a bat flew into the room. It rested on the wood floor, its wings spread out in the moonlight, its tiny heart thumping so hard its body quivered. A funnel of wind circled the room drawing dust up with it. The dust gathered in the center where the bat lay panting on the floorboards. The dust obscured everything, and the wind flew itself back out the window. In a pillar of moonlight, an old woman stood barefoot in the center of the room.

"I know you're there behind the curtain," she said. "I have the key to your room. So you can sleep."

Sleep. Sleep meant white feather pillows, no more buzzing, moonlight warm on the skin, a sheet and a blanket covering her completely.

"You do want to sleep?"

"Of course," Jennifer said.

"First you must go to the basement and help the mechanic fix this problem with our time."

Out the window the moon was punctured in the middle with a dark hole. The woman parted her bright lips. Her toothless mouth hung open. Her upturned face white, she sucked in the night air. Jennifer put her palms against the wall and made her way around the room, keeping clear of the moonlight. At the door she turned back to see the woman crouched on the window ledge.

Outside the door, the hallway became a series of S curves. Eyes the size of eggs with roaming red pupils poked out of the wall paper. The piano music grew louder and louder, eight, ten, twenty pianos all playing ragtime at once. A mouse peeked out from beneath the carpet. "Where are the hands?" it said.

Jennifer shook the doorknob of her room, but the doorknob came off in her palm. She knelt on the ground and pressed one eye over the keyhole. There was a small, red bed with a white pillow and a blue blanket. There was a wooden bed stand with a glass of water. There was a yellow candle in a candleholder with a saucer and handle. The flame flicked up and back down. She beat the door with her fists, but the door did not open. She put down the bag and slammed her body against the door. The mouse grabbed the strings of the bag in its teeth and scurried down the red carpet dragging the luggage behind.

"Come back here!" Jennifer shouted as she ran after the bag. The floor bubbled up and down again, and the rug slipped like it had when she'd climbed the tiresome stairs. All the pianos were playing different tunes. The laundry bag bumped down the crooked stairs, muted metal bashing against the banister posts.

The doorman was leaning against the spiraled leg of the banister at the bottom of the staircase.

"Where do you think you're going?" he said, grabbing Jennifer's arms as she tumbled down the steps. The music was deafening. The chandelier shook wildly above her head throwing out bright splinters of light that flicked across the room, spots on the velvet flowers embedded in the wall paper, across an occasional egg-sized eye.

"My bag!" she shouted as the white heap rounded a corner and disappeared.

"You've prepared your dance, I suppose?" Dots of light swirled across the doorman's face.

"I thought it was a song," she said.

"A song and a dance," he said. "A song and a dance. A song and a dance."

"Let me go."

"Not until we get our song and dance."

The doorman's fingers pressed deep into her skin and pushed against her bones. He pulled Jennifer across the Mongolian carpet, now speckled with light, and down the dark hallway from which the music was blaring.

A jury sat in the corner of a ballroom. The judge turned away from an enormous pipe organ which he had been playing with his hands, his feet, and his very long beard.

"Hello there," he said. On his puffed out cheeks were large, rose-colored dots.

"Song and dance song and dance song and dance song and dance!" shouted the jury.

"Okay, alright, okay, alright," Jennifer said glancing at the clock. But the clock was blank. No numbers. No hands.

"Song and dance song and dance!" The jury was made up of children, yelling pushing shoving children, their mighty little fists splintering the wood of the jury stand, mouths opening to a size larger than their heads.

"I'm thinking. Give me a moment," she said.

The judge turned back to the organ. His beard split into five six and seven points, and those points pounded on the blacks and whites. He looked over his shoulder as he was playing and raised his eyebrows up and down, up and down. "The girl has a song, the girl has a dance. Please wait, please wait, just give her a chance," he sang.

"You must let go of my arm," Jennifer said to the doorman. "I need my arms to dance."

He released his grip, and instantly five round bruises appeared. She swung out her elbows and crossed her fists in front of her chest, moving her arms back and forth like the arms of a marionette.

"In the mornings," she sang, "and this is the truth, the birds are always singing and the sky is always blue." Her feet, as if disconnected from her body, shuffled across the courtroom. She turned her face back to the judge, smiled, and ran.

She ran across the ballroom floor. Gunshots slammed into the wall just as she rounded a corner and ran down a dark hallway. Quite suddenly, she fell headfirst down a flight of stairs. She picked herself up from cement. Her bones ached. An egg-shaped bump materialized on her forehead.

In front of her was a giant clock with no hands. The mechanic was crouched on the floor surrounded by black numbers. He was opening Jennifer's laundry bag.

She lunged forward and snatched the bag out from under him. "You will not continue this!" she yelled. "You will not continue this!"

The mechanic, squatting, stared up at her, his red mouth hanging open. She turned and ran back up the stairs, the heavy bag clunk clunk clunk on the hollow steps. She ran down the dark hallway. She ran through the ballroom where the judge never again turned away from his organ and the doorman was reloading his gun. She ran down another hallway and across the Mongolian carpet speckled with light. She pulled open the heavy wooden door with her bruised arms and ran across the desert.

The sound of the falls filled her ears. With her laundry bag over her shoulder, she climbed as close to the water as she could. Finally, she stopped at a flat rock overlooking the falls. Spray landed on her arms and wet her face. The roar covered the alarms way back in her ear. She hung her knees over the cliff and rested the bag, which contained the heavy hands of the clock, across her legs. A familiar smell entered her. It crept inside her nose and warmed her all over inside. She turned and looked back at Dry Falls Lodge. Her room was a far away box of muted light in which a little candle flickered up and down.

The smell was coming from a room downstairs where a man in a chef's hat had just opened the window. It was the smell of pancakes. The same pancakes Jennifer ate every Saturday morning when she was a child. The same pancakes her mother had layered with small squares of butter and topped with hot maple syrup. The pancakes that came with the warm kitchen and the Saturday morning cartoons. This was the most wonderful smell Jennifer could ever imagine. It was the best thing she had ever smelled in her entire life. And it was not enough. She jumped. 📖

Crime or Something Like It

Mercedes Lawry

A handsome thief slides in the window
like the quick breath of a woman whose lover
has entered the room. The widow sleeps
under the spider's eye while none of the clocks
match their ticking, its chaos, this scatter
of time, hours lumped like soiled laundry,
seconds lost in the dust under the bed.
Where are the diamonds? Where is the platinum blonde,
the fast cars? I only want my share,
the thief tells the cat who could care less.
There is no moon tonight, no stars, right
on schedule. The water in the glass on the table
evaporates. This is far from a drought,
this is a crime scene now and a frisson of joy
sweeps through the neighbor who watches
from his kitchen, the glue of cold pie
in his mouth. Real life, he thinks, TV, 911,
guns. Or am I dreaming myself out of boredom?
The thief sweeps on, professional and alert.
Risk balanced on hope and clouds of money.
The widow's eyes open, unplanned.
The neighbor has another bite. The thief
decides on one more drawer.

The Cycle of Seasons

Avital Gad-Cykman

Robbin arrived in the fall. The early morning light painted the sky purple and drew an orange line over the dark hilltops. Raio Dourado, the Brazilian desert town, exhibited its perpetual floods of beauty. At different hours, bright rays of sunlight or of moonlight sprang from behind the hills and arched over the town like an exquisite necklace on an aging neck.

Robbin took his tattered backpack from the ground and waited until the bus disappeared. At the edge of the square, inside Café do Ponto, Mylla stood behind the counter and watched him. He was the first stranger the town had seen in years.

On his way down the road, Robbin came across a railway track that, strangely, emerged from the ground, running towards the sky. His gaze followed the track until a sunray dazzled him. He looked away, searching for street signs. There were none.

The few early risers ignored him. The town seemed drowned in an image of dreamers interlaced. Foreigners stayed away.

The sound of hurried footsteps mingled with low voices. The town's central square was waking up.

Peeping into the old café, Robbin drew invisible shapes on the glass wall that separated the café from the street. Mylla's smile lingered in her eyes before parting her lips. She noticed the restrained movement of the muscles under his skin. His bare chest looked tanned under his red coveralls. Around his red-cheeked, narrow face, his hair flowed long, dry, and blond like straw. His eyes, two slanted blue cuts, conveyed he had just found a treasure.

In a quick gesture, he took red, blue, yellow, white, and green balls out of his overalls' pockets. He started juggling, moving among the balls, under them, on their right side and on their left, making them his dancing partners.

She lowered her eyes and started to clean. Changes were not welcome, challenges not expected. She had already framed her days and nights with a melancholic acceptance. She watched the trees along the avenues as their leaves grew and died. Red and yellow leaves now covered what used to be a desert, and long branches filtered the light. The leaves were born and reborn from apparently dry trunks. Unlike people, the cycle of seasons never failed.

She stopped expecting the townspeople to embrace her. Neither her serene smile, nor her peach face could make her popular. They said she spoke alone and howled at the moon. It was not untrue. She accompanied the sounds of her yard, the desert, the ever-advancing sea waves.

Her speech was scarce.

She mostly said,

"What would you like to drink?"

"Sweets are thirty centavos."

"Here is your bill. Have a nice day."

The customers watched her stand behind the cash register the way they observed caged canaries.

During the fall, Robbin settled in the Café Square. In front of the café, he juggled every day with colorful balls and brilliant sticks. Standing among the dark wooden tables, Mylla watched him through the large windows. She studied his thin, stringy body, then noticed that the balls formed a heart in the air. His gentle tease invited her rare, open smile. Soon, the scenery was never whole without him. Even while crossing the square in the evening and strolling down the avenue, she thought of Robbin. He touched her days the way an artist's paintbrush stroked a canvas.

The desert expanded into his eyes: they still widened for a brighter sun. His hair had turned blazingly blond in dry winds. Mylla wondered why he had left the desert. She heard that Raio Dourado's hostel had opened for him, expecting a stream of strangers to follow. To the owner's disappointment, Robbin remained the only visitor. Her wooded town, the oasis created in the desert's heart by ambitious pioneers, did not attract the people of the vast desert. They were rough and direct, sometimes violent, and never ostentatious.

The air turned translucent as days touched evenings and evenings caught nights.

Whenever she opened the café's door, she caught his scent, that of a broken cactus.

They never spoke with each other.

Then, somehow, they did.

"Good evening," he said as she came out.

She considered it. "Yes," she finally agreed.

"I am Robbin."

"Mylla."

"Can we meet?"

"We'll see."

Mylla let most words slip over her body and stream away. The cruel words of the townspeople had accompanied her since the day she was born beautiful and fresh; a blossoming creature unlike most startled babies. Her mother held her to her body and put her cheek on the baby's warm, smooth head.

"She is her father's daughter!" the midwife announced in the corridor. "The family's shame painted the baby pink!" The word spread.

The new mother cradled the baby, trying to breast-feed her. Nestled between the soft arms, Mylla's demanding lips closed over the nipple. Mother and daughter lived on an island of two from which they would soon be exiled. The town pronounced Mylla sweet but guilty.

When Mylla's parents had discovered they were going to have a baby, they grasped that happiness hungrily. Their closest friend, Maria, brought them books about pregnancy and birth. She stretched her dark legs on their tiled floor and read for them. From her, they learned how a fetus developed its body and spirit. Excitement and apprehension filled them in equal measure. Their hope survived their worries and their love burst with sudden delights.

Mylla's father surrounded his wife with small gestures of attention. She woke up to find a cup of coffee, set between fresh azalea flowers. A warm bath welcomed her when she returned from teaching Bible at school. His body waited for her on their newly washed and pressed white sheets, ready for another summer night. Yet, it was his body that slowly betrayed him.

How can a carpenter work, bent down with pain? At times, his arms twisted like scorched branches. The sickness scared his customers away and poverty invaded their home as fast as a sandstorm. The town offered him charity but refused him work. They carried on the official compassion and the resolution to feed the poor. Raio Dourado's system exposed, secured, and insured the needy. Yet, in spite of that rigorous practice of aid, some people managed to suffer.

He wanted to work.

Since he could not count on people, he turned to God. He worked for entire days, preparing an offering. One day, everybody in town noticed a wooden railway track painted in a metallic color emerging from behind the carpentry store toward the sky. He continued working, but like the tower of Babel, his creation could not reach high enough.

However universal pain is, it cruelly clings to one man alone. Love turned into bodies holding desperately onto each other.

Mylla never ceased to hear the high tide of sounds of her mother's womb and the vibration filtered into her with the memory of her father.

His frustration burned her insides.

On the fifteenth night of the ninth month of her mother's pregnancy, neighbors heard the bank door cracking. A robbery?! Back then, nobody expected anyone from their town to commit a crime. It did not exist. Only afterwards would the town hire eight formerly unemployed guards. Astonished, the neighbors ran out to the bank. Before Mylla's father could advance inside, a forest of hands landed on his body and forced him to surrender.

"A criminal," respectful citizens commented.

"Stupid! Couldn't even steal," others said.

Mylla grew up in the shadows. His failure was a verdict she faced constantly. Shame and guilt were forced on her like a prisoner's uniform. People around her whispered that the railway track kept growing. "Like a tree," they said. "It's your family's tree," Maria told her.

At school, Mylla failed every test. Boys consoled her in hidden corners, becoming more daring as she grew wilder and quieter. Even after the school years, during occasional stolen nights, they lusted for her round beauty, desired her shy fire, and ignored her later.

After two years in jail, Mylla's father had disappeared. Rumors said that being well-educated and extremely rebellious, he became the prisoners' leader and later planned a smart escape and joined their gang in the desert. He might have died as well. Nobody in town looked for him or lent money to Mylla's mother to do so. She never found out.

"It wasn't your fault," the school principal said. He leaned over his table, his eyes bright and concentrated.

"He is my husband."

"Everyone forgives you," he said. "But I must ask you to quit Bible teaching."

Only Maria, the owner of Café do Ponto, offered Mylla's mother a job. Maria declared guilt was not a contagious illness, nor did it run in the family. But Maria had always been somewhat extravagant.

The café filled with colored women: Maria, tall and graceful and dark; Mylla's mother, thinner and redder every passing day; and Mylla, the baby girl, pink and round with glossy reddish-brown curls. Mylla witnessed her mother's face turn lifeless. From within her mother's body, bones scratched the skin that tightened over them. She died when Mylla was four. The girl was told to pray to a protective God.

People went on reminding Mylla who she was. She bumped in to the customers, got pinker and asked for forgiveness. She followed Maria like a pet, and Maria took her home, where no one ever counted how many appeared for dinner. It was nice to go unnoticed.

When Mylla asked for work, Maria hired her and told her the customers were always right. She had learnt it in a correspondence course. Mylla listened and smiled. No, they were not.

As years went by, she removed the weight of guilt and shame off her own shoulders to theirs. It remained her secret. Time taught her the delicate art of mistreatment. She served non-filtered tub water to the customers. According to her interpretation of biblical justice, the just people wouldn't have a stomach ache.

The past still darkened the present.

Monday morning, Mylla found Robbin, the desert man, at the closed café. He was coiled on the Peruvian carpet near the counter. Her fears raced. Had Robbin committed crimes? Had he failed someone and run away? She stumbled over a chair.

Robbin opened his eyes lazily, then sat up startled. "The hostel closed down last week," he said.

The café looked tidy, the cash register was closed, and the posters displaying the town in the old days watched over them as arrogantly as ever. How did he enter?

"Coffee?" she asked.

"Yes, please." He stretched his arms over his head. His eyes were soft. "You've never come this early," he said.

She studied him as he sipped the coffee. "So you watch me!" she said.

"I do."

"What if he's a runaway criminal?" Mylla asked Maria.

"Nonsense, child. Nothing's missing, right?"

"The door was locked. How do you think he entered?"

"Ask him."

Mylla's cheeks blushed

"Just follow your heart," Maria said with an unnerving smile. She watched soap operas every night.

The café closed in the afternoon.

The cool wind blew golden leaves and wrapped them around Robbin's body. He was juggling, but there was no one around to throw him coins. Mylla leaned against the café's door.

"It's cold," she told him. "Would you like to enter?"

He let the balls drop one by one into his hand and put them back into the pockets of his red coveralls.

While she brewed coffee, he watched the antique posters. The desert had already sneaked its head between the trees even in those old times.

"Good coffee." He wrapped his long fingers around the mug.

She inhaled his cactus scent. How would his hand feel against her face?

"More?" she asked.

She put her elbow on the table, her fingers on the warm skin of her forearm.

"Do you like it here?" he asked.

"I like Maria."

"I mean the town."

She bent forward. "Why?"

"You seem different from everyone else."

"I am not!" He, too?!

"You're a wild flower."

"Oh! That sounds beautiful." She smiled shyly. Then, she remembered. "I must leave the café ready for tonight."

They lifted chairs and landed them on the tables. She spread the tables and he passed a broom. He soaped the sponge, and she passed it over the cups he handed her, splashing water. He dried her arms and coated her fingers one by one with a velvety kitchen towel. They moved around each other, in measured steps.

He walked her home. She felt relief for his not taking long to lock his arms behind her back, pull her towards him, undress them both. The walls around them were beige and the bedcover red; all washed by fall colors. She held his desert-body, entangling her round lines into his straight ones. Their bodies hit the bed once too hard. The bed collapsed.

Mylla hugged herself, rolling on the broken bed. "The bed needs work," she said. Her laughter burst like a newborn's cry: insistent, full of life.

"I'll help you there," he got up and pulled the mattress, so she rolled down onto the floor.

She jumped back onto the mattress, fighting the air with her hands. "I dare you . . ."

He held her down, his slim body balancing itself on the uneven bed. Slowly, he set his knees on her sides. She wasn't laughing anymore. She heard a far wave. He could hear it as well.

"I wish the fall continued forever," Robbin said, lying on the bed, looking at the gray sky through the window.

"The cycle of seasons never fails, nor fallen angels."

"Too bad I am no angel." He rolled over.

"You fixed the roof, you changed the lock. The railway track is getting higher every day. The neighbors can't vandalize it! You're my angel." She stroked his hair.

"I do these things. I move from one place to another."

"What else can you do besides juggle?"

"Not much to be proud of. And how long can my juggling last here?"

Pain started pulsing in her head.

His juggling did last a few more nights and days. In the meantime they loved and talked, reciting old hurts and new hopes to the dark. In the mornings, she watched him sweep the yard, his naked back as brown as the tree trunks. She smiled.

He said there was something else he could do, if she agreed. "The fall can last a little longer."

Objects disappeared and reappeared in town, and then vanished again. A watch, jewelry, purses with money. He discovered entrances she never knew existed.

He closed a golden necklace around her young neck. "Here is your sunray," he said.

Outside, the trees revealed the fall's hurry to undress them.

Their day arrived, covered with clouds. Mylla and Robbin told Maria goodbye and received her blessings.

Raio Dourado slept peacefully that night. Only the bank's eight-soldier army stayed on guard. They never suspected the silhouettes moving in the dark. Colorful leaves flew over the roof and circled in the wind until dawn.

When the early risers arrived, they screamed and awoke the whole town. Red, green, yellow, and brown money notes landed over the square and flew to the desert. The bank had a new window torn among the roof tiles. The townspeople ran into the square to catch the bills, but they were slower than the wind.

And the wind blew into the hollow bamboo flutes placed above the old carpentry store. One by one, all raised their eyes.

They must have wondered at their Lord, watching Mylla and Robbin take the railway to the throne. 📖

Shadow Dance #86, photograph, 1993, by Glenda J. Guilmet

On Spilling the Paint

Marion Kimes

. . . too heavy for light work, too light for heavy
—Big Bill Estell, *The Pine Barrens*, by John McPhee

daily, a woman lawyer works the mess
on death penalty's tables. the doctor prays,
then teams separate twins. outside, gangs
of painted pigeons fly in great swirls
of wing. perched or moving, whatever we do
funerals proceed, dust collects, books,
enter & leave. chiselled, set one by one
until they glow, words carve & hold us.
in their cut & pasted pages I see myself,
heavy or light, slipping, sliding, spilling
the paint, a tenacious trashhound, often
raucous now, & leaning. loosely leaning.

here, in debris-filled air, honing in,
stooping for trash & leaves, we look
straight into homeless eyes. passing by,
we talk with the dogs—all laughing & lit
with their secret lives & the life we share—
tied up, short-leashed, curbed/on a precipice
(noxious fumes, bright moving traffic),
too-near but-not to food & chewing, eating
crumbs downwind & wingless. now, the crows—
they listen, they interrupt. struts & swaggers,
wings and landing gear—they get around.
survivors, cawing a mean mouthharp, crowing
ancient songs long fallen off the page,
they flourish in these soft Seattle rains.

The Scar Map

Jan Priddy

Twenty years ago, shortly before her death, Vera Pride came to live with the family of her great grandchild, Rosetha. She had once been tall, but now, small and gray, she told glorious stories of her life in South America, of soldiers and revolutions, the black market, young men who would kill to avenge an insult and who didn't believe in work, flags, and beautiful horses. It was impossible to doubt her. Asleep, her grandmother dreamed in Spanish and sometimes woke the house shouting, "Viva!" When Rosetha listened to her great grandmother's stories she wondered how anyone could leave Peru. In the night she listened, hoping for a disturbance. She slept on the back porch and lay awake trying to understand her great grandmother, but she also found her frightening.

"Where were you born?" she asked one evening after supper. The kitchen was heavy with steam, water boiling in a kettle and the water so hot in the dish pan that Rosetha could hardly bear to put her hands into the soapy water to scrub a cup. She looked around to see if Great Grandmother Vera had heard the question.

"The moon," the old woman snapped and shuffled off.

Rosetha snatched her reddened hands out of the dishwater. She supposed that the moon was not a likely place to be born, but many things that were unlikely about Vera turned out to be true. Rosetha had searched her great grandmother's luggage. The suitcases were stamped with labels from many cities and inside there were colored stones big as lima beans. And photographs. A young woman who looked a little like her own mother, laughing in a parade, astride a tall horse and another of soldiers with the same beautiful young woman, one hand pressed to a hat, her skirts short and blowing in the wind. There was a military officer, his uniform decorated with braid and bright trim, and another man in an open white shirt, his head thrown back, and another of sunshine and human shadows on a stone wall. She searched her great grandmother's face for traces of that beautiful, laughing woman who held the arms of the handsome men. She could see them both at once, the youth and the old woman. It made her want to cry.

A pale blue stone glittered on Vera's hand, and every Sunday for church she put on a strange red and white and dark gray fabric sewn into a skirt. It was long and bright and the family did not approve. But Vera was old. It wasn't right to question.

And that might have been all—a vague childhood memory of a great grandmother who went into the hospital while she was in school and never came out. Rosetha might have gone on about her days, married the boy on the corner, Davis, named for his grandfather who died fishing, and raised ordinary children herself, but something happened to change all that.

Her life turned.

Vera scarred her teenaged great granddaughter. Carrying a kettle for tea from stove to counter, she spilled boiling liquid on the neck and shoulder of Rosetha as she bent over to stroke the cat. Rosetha hardly knew what happened. She cried, her mother cried, she would never see Vera again, because the burn was serious, and took a long time to heal.

Her parents drove her to Portland because the burn was serious where the boiling water had pooled at her collar bone. The triangle of skin grafted onto her jaw required two trips to the Shriner's Hospital. There was surgery, and then a week later there was another surgery. Her mother stayed with her at first and then returned home after the second surgery to take care of her younger sisters, leaving Rosetha with long hours and nothing much to do. She peeled the bandage off the place on her thigh and looked at the wound. And then she did not look again. She read books from the children's book cart. She sneaked off the ward and stole magazines from waiting rooms in other parts of the hospital. She read pamphlets and the little cards posted on employee bulletin boards.

When Dr. Schuller checked on her, she asked to go home. And each week he would look at her surgical site and explain that while her shoulder healed quickly, if she went home she would have to return. Medical facilities nearer her home were not equipped to handle serious burns. There was a danger of infection.

She continued to read, to imagine odd things, to ask about things others had sense enough to leave alone. She seemed not to have changed who she was despite the nurses and doctors who were happy to help such a sweet child, such a poor girl from far away on the coast, whose mother slept in a chair by her bed and neither of them ever asked for a thing. Rosetha read books brought around by the book trolley. She smiled and stared into space, and sometimes asked difficult questions about other children on the ward, and even while blood was being drawn or bandages changed, perhaps especially then, she seemed to leave altogether. The girl's contemplative nature did not alter, but other things did.

Vera had left Rosetha with a permanent, though inconspicuous scar, showing a distinct seam and a raised patch, blushed as if Rosetha had stroked on pink face powder just at the elegant curve of jaw into throat, just there below her right ear.

And truth be told, the scar was small, the size and shape of the wedge of skin between lifeline and thumb. A plum pressed into a triangular mold. Rosetha found her hand drifting up along the side of her neck to stroke the peculiar grain of the skin which had been taken from her thigh to cover the burn. It felt velvety, a soothing one-way touch. Though her fingers felt the skin, the skin on her neck didn't quite feel her fingers back.

Her mother sighed in relief. She had feared any disfigurement would make a hermit of her daughter. When her husband argued that she could not be spared to travel with Rosetha to the Portland hospital, she pressed her lips in a firm line, lowered her eyes, and said, "It's needed." Rosetha already spent too much time alone reading books and staring into space. Too soft-hearted, a dreamer, a thinker.

There, Rosetha found work her classmates had completed that she did not remember starting. Her parents had not thought to send her assignments, and she would spend the entire summer catching up. In the fall, she asked her History teacher awkward questions.

At sixteen, Rosetha, who had cried after every haircut since the age of three, abruptly chose to have her dark mane scissored into fairy points, a style which accentuated her graceful neck and also revealed the burn.

The day came when she was allowed to return home. "You're done, you see," explained the night nurse who had her own troubles with a port wine stain across half her face. "There's nothing more to be done."

Both her parents appeared, grinning and grim.

"We're taking you home today," her mama said.

The bandages were removed that afternoon. The triangle of skin was not bloody, the skin no longer inflamed along the edges or blue in the middle, which she had seen a month before. She should be careful not to expose the area to the sun, or in any other way to injury. The girl was so relieved she cried. Her mother cried. Her father looked away and waited for them to stop, and then they drove the long journey home.

The scar itself was not so large or noticeable that boys would mind, the nurses assured her, but the girl smiled and looked away as they tried to tell her about what a little foundation and powder might do. Instead she tilted her head and looked at them out of the corner of her eyes in a way that made them fumble their words like children themselves. "Oh, never mind," they said. "You'll be fine."

And so she went home to Coos Bay and started high school and the boys were all bothered by the new girl who was not quite new, but someone who used to swing her legs and jump off the train trestle out on the river. Girls wanted to hold her hands and boys wanted something else they could not name.

But it was the effect of Rosetha stroking her scar that most unsettled the neighborhood. She'd sit on the bench outside church while her mother talked to her own friends, lean her cheek on her palm and seem to leave the continent. One finger would run over the scar, back and forth. Eyes half closed, her body glowed as though the stroke blew air onto a fire. Her mouth relaxed and widened into a tender face no one could see unmoved. Most observers looked away as though catching her naked or feeling the nakedness in their own hearts and burning, burning with each soft stroke of fingertip on flesh.

The remembered heat triggered a similar heat in others, a peculiar alchemy. Boys who'd never noticed her before, began following her about like hungry hounds. A senior in her high school library dropped his Spanish dictionary and stood with his mouth hanging open as she sat, right elbow pinning her book to the table, stroking the scar while reading. A compliment she hardly noticed.

She did begin to notice the scars of other people, tracing the marks of dog bites and old infection, knife wounds and blows on flesh. Scars are a map of our true passions, Rosetha thought. Not the injury, but the manner of healing. She walked up the long, winding road to the hospital on the hill and spent many hours walking the wards, and nurses invited her to talk to troubled patients, while some doctors found her presence disturbing and avoided her. She would sit beside someone, her fingertip along the line of some recent scar, and she would tell the entire story of a person's life—all the way to the end as though she had her finger on their life line and could see all the winding and twisting and splitting off that life would achieve. Always a happy ending.

One afternoon absorbed by a text in the medical library, she looked up to find three surgical residents standing over her, watching her stroke her neck as if in a dream. Out of consideration for their fire, she placed both hands before her on the table, looked into their eyes, and set them free.

Family legend placed Vera Pride always in settings of conflict, in the midst of marches, disasters, revolution, and theft. But her great granddaughter Rosetha followed a different map, to the wounded, the marked, the scarred, and all the way to healing. 📖

Grace Baking

Ronda Piszk Broatch

                    Yesterday
Jesus was a woman,
    her disheveled hair falling
from a hairnet onto square shoulders.
She bagged loaves in pairs:
    potato rosemary, pugliese, garlic—soft
whole cloves embedded in a porous
        body of wheat.
Near the fish counter and crates of wine

we spoke of children, of school starting.
        God'll bless you, she said,
wiping floured hands on a floral apron,
    and I agreed *Amen.*
We sampled bread, skin still crackling,
warm, as she pressed bags of fresh-

baked rolls against her breasts.
        *It's the music that gets
        the menfolk to church*, she stated,
not missing a beat, slipping baguettes
into sacks marked Grace Baking on the outside.
        Grace is the name of our church,
I pointed out, and she smiled at me.
        Have some more bread, she said.
Amen.

XII

Volume 10, Number 4
Summer 2003
This Neutral Air: 9/11

Untitled, 2001, Acrylic on Masonite, by Scott Martin

Canal and Lafayette, September 11, 2001,
photograph by Whitney Pastorek

After

Thursday, September 13, 2001

Whitney Pastorek

The day after, the streets of New York City were silent, but the skies were choked with a light brown dust. It infiltrated every inch of the city, and the smell of something burning was unavoidable. As high as 34th Street, people were wearing respirator masks—some real, some made of shirtsleeves or napkins—to block out the putrid air. Looking down the wide, empty avenues, the buildings of downtown disappeared into the haze, almost obscuring what wasn't there from sight. But from a rooftop in Brooklyn, the change in skyline was horrifyingly apparent, and the plume of smoke a landmark of its own.

Many New Yorkers spent the day being evacuated from their offices, train stations, libraries, and neighborhoods due to bomb scare after bomb scare brought on by unattended briefcases and much-appreciated paranoia. Police officers stood in the major intersections, not so much to guide traffic as to guide pedestrians, and few people jaywalked across the larger streets. The occasional photographer darted into the middle of the road to snap a southward shot. The occasional police car zoomed past, lights blazing.

A man walked through the garment district, wearing a homemade sandwich board with two photographs, a name, and a series of phone numbers to call if you had seen his lost friend—the man was blanketing the city, walking north by degrees. His eyes were vacant. As I passed, he stopped to take a call on his cell phone.

Cell phones were omnipresent; although service was spotty and the network was busy and, in general, people seemed to be calling more in search of something to do than out of any real necessity. Human contact was at a premium.

In Union Square Park, long rolls of paper had been put down, markers strewn about, and a makeshift quilt of remembrances and flowers and photographs was in process. Love will overcome, said one message. Don't give up, said another. No one seemed concerned with cliché. Somewhere, a group of people were singing the National Anthem. Hundreds of mourners milled about, reading the words on the ground. Several people left pictures of the skyline as it was. One person wrote the word *Tomorrow* and then drew a sketch of three tall towers rising over the island. Across 14th Street, National Guardsmen checked IDs and the bags of anyone needing to enter Greenwich Village.

Men walked up and down the avenues with armfuls of American flags for sale. People bought New York City postcards and air purifiers. There wasn't a *Times* to be found after 11 am, and a crowd of fifty waited outside their Times Square office for the reprint to arrive. The first section was filled with images already pounded into the mind of anyone who had spent the past twenty-four hours watching television, and the feeling of past history and present moment being one and the same was overwhelming.

Televisions blared out of every window, radios out of every car.

Today, lampposts are covered with fliers begging for information, any information, about missing family members and coworkers. People are turning off the TVs and going out with friends instead, or simply walking block after block of their city, cameras and masks around their necks. Street corners are filled with people taking donations of clothing, money, time. Most relief organizations have put out word that no more volunteers are needed, come back tomorrow. The air has cleared somewhat, and downtown you can see the Woolworth Building, a proud survivor, standing strong against a bright blue sky.

Out of the rubble came survivors, buried for two days, but alive.

The city, too, is alive. People look at each other now, really see each other. Old friends meet by chance on the street and hug for an eternity, no longer squealing in fake delight at the sight of one another or promising to call, really, I swear I'll call—in fact, sometimes we say nothing at all. But we are together, and we are okay, and we grasp each other tightly in remembrance of those who are not. 📖

The Memento

Tuesday, September 25, 2001

Whitney Pastorek

I'm in a bagel shop last night, late, heading to a bar, when I catch the eye of the man next to me at the counter. He's dressed head to toe in American flag merchandise—hat, shirt, bandanna hanging out of his pocket—and around his neck he wears a complex series of badges, pagers, and ID cards.

"How are you?" I say.

"How long you got?" is his reply. "You got a couple days?"

"Yeah, really," I say. I nod compassionately. I've talked to a lot of strangers this week. I turn back to the counter.

"I been down at the site," he says, "since Tuesday."

The counter is less interesting now. Now, I'm really looking at him. "Oh, god," I say. "How—um—wow. You must be exhausted."

"I been working eighteen, twenty hour days," he says, rubbing his arms that I now see are a little black, a little swollen. "This is my first day off."

"Did you sleep down there?" I ask.

"Yeah, an hour here, an hour there," he says, adjusting the ID card around his neck, that I now notice says Office of Emergency Management. "I been running a command post, and today I just sat and pointed, 'You go there, you go there.' I just couldn't move anymore, today."

I am speechless in the way I get when there are too many questions, or when rather than talking I just want to crawl inside someone's brain and curl up to understand. I ask him how it's going, he says slow. I ask him what, if anything, people talk about down there, he says it's quiet. They did bring in musicians to play, he says, to try and keep up morale.

"You been down there?" he asks me.

"No. I mean, no," I stammer. "I don't want to. I don't want to get in the way. I had a friend who went down to work last Friday"—and I tell him the story of my friend the volunteer fireman who was rendered speechless by a day on the site, a story that seems awfully insignificant in the light of this man's close-to-two-weeks-straight of work until I tell myself that's stupid and go on—"I can't believe people are going down and taking pictures. It doesn't seem right." I scan his face, which I now notice is pockmarked and drooping.

"They're confiscating cameras now," he says. "People should just stay away." I nod again.

All I can do is nod as he tells me that they found seventeen bodies yesterday, because they finally unearthed a staircase. That he's seen things that would make a seven-foot gorilla black out, do I know what he means? That the cadaver-sniffing dogs are doing their best, do I know what he means, cadaver? I nod. That when you find a body, all you can do is step over it and keep going. But he's been all over the country doing this kind of thing—setting up command posts—he was in Oklahoma City, he thought he'd seen it all in thirty years of working for the O.E.M, and he thinks—no, he knows—that there are still pockets of air down there, in the basement, and there could be people alive. The ultrasound scanners might be picking up life. There are restaurants down there, you know, he says. I nod.

"What's your name?" I ask.

"Eddie," he says.

His partner, sitting silently at a table behind us, bites into his bagel. His shirt reads New York Housing Authority, and his badge is flipped in towards his chest.

Eddie clasps my hand, and then reaches into his pocket (which I now see is overflowing with work gloves and plastic bags) and pulls out a shrink-wrapped packet that looks a bit like what comes with my Chinese food delivery except it's not filled with duck sauce or a fortune cookie; as I turn it over in my hand, the vaguely yellowed bag crackling, I see within instant coffee, a teabag, a wetnap, gum, a tiny bottle of Tabasco sauce.

"It's called a Survivor Pack," Eddie says. "They hand'em out in combat, and everyone's getting'em down at the site." He presses it into my hands. "It can be your memento."

I nod, feverishly. "What's the Tabasco sauce for?"

"Cleans out germs," Eddie says.

"Thank you," I say.

"Thank you," he says back.

Later, walking home, I pass by Union Square Park. So much time and love and respect and pain have been deposited here in the form of candles and flowers and posters, extending into the sky in the form of flags and banners and chalked messages on the George Washington statue in the center of the plaza.

But now, it's raining, and the piles have wilted into the gray stone. Someone has taken the time to place cardboard boxes and umbrellas over the candles to keep the rain out, but the candles have instead lit the boxes and umbrellas on fire and a small bonfire is blazing at the foot of the statue. As I walk up the stairs, five or six policeman and a couple of people with cameras are standing, staring at the blaze, no one moving to do much of anything to put it out or contain it. A tattooed skate punk kid walks gingerly around the circle, blowing out the remaining candles before they can do any more damage. We watch the fire in silence, except for the clicking of shutters. Someone bums a cigarette, we struggle to get it lit in the wind and rain.

Two police officers come up out of the subway carrying fire extinguishers, walk to the middle of the memorial, and put out the fire. It only takes a few blasts from the extinguishers, with a few extra blasts for good measure. The smoke carries up into the sky, bright white in the neon of Union Square.

The tiny crowd disperses. As I walk down into the subway, a fire truck pulls up on 14th Street, and I see a man wave it off. The sirens disappear, the red lights stop turning, and the truck drives away. I try not to look at the gray ash covering the flowers.

* * *

Since this was written, over a week ago, Union Square Park has been cleaned, scraped free of wax, scrubbed free of graffiti. A few candles and memorials have returned, but nothing close to the carnival atmosphere of the immediate aftermath. Here and there, fliers are popping up protesting the cleaning, accusing the city of forcing a fascist "return to normalcy." The truth is, that fire begot fire. We came full circle. It was time to move on. 📖

Lower Broadway, September 11, 2001,
photograph by Whitney Pastorek

Terror

Anna Bálint

Outside, the plumes of smoke,
the heat of the fireball,
have subsided.
Now the air is ash.
Now there is stillness.
Never before have I known such quiet.
Never before have I lain so still.

This morning, early,
while the children slept,
I readied for the day.
I washed and dressed.
I brushed my hair.
I heated water for tea.
Later I called the children awake
and the little one yawned,
her pink mouth wide.

Now my children's faces
float inside my mind
like dust in sunlight.
Here, beneath the rubble
there is no sun, only dust.
If there is a difference
between death
and awaiting rescue
I do not know it.

I heard the plane.
First the drone
and then the roar of it,
the rest a confusion.

Sudden heat and screams,
a rush of fire, black smoke,
fire and smoke
rushing into my lungs
as everything
everything
gave way: no floor,
no walls, no doors,
just falling,
endlessly falling,
everything red,
the red of fire,
the red of my own blood,
my heart and lungs exploding,
a terrible snapping
and cracking of bones,
my bones, and the bones
of this building.
And then the silence.

There came a moment,
lying here so still,
when I imagined I heard a sound.
I imagined I heard the voices
of my rescuers. They came
with shovels and bravery
and picked through rubble.
They shouted my name.
Later I imagined I heard
my children crying their desolation.
There was nothing of me left
to answer them.

I do not know
whether this is the the same day
of the morning my children set out,
the oldest holding tight

the hand of the youngest,
sunlight warm upon their faces
as they turned to wave to me.
I do not know
whether this is that same day,
or the night of that day,
or another day or night entirely.
I do not know.

I do not know
the men who did this thing,
or their morning thoughts
as they shaved or combed
their beards, or whether
they dressed in fresh shirts
in readiness of this day.
I do not know
the color of their eyes,
or what light they held.

Outside, the plumes of smoke,
the heat of the fireball,
have subsided.
Now it rains dust,
the air is ash,
and my children are shadows.
Now my scorched skin
drifts over the city like feathers.

I am thirty years old
and the mother of three.
This morning
American bombs fell on my city.
I live in Hiroshima, Japan.
I live in Baghdad. I live in Beirut.
I heard the planes coming.
I live in a village in Vietnam.

I live on the West Bank.
I live in the highlands of Guatemala.
The soldiers who came to my village
carried American guns.
I live on the Oklahoma Plains,
I journeyed here along the Trail of Tears.
I live in New York. I arrived by slave ship.
I live in Afghanistan.
I am thirty years old,
I pray facing east,
I fear for my children.

Suspend

Suzannah Dalzell

"But now there is hope, and pain is implanted in hope."
—Marguerite Duras

SUSPEND: To keep from falling or sinking by some invisible support as if by hanging.

I am staring at the image of the second plane suspended in the air as it careens toward the second World Trade Tower. The upper portion of the first tower is engulfed in black smoke. The sky is very blue. For those who saw it on television this was a split second event, one frame of an unfolding drama. But I am far away from a television. What I see first is still pictures. I see men in business suits carrying brief cases, walking out of the cream colored dust; a ghostlike woman in pearls frozen by fear; red fire trucks and acid-green-striped firefighters blooming out of the rubble; small twisted bodies caught by the camera as they plummet down the face of the building.

SUSPENDED ANIMATION: A state of temporary cessation of vital functions.

My mother is suspended between life and death. She was taken to the hospital in January of 2002. It is now March, six months after the event, which we refer to tersely as 9/11. Because my mother was unable and unwilling to communicate with her doctor, an esophageal ulcer went untreated and began to affect the surrounding systems. She ate and drank very little to minimize the pain and became severely dehydrated, which in turn affected her brain function. Although her health has been compromised for the last twenty-five years, due to a stroke at the age of fifty, she has been declining rapidly since September.

I have not seen my mother for twelve years. Occasionally one of my siblings will send me a photograph. Most are of both my parents, because my mother shies away from the camera. There is a picture of the two of them sitting side by side on the piano bench. My father is playing from a piece that is laid on the closed lid. My mother is looking at the music also; her good hand poised ready to turn the page, her crippled hand out of sight, hidden by the bulk of the piano. There is a picture of the two of them taken on their 50th anniversary. They are looking at each other, but only my father's face is visible. My mother is turned toward him. I am told it is my father's favorite picture.

In my favorite photograph she is looking directly at the camera. Her eyes are dancing over her reading glasses and she is grinning broadly. The last picture, the one I received most recently, was taken a couple of months before she went to the hospital. My mother is sitting in her wheelchair. Her crippled hand is sliding off her lap. Her clothes are all askew and her reading glasses are hanging awkwardly from her neck. Again she is facing the camera, but she is not smiling. Her mouth is a flat line. Her eyes stare out blankly like a blind pet that turns toward the sound of your voice, but cannot see you anymore.

SUSPENSIVE: Having the effect of suspending the operation of something.

I spent a good part of my life cloaked in hope and anticipation, longing for a better world. During the 1980s this sense of hopefulness kept expanding. I was filled with hope for true communication and healing in my family, hope for true communication between the people of the world and the healing of the planet. Global warming was being taken seriously. Gorbachev's glasnost made cultural exchanges with children from Russia possible. The Berlin wall came down and my right-wing neighbors were recycling with gusto. Two violent events blew apart this optimistic bubble.

The first event in August of 1989 was of my own doing. I flew the plane carrying the bomb. I pushed the button that released the bomb into the heart of my family. I wrote letters to my parents and siblings. I firmly believed there would be harmony in my family, if the closet doors were thrown open and all the skeletons were brought into the light. I was on a peacekeeping mission, a nation-building mission.

SUSPEND: To hold over one or more musical tones of a chord into the following chord producing a temporary dissonance or discord.

The second event, which happened a year and a half later, was not my doing. On January 17th the first air attacks on Iraq began. This event I did watch on television. I watched jet fighters taking off, bombs exploding, tracer lights in the night sky, the oil fields burning and burning and burning. All that I had been working for was going up in smoke.

Squashed into a corner of the couch, my thirteen-year-old daughter asked how long the war would last. I flashed back to the Viet Nam war, my coming of age war, which dragged on for years. The World Wars of the twentieth century, my parent's and grandparent's wars, were long drawn-out conflicts connected by economic disaster and civil unrest.

Again my daughter asked how long the war would last. She wondered whether she would be drafted, if the fighting continued. I turned to look at her. Her eyes, locked on the TV images, were animated by equal measures of fear and excitement. I turned the television off.

SUSPENSION: The state of a substance when its particles are mixed with but undissolved in a fluid and kept dispersed by agitation.

Initially there was a great deal of movement in my family. Letters and phone calls flew back and forth, carrying accusations and pleas for understanding. My father took the offensive position. He attempted to obtain my childhood psychiatric records in order to prove that I was delusional, which made me feel violated all over again. My mother, caught in the crossfire, sought refuge in her marriage. A few last angry words were spoken and then there was a long silence.

I was determined not to return to the crippling coping mechanisms of the past, but could not envision a future either. The only way I could survive was to kill off hope, to kill off longing. Hope is an addiction without a twelve-step program and many of my friends were afraid to walk with me. At first I was very lonely, but then I got used to the solitude. I started writing.

SUSPENSE: A state of mental uncertainty as in awaiting a decision or outcome, accompanied by anxiety.

On September 11, I was attending a silent meditation retreat on Cortez Island off the coast of British Columbia. After ascertaining that my family and friends were all safe, I decided to stay. I was too depleted from a difficult summer to be of any use to anyone. I spent the week sitting in meditation, walking mindfully in the woods, and staring out over the calm gray water.

When I did re-enter, my writing dried up. I started reading. I read the New York Times every day, clipping articles and highlighting passages. I spent hours on the web downloading essays and sending them on to friends. I stopped sleeping. I worried constantly about what I should do to help solve the world's problems. Should I fly to Afghanistan and join an aid agency? Should I march in an anti-war protest? Should I return to the island and meditate on peace? In the end, I went to my doctor and upped my anti-anxiety medication.

SUSPENSORY LIGAMENT: An annular- or ring-shaped transparent membrane holding the lens of the eye in place.

It is April and my mother's condition has stabilized. She hopes to be home by Easter. At Ground Zero the search for identifiable remains continues and the "war on terrorism" is raging in the mountains and deserts of Afghanistan. But my mother and I have suspended our disagreement. We are putting aside the rhetoric of détente and learning the language of forgiveness. Three years ago we began a written correspondence and although we were growing closer, she firmly rejected my periodic requests to get together. When she became ill, I longed to be with her, but did not want to cause her any additional distress. At the urging of close friends, I wrote to her and she agreed to see me.

See is perhaps the wrong word, since my mother has been going blind for five years. Until recently she kept this fact a secret from everyone including her doctor and my father. Fiercely independent, my mother hides her infirmities, like a feral animal that tries to outwit potential predators.

I made two trips back to visit my mother in the nursing home, bringing one of her granddaughters each time. During the first visit our conversation was very careful, very guarded, but the anger in her voice was gone. The second visit went more smoothly. She was truly glad to see me and greeted me warmly. To my daughter's astonishment, we lapsed into old conversation patterns anticipating each other's thoughts and finishing each other's sentences.

As we were leaving I hugged my mother lightly. She did not hug me back, but she did not stiffen or pull away either. At her request, I left the door to her room open.

SUSPENSOR: A structure in seed-bearing plants that bears the embryo and carries it to a food source by elongation. 📖

Faith and Urban Life, Photograph by Manit Chaotragoongit

A Better Way

David Warren Paul

*"If I see someone come in and he's got a diaper on his head and
a fan belt wrapped around the diaper on his head, that guy
needs to be pulled over and checked."*

—U.S. Rep. John Cooksey (R-La), responding to reports that Muslims
were being investigated and harassed in America following the attacks
on the Pentagon and World Trade Center.

"On Saturday, September 15, 2001, an unplanned visit to the
Idriss Mosque in North Seattle lifted me out of the gloom I
was feeling. Afterward, I wrote an email message to a list of
friends and relatives, describing the experience and expressing
some thoughts about it. What I wrote came straight from the
heart and was not intended as literature; I was merely reporting
on something I stumbled into while feeling anger at the attacks
on Muslims that had taken place in Seattle and elsewhere in the
wake of 9/11. Many who received my message wrote back and
told me it had helped them, somehow, and they were forwarding
it to others around the country and around the world.

Among the responses was a personal email message
from Jimmy Kolker, then U.S. Ambassador to Burkina Faso.
Ambassador Kolker thanked me and reported that he had read
my words to an assembly of Muslims at the largest mosque in
Ouagadougou, the capital city, which he visited in a gesture aimed
at assuring Burkina Faso's Muslim majority that the United States
harbored no ill will against them or their religion.

The responses surprised me. All I meant to say in my email—
and all I mean to say by offering it in this chapbook as a new form
of literature, the "open e-mail message"—is that there are times
when we may feel helpless in the wake of tragedy and injustice,
but in fact we are not. No matter what is happening around us,
we can find a way to do something useful if we keep our eyes and
hearts open.

Subject: A better way
Date: Sat, 15 Sep 2001 14:49:33 -0700
From: "David W. Paul"
<davudwoayk@Home.com.
To: Friends and relatives

On my way to the Northgate post office in Seattle just after noon today, I saw a small crowd of people gathered at the Idriss Mosque at 15th Avenue Northeast. My first thought was Oh, no. As I drew near, however, I saw smiling faces, signs that read "Peace" and "Honk to show support." Flowers were piled up on the steps, and fifteen or twenty people were milling around. I honked. The car behind me honked. Cars from all directions honked. The people standing and sitting in front of the mosques waved, yelled, flashed the "peace" sign; or was it "V" for victory?—same thing, in this context.

I continued to the post office and dropped my letters. On my way back, I turned the idea over in my head. Do I want to get involved? Don't I have other things to do? Is it dangerous there? Will I be on an FBI list?

I decided there was no better way of spending some time in the middle of a gorgeous September Saturday, just four days after a national catastrophe killed thousands of Americans and a couple days after our own neighbors, our friends, our fellow Americans, became victims of sporadic outbursts of hatred, than to stop and show my support.

I had no idea what to do or say.

When I reached the mosque, people welcomed me. Muslims and non-Muslims. The heap of flowers was bigger and more beautiful. Still more people were coming to lay bouquets on the steps. There were American flags, and signs that said, "We are Americans" and "Islam = Peace" and "We are one." I shook some hands and said hello to a few people outside, told them how glad I was to see this happening, and asked if I could join them. Yes, of course, and would you like to see our mosque?

I took my shoes off at the door. Inside, the man who ushered me in called to a boy, about 14, who showed me around. He pointed out the *minbar*, or pulpit, and the wall lined with holy books; he explained how the mosque is used and the schedule of daily prayers. We talked for a short while. The mosque is of simple design, by no means as ornate as some I've seen, but it is a holy place. It made me both sad and outraged to recall that just two nights earlier, some ignorant and hate-filled person had tried to burn it down. There were no signs of damage; the firebug was arrested in the act of throwing gasoline on the outside walls; he had not yet lit a match.

I joined some of the people sitting on chairs at curbside, waving to motorists passing by. The response was tremendous, heartwarming. Horns honking, people waving and calling out their support. Only one instance of an extended middle finger the whole time I was there, about an hour. It's been days since I smiled like that.

In a time when it is so difficult to find ways of doing something helpful, something to take our focus away from anger and turn it to our common humanity, our little group at 15th and Northgate Way may have done some marginal amount of good today.

I don't know how to conclude this. Maybe it's best not to conclude it, but to hope that this spirit is replicated a thousandfold across the USA, and that it helps us remember who we are as we face the troubled times that lie before us. Whatever action we as a nation take, it will have no positive outcome if we are a people divided by prejudice and hatred. 📖

At the Reading

Robert Gregory

While he stood at the gleaming podium
in front of the two brand-new windows
in the unmarked room with its mild
smooth carpet and ranks of identical chairs
speaking slowly and gravely about the loneliness
of his childhood, big ragged flakes of snow,
some of them joined as if holding hands,
began to race past the windows behind him
horizontally, just a few fragments at first
and then many thousands. Some in his audience
saw the snow going past (pretty); some
saw small gleeful beings rushing by, their freedom
to fly a cheerful mockery of the speaker
and his gravity, and his motionless audience as well,
and the words that moved so slowly and carefully
out of him and disappeared into the space
of the room; some saw a reminder of the things
that can happen: something solid and permanent
just up the street disintegrates in distance and silence,
and a roaring wind from the unheard blast comes
running past us with the ragged torn fragments
of paper and skin, some of them still joined, racing them away
to scatter them so that although lonely and broken
and gone forever they will be everywhere and anything now

Letter to Myself

Amontaine Aurore

I tell myself that I am a good person; that I am a good citizen. After all, I work, pay my bills, try to eat right, try not to hurt others. I tell myself that one day when I get some time I really must do something about the starving children, the war torn countries, those many men who rot away in hopelessness behind prison walls, and the homeless people discarded like garbage through our streets. And then one day across my television screen I see towers exploding in flames, exploding not that far from me, leaving a heap of destruction and awe in its wake. I see desperate people carrying pictures of their loved ones through the streets, their trembling hands holding cherished family photos to the television cameras, crying, "*Has anyone seen my father? My husband? My wife? My beautiful, young daughter? Has anybody seen my world?*" And I turn away in shame and try to figure how it is I have done so little to alleviate the suffering all around, for the suffering is not new, only more unique and closer to home.

I am not a religious person. Not in the traditional sense of getting down on my knees every night or blessing my food at every meal. I do not go to church on Sunday . . . any Sunday. I cannot quote the Bible, for I've never read it. Nevertheless, I am aware of a spiritual presence, a divine being that permeates everything, though much of the time I fool myself into thinking I can function just fine without it, that my human intellect is all I need to see me through. And then fire and ashes and black billowing smoke rain down on New York City, and I realize that in this world of pundits and politicians and experts and geniuses, our intellect has severe limitations. For all of our extraordinary technological advances, we are still like emotionally and spiritually crippled children. We have polluted and desecrated our planet. We have destroyed untold numbers of species. We have developed more and more sophisticated means in which to hurt and kill one another, including germ warfare. But we have spent comparably little time trying to figure out how we can learn to get along together. And so I turn humbly towards that which cannot be seen, saying, *mother, father, this world of ours cannot possibly be all there is to the story.*

Perhaps Martin Luther King, Jr. was wrong when he said that violence was not the answer. One would think so after watching our leaders prance up and down with hands on hips and "kick ass" grimaces, words of retaliation and war tripping far too easily off their tongues. However, every year on January 15th we celebrate Dr. King's birthday. Because we say he deserves to be honored for his deep commitment to peace. Because he moved us with his philosophy of love . . . love . . .

Jesus is love. Not that I would know anything about that personally, for I have never read the "New Testament," but have many times heard this nation of so many Christians describe Him as such. So tell me, what is love? It probably sounds like a stupid question, but I am beginning to realize it is those concepts we take for granted, those things we never bother to question but mouth in robotic, half-sleep states, that are the culprits in our demise.

Is love a concept or a practice? The domain of poets and artists only? Is it really a driving force bringing two people together so that the generations will continue? Does it have any place in our national and foreign policies? Does it have a practical application that can be used to take us to higher levels of consciousness and existence? Or is it something for stupid people? Something for those Blacks to adhere to when they get out of line? Something to mouth on Sundays so we can feel good and clean and right and pure?

If there are those who still question that we physically exist in a unified energy field, they surely cannot deny that the revolution in our global telecommunications has done much to tie us together psychologically. It has been said that humanity is "a single species, sharing a common home and a common destiny." There are no walls between us, save the ones we continue to erect in the name of racial, religious, and national pride, which when you examine, begins to look a lot like fear.

I wish we had a global flag—one we could wave for the whole of our world. I wish we had an understanding of love that wasn't compartmentalized like a TV dinner tray. For can we truly have peace and security and happiness that is roped off and kept within the boundaries of our nation? Can we secure freedom for ourselves, while we deny it to others? Can we ask God to bless America and forget about the rest of the world? Can we wage war, and call ourselves "winners" even as we trudge through the refuse of lifeless bodies and watch the boundless tears of parents who will pray every day to die because they have experienced the ultimate suffering of outliving their children?

I tell myself that I am a good person. I work and pay bills and try not to hurt anyone. But in reflecting upon the Eleventh day of September, I realize that I am not the harmless being I like to think I am. Like many of us, I have been silent, and that silence has hurt us all. I have learned to accept the hypocrisies and incongruities witnessed all around because I believed there was nothing I could do about them. But I can begin to speak up. I can question. I can demand to know why there is such inconsistency between our leaders' words and actions.

Like the heap of rubble and death that piled up before our eyes, our challenges are mounting . . . mounting. We don't need greater technology, for it will take more than mere intellectual wizardry to free us now. A spiritual crisis demands a spiritual solution. We have work to do. 📖

XIII

Volume 11, Number 1
2003-2004
Wealth, Economy & Madness

Medicine Bearer, Woven Mask
by Gail E. Tremblay

Another Cousin

Keith Egawa

Hey Cousin Dogface, did I ever tell you I was ten years old the day I met your father? This is back when you must've still been in diapers, though you stayed in that stage a little longer than the norm. Let's see . . . he was my second cousin, once removed. That makes you my second cousin twice removed, which is pretty close in the Indian way—something that obligates giving second, even third chances to those who let you down now and again. Give me a minute and let me tell you about that day.

I remember my dad and I were standing next to the porch of Great Grandma's house, looking over the oysters we'd gotten from Gooseberry Point. It was a hot day and the oysters were spread out on the yellow lawn. I was watching the tiny crabs and sea bugs scurrying around on the shells as my dad buffeted them with the hose. That's when the big sedan rolled into the driveway, rust eating it alive. The driver stomped the brake just short of ramming our station wagon, the two faces in the windshield lurching forward.

My dad let the garden hose fall to the ground. Water bubbled and hissed from beneath the weak seal of the attachment. A smile spread across his face. Two men got out of the car, your father on the passenger side. He was the first one out, the first to approach. The way he lowered his head, turning it nearly sideways, made me think of captured wolves at feeding time, running back and forth at the fence. Injured wolves waiting to heal up and be released. I could tell he'd had a bunch of beers the way his feet stepped with a little too much care, boots thumping on the asphalt.

"Hey, Cousin!" his voice boomed for the distant neighbors to hear. He led with his arm raised to deliver one hell of a slap on the back then dropped his hand into my father's. He pulled their bodies together, pounding my dad's shoulder several times. Then they stepped back from one another. Their speechless pause said that it had been a long time. In their eyes, for one quick moment, you could see all that humor of their shared beginnings coming right back. Even all the scary stuff—all the bad shit coming with it. And that was something to smile about too, because it had been such a long time.

Your father flung his arm toward his buddy who was now seated on the hood of the car eating a corndog. "You know Beer-can, dontcha'?" he said to my dad, more statement of fact than question. "Sometimes he goes by 'Loogie' if he's in mixed company."

Too polite to speak with his mouth full, Loogie saluted us with the corndog.

My dad placed his hand on my shoulder without looking back. "This is my son, Henry," he said. Then he turned to face me. "Henry, that's Loogie Beer-can and this is your cousin . . ."

"C.J.!" your father interrupted loudly. He reached for my hand, stepping forward right onto the nozzle of the hose that rolled beneath his foot. He made a quick recovery, laughing it off, directed at himself, dispelling focus from the drunken jackass move. He was wearing a heavy military jacket, washed-out army green. He looked tough with the heavy zippers stitched across the pockets and flipped-up collar.

"H.C." I said, giving my initials in return. He thought this was clever, or maybe smart-assed, which I bet, to him, was even better. His smile crept from suspicion to approval like we'd made a secret bond; he'd caught me stealing his material and appreciated the hell out of it. His hand was solid, with big, hard labor knuckles. But his handshake was Indian. He just placed his hand in mine. He didn't crush my fingers like he could have, but it felt as if I had grabbed a piece of machinery—part of a car engine or a tool off the workbench. That's how I remember it. His smile lines pointed to the sky, to the ground, in every direction around him, though I know now that he was only in his mid-thirties at the time. His eyes were very dark, even when he was laughing. Like yours and mine.

He held the handshake a long time for effect, his smile closing his eyes down until they were nearly shut, holding my gaze like some ridiculous challenge between man and boy. Then finally, "So, what's your story, Chief?"

I felt embarrassed over the prolonged attention, and at being called Chief. I glanced down at my ten-dollar shoes that would later give me tendonitis, and then back up at him. "What do you mean?"

"I mean, what are you doin' with your life?"

Sure, I was only ten, but I was above average, quick. I could think of something I was doing with my life, aside from watching cartoons and eating candy. I was scribbling and misspelling stories that anyone in the family might volunteer about themselves, or about someone else—a sure cause for future dismay.

"I'm writing down family stories," I said, "so no one will forget 'em."

He leaned in with interest and his smile grew like he really couldn't help it. His teeth were as white as pieces of polished stone off the beach—big round teeth trying to show you that all is well, like my dad's, though my dad was putting his at risk with chain smoking.

"Right!" said C.J. "Cultural preservation! I got some stories for you."

Now I was doing even better. I was more than smartass stealing his material; I was a tribal historian. I tried to look all serious. "Let's hear 'em."

C.J. ended the handshake. "In good time, boy," he said, backing up and turning his body to include my dad once again. Then, "So you got some oysters? Why don't you shuck one for me there, Guy. Don't bother with the small ones neither."

My dad squatted down over the catch, his wide shoulders hunched up under his ears. I could hear the clacking of shells as he flipped them around. Then he rose holding an oyster about as big as a flattened softball. He worked a paring knife into its strong muscle. The oyster gave way with a crack and hiss as the seal broke. He discarded the top shell and handed the other half with the oyster to C.J.

Loogie remained mute and grinning, perched on the hood of his junker, satisfied to sit back and watch the behavior of his buddy, a man with charisma enough to take up all available space.

C.J. paused for effect, foreboding and humor unified in his eyes, as if he were playing Russian roulette and was so completely reckless that he found the stakes to be laughable. "So you decided to come in from the big city, eh, Guy?" he asked my dad, the oyster jiggling a little in its shell, inches from his face.

My dad just smiled at the question. Our house in Seattle was about two hours from Great Grandma's front yard. We didn't make the trip down I-5 that often, passing the sign that reads, *You are now subject to the laws of the Lummi Indian Nation.*

C.J. tipped the shell and sucked the cold fist-sized oyster into his mouth. Then he took turns making eye contact with me and my dad, rotating the huge blob from cheek to cheek, barely containing the milky sea water from running out the corners of his mouth. It took him a good while to chew it up and get it down his throat.

My dad laughed the whole while. I thought it was pretty cool too.

I asked my dad to shuck another one for me. I sensed that this was one of the important things to be learned from the men of the family. I was a kid who would eat anything from out of the water or crawling on the ground; a cold slab of wildlife from the mud of low tide was just fine by me. Although it was as big as a hard-boiled goose egg the flavor wasn't so bad. It was triumph more than taste. I chewed the animal until I was sure it had given up the ghost then gulped it down. Your dad slapped me on the back. My dad said "way to go," and hit my Sears and Roebuck sneaker with a blast from the hose. I was accepted. You know that feeling down inside. Remember when uncle Gunny carried you up the beach on his shoulders the year his canoe won at Stomish? Pride coming down on you like sun on your face. He reached back and lifted you up, hollering, "This squirt'll be pullin' in my place next year!" At the time you were less than four feet tall with Kool Aid stains up to your eyeballs, bur your expression said that if Gunny thought so then it must be true.

The second and last time I saw C.J., he was standing at the side of the road in front of your house. I think you might have been on the porch with a runny nose, bouncing in one of those Johnny Jump-ups. C.J. saw us across the street visiting the McCluskys, and he walked over without his shoes on to talk with my dad. I went over to where they stood, wanting to be a part of what they were saying, wanting to stand by them. C.J. said his boat and nets had been impounded by the state for illegal fishing.

"They're waiting for us to just go away, Guy," said C.J. "But I'll tell you what. When they gimme a silver bullet I'll shoot myself with it. 'Cause nothin' else they got is gonna kill me, Cousin." That's what he said. I didn't ask him to tell me any of the stories like he'd promised before. He seemed awfully distracted. When he spoke he was looking down at his bare feet. There was a teenager on a motorcycle racing up and down the street. After making several passes, C.J. picked up a rock and threw it at him lackadaisically like a boy skipping stones across a lake. He missed on purpose.

He yelled after the teenager, "Slow it up a little, Buddy! There's kids on this road!"

A few weeks later I asked my dad if we could go up to the Res that upcoming weekend to get some oysters and eat a few raw ones with C.J.

"Sure we can," said my dad. And he laughed at the memory.

But the weekend was too late. It didn't come in time. Your mom called, telling us that C.J. was dead. He'd been driving drunk and had hit a telephone pole. Hit it so hard he'd sheared the damned thing right off. But he survived the crash. Supposedly he was just fine. Then, when he got out of the car, he stepped on one of the fallen wires, lying there in the dark—a mean ending to a generous string of second chances, coiled and waiting. There are fields of corn and muddy plains all around the road where he died; there's that fireworks stand there now with the sign, bombs, rockets, crabs, and salmon. It's one of the roads that lead off the reservation.

I bet it was quiet when he got out of the car, when the power racing through rubber cords above the Res floated to the ground to take him. I wonder if the moon was out for him to see one more time, illuminating the contours of his land, dark blue shadows hiding the bottles, cans and paper, making his last look at it beautiful. I bet he actually might have smiled one more time, standing in disbelief of living, of being spared to get back into his boat and put out his nets. Did he thank the Creator for watching out for him? Did he ask why things turned out the way they did?

"C.J.!" I can hear the way he announced his name like everyone was waiting for him and he had finally arrived. Or maybe it was just to reassure himself out loud—*Damn, look at this, I'm still here.*

I wonder if the air outside the car was cool. I wonder if he smiled. I don't know the answers to these questions, nor will I ever, because C.J. died before he could tell us. I don't mean to stir things up for you with all this. I just thought I should let you know I met your father. I thought I might tell you what I felt.

My dad said, "I'm glad you liked him. He had a tough go of it. Just remember that he..." Then he trailed off, and I could sense he meant to mention that C.J. had been drunk, to work a lesson into the whole thing. But he didn't. He just took a sip of his coffee and made a face like he had burned his mouth. Then he went over to the sink and kept his back to me. He repeated himself. "I'm glad you liked him." I can still see that scene.

My parents separated not even a month after C.J.'s death, shortly after my dad had come home in the middle of the night with soot on his hands and face, his eyelashes singed. It wasn't until at least ten years later, when I was in college, that I found out what had happened. He had gone to the yard where C.J.'s boat and nets were imprisoned, impounded. He climbed the fence, poured gas into the hull of the boat where the nets were piled, and set the whole thing ablaze. Can't you just see him rattling over that fence, damn near torching himself in the process?

By the time my mother decided to tell me all those years later that that's what he had done, I'd forgotten all about that distant night when I'd sneaked out of bed and seen her chewing him out in the living room while he sat there charred as a pork rib. When Mom finally told me I was eighteen and must've been ready, I suppose. My older sisters had already known. Of course I went straight to my father to ask about it.

I was wondering if that'd ever come up," he said. "It was a lot of anger over a lot of years and memories. They took so much from C.J. even before he was born; a type of hurt that kept taking while he was alive. I figured I wouldn't let them take some more after he was dead. It was stupid though, Henry. Really stupid and unfair to your mother and you kids. I didn't get caught but I coulda' gone to jail."

"Sounds like something I'd do," I told him.

"Oh man, don't say that," he laughed. "Keep in mind I was only in my early thirties. It was rash and stupid. You're beyond that."

I'd reminded him that I was only eighteen.

"Oh, yeah," he said. "Good lord. Well, you're a lot smarter than me."

"Yeah," I agreed. "I suppose that's true."

"Look," he said. "I'm not proud of it. But I'm not exactly ashamed either. It just is. Maybe in a way your mom and I ended up splittin' 'cause she couldn't really get it. Not that she needed to forgive me for putting us all in jeopardy like that, 'cause it was wrong. But maybe she couldn't understand, really know why it all hurt so damn bad. And maybe we ended up splittin' 'cause I wouldn't let her."

There's an energy that young boys watch for, seeking it out in their fathers, their uncles, their cousins. Anywhere, I guess. I caught a glimpse of it that one day, moving a few feet ahead of C.J., brave and distracted, towing death on a leash, completely certain and without a clue about what's coming next. It's a charisma that seems to overshadow the dangerous parts—those patches of darkness that even a boy can see. Those patches coming through despite the smile, revealing a man moving too quickly toward the day when the men and boys of his tribe line up to throw in a shovel-full of dirt and say goodbye. *A silver bullet—nothing else they got is gonna' kill me.* That's what your daddy said. He was wrong. They got plenty more than that.

Is it true you and the rest of the boys are getting jobs with the forest service? Your brother was telling me you're going to have to quit relying on fishing to pay the bills. Lots of policymaking on the horizon. Regulations over a big empty ocean. Time to back off and let the salmon come up stream. I don't know, Cousin. When the last living human beings finally succumb to their homemade cancers and self-imposed starvation, the planet is going to make a sound like a tremendous and lonely gust of wind as the last souls of the most intelligent species evacuate the globe. Maybe it will be sorrowful, or maybe it will mean something quite different, like *good fucking riddance.*

Cousin, I don't know what things your father did in life, good or bad. I don't really know much about him at all. Not much beyond the admiration that I had for him as a boy during one of those flashing instants free from knowledge of history or the future. He never got to tell me all the stories like he'd promised. He didn't get to tell all the stories that he owed you. But I'll remember him as my older cousin, a Lummi Indian. The man who ate the oyster. I will love that memory and his part in it. And if I don't tell the one story he gave me, it will simply go away. You see, when living things are gone, stories are all you got. Now tell me, can you smell that salt and seaweed, the rocky silt warmed under the cloudless sky at low tide? Can you hear the sound of those rubber boots on the linoleum, in the darkness of the kitchen at 5:00 a.m. on opening day—everyone heading down to their fishing boats? Can you feel the edge of the bay where the reservation stops, when you look out across that entire deep green to the rest of the world? Can you see the accumulation of life's expressions on all those faces dead and gone? Will you remember them? 📖

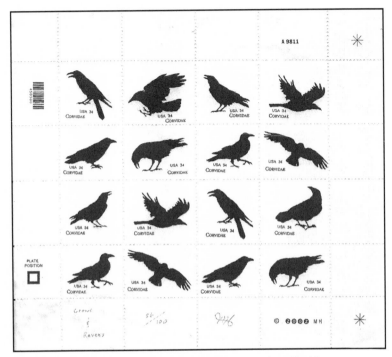

Crows & Ravens, #56/100, 2002, Stamp Art, by Mike Hess

Procession

Joan Fitzgerald

The Pritchetts rode horses one brilliant summer
      in the Fourth of July Parade
buttermilk tails flicking dust over people in webbed lawn chairs
along the road, and clopped swaying, high above the crowd,
between the Silver Prince Drum Corps and a Four H Troop.
No banner was as bright and arrogant as this family.

They mismanaged their farm.
Ignoring the hired hands who smashed tavern windows
      with bar stools
fell drunkenly off tractors and lay vomiting in ditches
while the cows stood up to their knees in manure in the barn
next to a cache of CDs and tapes that the girls had
      boosted from Record Shack.

The parents gave parties where guests pulled the hostess's
      dress down
and sprayed her snowy Alps with whipped cream
as her husband French-kissed her best friend in the kitchen
with the children watching from the stairway landing
waiting for sirens, fistfights.

The fourteen-year old drove her parent's SUV
into the front of a house on the main road and gazed in surprise
through a windshield wreathed in broccoli and lettuce
at the family cowering over their roast beef dinner.
The oldest boy carried a shotgun onto the school bus
      wrapped in newspaper
hoping to shoot his Social Studies teacher.

Barmaids, car salesman, and tumescent neighbors
invaded the wreckage of their nights
while the parties got louder and the drinks stronger
time gutted their glittering, solipsistic beauty.
The divorce was not pretty.

The second boy perished in a motorcycle accident at twenty-two.
His sister wore gold sandals and a heliotrope satin blouse
          at his wake.
The following spring she was shot to death outside
          a Nevada casino.
The other children married, separated, started repair shops,
          got fat.

And now, no one remembers that lambent summer
when in boots and fringes, turquoise and silver, taller than mortals,
they rode horses in the Fourth of July parade.

Mrs. Morrissey

Priscilla Long

Rosalie Morrissey had never robbed anyone before. Oh, as a girl in the 1930s she'd snitched Padraic's marbles, one at a time, and kept a nice stash. And once, she and Paddy had pilfered quarters from their father's change purse. They'd run down 40th Street with their loot and bought Blue Bunny Ice Cream Sandwiches from the Durn Good Grocer. Her old friend Mary Rothstein, who'd died of breast cancer last year, shoplifted all her life and boasted about it to anyone. Mary had purloined her entire wardrobe, gaudy and mismatched as it was. She used to laugh and say she never understood why anyone would pay for clothes. But Mary had not come from a good family.

Mrs. Morrissey *had* come from a good family and besides, a third-grade teacher, even if retired, had to set a standard. She was a good woman who did good deeds. Not that she was a churchgoer. But she bought Girl Scout cookies. She canvassed in voter registration drives. She collected clothing for the less fortunate, even after she herself had become less fortunate after Robert died. She purchased her garments in thrift stores and bought groceries within a strict weekly budget, which she meticulously inked into a green ledger. She volunteered once a week at Harborview Hospital. Her only deviation from perfect goodness—and she had no regrets about this—was her friendship with the irascible Mary Rothstein. But now Mary was gone and Rosalie Morrissey was being evicted.

Rosalie had not planned to hold up the Durn Good Grocery. If she had given it a moment's thought, she would not have held it up. But she didn't give it a moment's thought. She opened the eviction letter and read it and sat down. She didn't know how long she sat there. But gradually all the hand-wringing and anxiety of the past months drained away. They had raised the rent, and raised it again, until she had become distraught. The days had become an anxious search for ways to economize, to cut back, to gather sufficient funds for the next rent. Now she was distraught no more. She was simply at the end of her rope.

And it *was* simple. It was as if a decision had been taken by God or the Devil, not by Rosalie Morrissey. She allowed the letter to float from her hand to the floor. She went to Robert's sock drawer and took out the pistol she'd left there undisturbed after he died. It was surprisingly heavy. She slung on her shoulder bag and placed the pistol into it. She walked out the door, not even bothering to lock it behind her. It was evening, hot and dusty, about 9 o'clock, still light. She walked down North 40th Street, past the wood-clad houses with their porches and brick chimneys, past the topped sweetgum trees and scarlet oaks that she herself had helped to plant back when they thought the city was going to bury the power lines. Now the trees were dying, beheaded by City Light for tangling in the overhead wires. She'd walked this walk a thousand times, but on this hot August evening everything looked different. Dusty maple leaves seemed to curl at the edges and the purple dahlias and orange poppies in the yard at the corner of Burke Street glowed in a greenish, sick-looking light. As for Mrs. Morrissey, she felt fine, almost cheerful.

She entered the Durn Good Grocery. The cash register was jingling and clacking and spitting out its long white tongue of the day's transactions.

"Why, good evening Mrs. Morrissey. You're just in time." Benjamin Zaslavsky had perched himself on the stool behind the register. He was closing out the day's receipts. He was a stout, balding, red-faced man wearing a white shirt and trousers upheld by suspenders. He was studying the receipts through a pair of round-eyed, wire-rimmed glasses.

"Good evening Benjamin." Rosalie removed the pistol from her shoulder bag and pointed it at him. She had known him ever since he was an eight-year-old pupil in her third-grade class. Indeed, it was she who'd taught him to make change.

"What can I get for you this evening?" Benjamin glanced up absently and then returned to his task. Then the information that she was pointing a gun at him registered in his face. He glanced at it and frowned.

"Oh do be careful with that, Mrs. Morrissey. You could hurt yourself."

"Benjamin, dear, this is a holdup. Please be so kind as to hand over the cash." The pistol shook in her hand.

"Mrs. Morrissey, what's the matter?" There was genuine concern in Benjamin's voice.

"What's the matter?" She took a breath. "I'm getting evicted! Just as if I hadn't lived in this neighborhood all my life! I bought gumdrops from your father!" Her voice quavered with indignation.

"Evicted!" said Benjamin. He stood up and leaned on the counter with both hands and looked at her closely. Then he looked down at the gun.

"Evicted!" Mrs. Morrissey repeated. "I helped plant those red oaks out there, I registered these people to vote!" She waved the gun at the wooden houses visible out the window of the corner grocery.

Benjamin squinted at the weapon as she waved it. "That's a Colt 45 semi-automatic pistol! Dad used to have one."

"They want to put me into some sort of home like I was a piece of furniture," Mrs. Morrissey continued, "or maybe they think I can live under the I-5 bridge." With the muzzle, she brushed the box of Extra Tall Licorice Ropes to the floor. "Why don't you start with the safe," she suggested.

Benjamin sighed. "But Mrs. Morrissey, it wasn't me who evicted you."

"Oh it's not your fault. You're just having—What did that letter say?—the luck of the draw. You are having the luck of the draw. And they're terribly sorry, and there's nothing they can do about it." She raised the gun with both hands, pointed it, and shot the safe. The gun popped and her arm jerked back and behind her the bullet case *pinged*.

Benjamin jumped. "Mrs. Morrissey!" He put up his hand as if to bless her. "Remain calm. I'm going to open the safe. My goodness! I've known you all my life." He turned his back and got down on his painful arthritic knee, and knelt before the safe as if to pray.

"Benjamin, it was me—taught you to make change." She

looked at the jumble of Juicy Fruit Gums and M & Ms and Clark's Bars and Power Bars and Chesterfield Lights and Chiclets and Fritos and frozen burritos and Bazooka Bubble Gums with their twisted waxed papers. My star pupil, she thought. I felt sure he would make a scholar.

"If you can count, you can make change," Benjamin Zaslavsky recited. He turned the combination of the safe. "Be careful Mrs. Morrissey. That pistol is already loaded for another shot."

"You have a brilliant mind, Benji, dear. I've always been sorry your Dad died just when he did. You would have made a scholar." Al Zaslavsky had opposed Benjamin's going to Harvard, even with a full scholarship. He'd wanted his boy to join the family business. He'd gotten the last word, too, by dropping dead the summer after Benjamin's one glorious year at Harvard.

He half turned to look up at her. "I've just now read Seamus Heaney's *Beowulf*. Have you read it?"

"I just returned it to the library! It's delicious, isn't it?" Mrs. Morrissey set the pistol down on the counter and took a handkerchief from her bag and mopped her face. "Doing hold-ups is exhausting," she confided.

"Oh, I should say so. You wouldn't want to hold up a store every day, that's for sure." Benjamin heaved himself up and plopped the bank-bag of money on the counter.

"It's never too late to return to school. When you turn 60, you know, you can take courses at the University of Washington free of charge."

"Is that right?" He opened the cash register and with both pudgy white hands lifted out the money drawer. "I'll be 60 in five years."

"Well then. No one with a mind like yours should let it deteriorate. Brains atrophy, you know. They die down."

"I was good at the classics." Benjamin set the money drawer on the counter. "Well, there's your loot, Mrs. Morrissey. Funny how I don't much care. This saves me from having to close out tonight. I suppose I'll have to call the police though. Where're you off to now?"

The old lady dropped the pistol into her shoulder bag, and

looked at the cash drawer and cash bag. "I'm going home," she said. "I have no place else to go."

"Can I get you a bag?"

"Thank you Benjamin, dear."

Benjamin bagged the bank bag and then he bagged the contents of the cash drawer. He folded down and creased the top of the brown bag three times and handed it to her. "What are you planning to do with that money, Mrs. Morrissey?"

Rosalie Morrissey took the bag. Tears came to her eyes. She said, "I'm going to pay my rent. Then I'm going to shoot myself in the head."

Benjamin's eyes widened. "Oh, you mustn't do that."

"Mustn't I? And why not? What would you do under the circumstances?"

"I wouldn't shoot myself in the head, certainly not."

"They're planning to evict me," Mrs. Morrissey repeated, this time with quiet dignity. She turned to go.

"Mrs. Morrissey!" Benjamin raised his hand as if he was back in the third grade and needed to go to the restroom.

"Yes, Benji?" She half turned to look at him.

"You've got a fighting spirit."

"I'm afraid I don't have a fighting spirit," she corrected. "I see now that I've lived my entire life as a sweet old lady. I was a sweet old lady when I was 23. Robert used to tease me about it. So did Mary. I can't change now. I'm 85 years old."

They both stood there. The ceiling fan made a breathy sound. Outside dusk was fading to darkness. The cars passing on 40th Street had turned on their headlights. Finally Benjamin said in a shy voice, "You can hold up a store when you put your mind to it."

"Well," said Mrs. Morrissey. She pressed her lips together. Then she said. "And you, Benji, can go back to school and become the scholar you were meant to be."

"I suppose I could," he nodded thoughtfully. "Maybe I will do that."

"You are wasting your brains." Mrs. Morrissey spoke in her best gently chiding voice. "Your dad would have relented in a couple of years."

Benjamin got a look of concentration on his face. She remembered that look from when he was in the third grade winning mathematics bees, doing long division in his head. He said, "And you're wasting the rest of your life by putting a bullet through your brains."

Mrs. Morrissey looked at him for a considerable length of time.

Benjamin spoke again. "Mrs. Morrissey, why don't you put up a fight?

"Put up a fight," she repeated after him.

"Organize the tenants in your building. Don't go shooting yourself—maybe they'd be sorry, but it would solve a problem for them. One less tenant to worry about. Mrs. Morrissey, I believe you have it in you to make them rue the day they ever sent that letter."

She sighed. "Maybe so," she said.

"I'll help you," he offered. "The Durn Good is getting evicted too."

"The Durn Good Grocery is getting evicted?"

"The whole block's getting bought up. This neighborhood is history." He swept his hand through the air as if to dispense with the neighborhood.

Mrs. Morrissey clutched the brown bag containing the day's take at the Durn Good. "Paddy and I used to buy Blue Bunny Ice Cream Sandwiches here," she said. "Before you were born," she added.

Benjamin pointed to a row of baseball caps he'd agreed to sell on behalf of the King County Labor Council. They were camouflage green caps with a motto stitched behind the bills. He quoted, "United We Fight, Divided We Beg."

Mrs. Morrissey suddenly felt exhausted and confused. "You may have a point," she said.

"Think it over. Here, let me keep that pistol." He put out his hand.

Mrs. Morrissey looked at his hand. Suddenly she began to cry. "It was Robert's," she said. Then she stopped crying.

Benjamin kept his hand out. "We'll keep it safe for you. That way, you won't be tempted. You can get it in the morning."

"All right then." Mrs. Morrissey set down the grocery bag and fumbled in her bag for the pistol. She handed it to him.

Benjamin took the pistol and pointed it toward the floor. He dropped the magazine and pulled it out. Then he racked the slide. The bullet popped out the back. He uncocked the gun. Then he got down on his painful arthritic knee for the second time, and placed the pistol and the magazine and the loose bullet in the safe. Then he stood up once again.

"Good night then, young man," said Mrs. Morrissey.

"Until tomorrow, Mrs. Morrissey."

She walked out into the hot August night.

Now it was Benjamin Zaslavsky's turn to draw out his handkerchief and mop his face. 📖

Star, 2017, photograph by Michelle Brooks

The New Gold Rush

or *How to Become a Landlord*

Andrena Zawinski

Get a job. Get a good job. A really good job—
    in the Cyberspace Gold Rush.
One with DotCom stock options. Struggle it out working even
    in your sleep,
just until you get vested. Spend a lot. Spend a lot of money
    you don't have.
But spend it anyway. Spend it on tapas and martinis,
    and in upscale clothiers
specializing in downwardly mobile chic. You can afford to pay
    later.

Cash in. Cash in your stock options. Buy a house.
    Pay too much for it. But buy it
anyway because you want it, you want it now. Fix it up.
    Or have someone else fix it
up. Doll it up with Art Deco fixtures and Victorian frills,
    all the accoutrements of excess;
Chop it up. Chop it in half, maybe less, to get some rent;
    and cut those corners—
skip that laundry or bathtub, park your car in the backyard
    until someday later.

Advertise it. Use creative language. Put years of training in
    the practice and use
of English to work. If the place has a tool shed or garage,
    call it a cozy cottage
or even atelier. A root cellar can become a ground floor in-law.
    A crawl space can be
an efficiency, studio, junior bedroom, even a small flat.
    Suggest it's a deal for professional
couples. (DINKS, double-income-no-kids, preferred.)
    Suggest it is near

transportation, even if it is only a troll mound under a freeway.
          Call that din and dark:
kinetic art. Claim it is convenient to all points; so what if it's a
          twenty-minute walk
to an infrequently running bus to a so-called Rapid Transit
          stop with limited service.

Advertise it at what The Market will bear. Check salaries
          nonprofits offer, then
make the rent equal so that no artists or humanitarians need
          apply. (They can bail
themselves out begging for some tax dime.) But do treat this
          seriously. Treat it like
an application for employment. Require rental resumes that
          itemize aromatic spices
favored, radio stations played, year/make/model of vacuum
          cleaner used, as well as
all waking hours applicants will find it necessary to occupy
          the premises. Require
on-the-spot, handwritten essays on why each would be
          your perfect tenant.

Try to be honest. Let them know the apartment may come
          partially furnished—why
should you pay some Stash'n Store to keep your old office bean
          bags and broken
foosball table? After all, you are the landlord. You'll be living
          there while they pay
your mortgage. And don't forget to say the neighborhood is
          up-and-coming
so they will not question those pawnshop lockup bars
          decorating local homes.

Do have fun with it. You are like a movie producer—hold an
          Open House cattle call,
roping off a portion of sidewalk around the block for those who
          can afford to arrive

on a frigid December Friday between ten and noon.
     Charge a cash, non-refundable
application fee from everyone in line. Refuse credit reports
     already paid for they
may have in hand. Someone's got to cover the cost of
     advertising it and your time.

And when you send them off wringing their hands wondering
     if they will make
the final cut, offer it to someone who makes more money than
     you do. Offer it
above the original advertised price due to unanticipated
     popularity. Make it available immediately.
Make it available within the week of showing so you can
     collect rent
on the key. That way tenants can prove they can afford to pay
     you while honoring
a current lease plus any future increases as might be demanded
     by The Market.

Aspire to greatness. Become that landlord dressed up in a
     month-to-month lease,
flying a petition against tenants' rights and living on the
     expense account of the soul
of a city. Then sell. Sell the place to a relative who will sell it
     back to you in a year.
Evict everyone. Put in that tub or laundry you skipped. Turn
     that backyard into
a detached office with solar lighting: shed, no electricity.
     Then double the rent!

The Medicine Bundle

Anita Endrezze

It was five minutes after closing time when the museum curator, Margaret Winther, walked past the glass cabinet and saw that it was empty. At first, she couldn't believe her eyes. She closed them, then looked again.

"I haven't authorized any ..." Her voice trailed off. The cabinet was definitely empty. She could even see a layer of dust defining the missing article. Briefly, she thought of berating the staff for failing to clean properly, and then would've laughed at her own absurdity in the situation, but she suddenly felt sick to her stomach. Nine years ago, when she was just starting her position as curator, she had argued for the acquisition of the missing object. Her museum (for that's how she thought of it) had bought the artifact when another museum had financial troubles and was looking for money more than history. The purchase had been the major expenditure for the last decade and much worried over by the board of trustees.

It wasn't that the item cost so much, but rather that the museum had so little money. Located in a mid-sized city, Ms. Winther had hopes of it becoming a regional museum of enviable quality.

Now, hands shaking, she pressed her face against the glass. The exhibit backdrop was a lurid painting showing a Plains warrior, in full battle regalia, astride a galloping, wild-eyed horse. It was especially inappropriate for what should have been there: a sacred Kiowa medicine bag. A bundle made of bison skin enveloping one hundred and twenty-five-year old objects used for healing and spiritual matters. Now it was missing from a locked case.

She ran to the front desk. Unless an employee had some good reason ... cleaning? No, of course not. She forced herself to say it mentally: it had been stolen by someone she had worked with and trusted.

She spoke breathlessly, urgently, to her staff. They all seemed shocked. She looked at each one of them carefully, wondering who the thief was, who had betrayed her dream, a dream she thought she had shared with them all.

The police came. They questioned the staff and dusted for fingerprints. What would that prove, Ms. Winther wondered bitterly. They all wore gloves when they handled exhibit items; she had insisted on it. They lacked any sophisticated security arrangements, a situation she had railed against at every board meeting, but the budget precluded anything more fancy than a burglar alarm at every door and window.

She began calling other museums, art galleries, pawn shops, tribal centers, alerting them to the theft. She had no doubt it had been sold to a private collector, but it was possible that the thief had a more altruistic motive. Many Indians didn't believe their heritage belonged in public museums. Ms. Winther concluded that they might have a point, although she could have argued America's history belonged to everyone, and particularly, to her museum.

The police gave up looking for it.

The empty spot in the glass case irritated her, like a missing tooth or one broken fingernail on an otherwise perfectly manicured hand. She checked on the exhibit every hour, an obsession formed from anguish and loss and having no personal life to speak of.

Eventually, she replaced the stolen medicine bag with a display of a Cheyenne war shield. At least, it went with the backdrop painting and, therefore, required no further expense.

In Germany, Helmut Trautmann gazed excitedly at the new acquisition to his private collection. The medicine bundle looked wonderfully authentic, like something from a John Wayne movie, he thought. The leather was gray with age. Thongs made from the immense sides of bison wrapped the bag tightly. Ragged feathers were tucked into the knots at four corners. He imagined they were the feathers of eagles, noble birds with wings as wide as the

American prairies. Strips of faded red trade cloth further bound the bundle. When he twisted one end of the cloth, he could see the dark crimson fabric underneath, like blood opened in a vein, undimmed and vibrant.

He was eager to open the bundle. He wanted to touch the objects within, not because they were holy (he wasn't sure he believed in a god beyond Good Fortune), but because they were old and from an extraordinary savage people (that somehow struck a chord in his own Teutonic soul) and because it reminded him of his childhood. He had played "Wild Indians" with the other schoolboys, crafting arrows from the willows that grew by the river. Sneaking Indian-style, which involved placing one foot silently in front of the other, he had crept through the long fronds of willow, his face smeared with river mud. He had perfected a blood-curdling cry, much to his mother's distress. He helped himself to one of her cream-colored handkerchiefs and dyed it red from berries plucked by the roadside. His medicine bag was filled with the magic of his lost childhood: a duck feather, a round white pebble, a pig bone that he variously pretended was human or bison or bear, and an arrowhead he'd found in a field his father rented out to a farmer. Although the arrowhead was marvelous in its own right, being from his ice-age ancestors, he had instilled it with the mystery and mastery of new makers, ones who wore bison robes and painted red circles around the eyes of their war ponies.

Long ago, Herr Trautmann had discarded his own medicine bundle. Now he had it back.

But he didn't open it. The knots were tight and the seller had supplied him with an X-ray of the interior. The seller had advised him to keep it unopened, thereby increasing its resale value. Untouched, the seller insisted, it retained its provenance, its power, its mystery. Herr Trautmann didn't care about its resale value since he intended on keeping it forever, but he was thoughtful. He could see the objects within by viewing the X-ray, a negative of what was holy, the light transformed to dark, the long shapes that could be bones or flutes or the nerve endings of trees shattered by lightning. The round shapes could be small skulls, creatures of the grasslands, or balls of bison hair, or even the essence of earth's curvature seen from a shaman's entranced eye.

Who knows what magic was potent enough to turn away bullets or heal the wounds caused by life turning as dark as soldiers' coats? The irregular shapes in the bundle made him feel as if he had entered a cave and found his whole body covered with black hand prints; or that he had fallen off the edge of a cliff and found himself broken at the bottom, dark-skinned people pulling the meat off his bones, singing in a language that sounded like chips of flint.

No, he decided, he wouldn't open it, considering himself already open to it. Herr Trautmann had a mystical bent, a side of himself he didn't like to think about too often. As chairman and owner of Germany's largest textile company, he was used to numbers and considered himself cut out of cloth of the highest and rarest quality. That he was successful only proved his point, and like the bundle, he kept himself tightly contained, lest his emotions and dreams escape, unraveling the man he patterned himself to be.

Weeks later, Herr Trautmann was mulling over the name for a new line of athletic shoes for one of his subsidiary companies. He doodled lines and circles on his notepad as he listened to his marketing team toss around ideas. He realized suddenly that he was drawing arrows. That brought to mind the medicine bundle.

Why not the Kiowa shoe, he asked himself. No, that might bring attention to himself and, besides, it wasn't a well-known tribe. But what about the Apache? Most Europeans had heard of that tribe from watching Hollywood movies. Everyone knew about the most famous Apache of them all: Geronimo. Now there was a name for a shoe! It would suggest to the customer an image of a warrior. The wearer of this shoe would imagine himself to be strong and fearless, with great endurance, an invincible urban renegade!

"Gentlemen! Our new line of shoes will be the Apache. Top

of the line will be the Geronimo," he announced, straightening the knot of his tie. "I'm sure you can think of a number of marketing strategies."

Everyone agreed it was an excellent image. They discussed it feverishly while Herr Trautmann listened indulgently. These advertising types were of an excitable nature. They all agreed they needed a logo, one that would identify the shoe immediately to the consumer.

Herr Trautmann stood up. He had just the thing, something he'd seen in the X-ray of the bundle, or maybe in his dreams. He brushed aside his uncertainty and quickly drew the symbol on a sheet of paper with a black felt pen. Nodding, the group agreed it had power, although everyone seemed to have a different opinion on what it was: lightning or an arrow or a cosmic music note or a tree branch divided by the sky.

The shoes were manufactured in Mexico, in a polluted border town where labor was cheap, and the workers, descendants of Apaches and other tribes, would never be able to afford the shoes they made. Then the shoes were shipped to stores in Europe and the States.

1.

Jimmy, "the Snowman," bought a pair of Geronimos for $195 in Buffalo, New York. He liked the logo, which was emblazoned on the heel in designer graphics. He liked the price; it showed the world that he was someone. There's not much to know about the Snowman. He had two emotions by which he experienced life—rage and lust—and it was often difficult to tell the difference between the two by his actions.

He seldom thought about himself, partly because he was young and partly because he didn't understand the concept of introspection. His life was based on action, his world the one of physical push-and-shove. He had a couple of girls he called "his bitches" and he had fathered several children by them, without any sense of responsibility for their lives.

He considered himself an entrepreneur. His merchandise

was drugs, especially heroin. High quality stuff. But it was the dealing that gave him a rush: the dimly lit alleys where he was only one more shadow, the competitors who wanted a piece of the business, the cops who were waiting for an excuse to bust him. It was a tough world and the Snowman was tougher.

That night, he wore a silk shirt, jeans, and his new shoes. As he drove he noticed a car following him. It pissed him off. He stepped on the gas and skidded around a corner. It followed. He hit the brakes and whipped his car around in the middle of an intersection. He headed straight for the other car and pulled out his gun. As the car sped past him, he shot. Laughing, he turned the corner and cruised a few blocks. Show that sucker! He zoomed through a red light, cars honking at him, and swung quickly down a side street. In his rearview mirror, he saw that the car was back. Shit! He drove faster. As he skidded around another corner, passing a tavern called Ten White Horses, his rear tire blew. His car side-swiped a blue van then skipped the curb and smashed into the building. The windshield exploded, tiny pieces of glass embedding in the Snowman's eyelids. His head snapped forward and the car burst into flames, the imported silk shirt flashing into instant threads of fire.

The car was a bundle of flames and metal. His shoes began smoking; that logo with its ancient symbol burned steadily into the bone of night.

In Germany, the stolen bundle was locked in an airless glass box, inside the safe which was in a hidden room in Herr Trautmann's house. If he had attached some kind of security weighing device, it would've revealed that suddenly the bag weighed less. But there is no machine that can weigh spirit, nor explain the quick bright light that flamed for a second over the bundle.

This was fire. This was East.

2.

Pamela Ford paused to glance at her watch. Forty-five minutes before her plane left to continue her journey to Seattle, Washington. She stood in front of a Kansas airport gift shop and figured she'd have enough time to browse a bit.

She wandered up and down the aisles. There were rattle-snake eggs, Dorothy and Toto T-shirts, giant pencils, "incredible drinking stone" coasters, rubber Indian drums with neon pink feathers, smokeless ash trays, rolls of breath mints, and stands of magazines, books, and newspapers. She paged through a fashion magazine then put it back, adverse to paying good money for the privilege of reading ads.

She turned to a display with Indian jewelry. There was a beautiful silver bracelet with a large chunk of turquoise balanced on a filagree center. It was very unusual, both masculine and feminine, strong and delicate. And the stone had a curious natural marking that looked like starry waves or lightning.

She asked the clerk if she could try it on. As the clerk handed it to her, she noticed an attached tag, which read, "This is genuine pawned Indian jewelry," and noted that the buyer should, "keep this pawn ticket to increase the value of the piece." Well, really, she thought, half-amused and half-irritated. What was she supposed to do, wear the damn tag? And what was so special about jewelry pawned by some down-on-his-luck Indian? She put the bracelet back, then paused and picked it up again. She put it around her wrist. She supposed it was all a scam; there was no poor Indian selling his last asset to feed his family. Instead, some enterpris-ing white guy was probably printing fake pawn tickets to cover stolen goods. She shook herself; she had a tendency towards the dramatic. It was most likely just what it seemed and she liked the bracelet well enough to buy it.

Later on the plane, she fell asleep. She had a strange dream, disjointed but filled with sparkling images.

. . . long degrees of falling earth . . . into the geography of garnets, tiny red suns burning, water and sky solidified into turquoise deep in

the mountains . . . twin heroes with the glass eyes of stars and with the mouths of fiery opals . . . it was midnight black, a carbon moon over her face of mica and snow . . . she was struggling to climb up from the center of the world . . . there were monsters with long tails and people made of mud . . . arrows made out of falling stars and a woman making pots from many colors of clay.

When Pamela Ford woke up, she rubbed her neck. What a dream, she mused. So vivid and yet meaningless. Her sister, Chris, would've written it all down. She was really into that kind of thing. Well, maybe she'd tell her all about it when she got home. But now she thought she'd better review her notes for tomorrow's business meeting. She reached down and pulled her bag out from under the seat in front of her. As she did, she noticed how icy one hand felt. Perhaps the bracelet was on too tight. She regretted her extravagance in buying it now. Maybe she'd give it to Chris for her birthday next month. Then, at least the money would've been spent on someone else. That seemed more worthy to Pamela somehow. She shook her hand and removed the bracelet, wrapping it in a scarf she had in her purse, and tucked it into one of the purse's inner pockets.

In Seattle, she took a taxi to her hotel. It was later than she expected. She was tired. All she wanted to do was climb into a clean, soft bed. As she stepped out of her taxi and turned toward the hotel entrance, she was pushed roughly to the pavement. All she saw was the designer logo heels of the retreating thief's shoes. The doorman rushed to help her. She was shaking; her stockings torn. She'd never been mugged before.

The thief ran down toward Pike Market. At night, there were many dark places under the Viaduct stairs that led down to the Sound. He rooted in the leather purse and grabbed the wallet, then threw away the purse. He didn't notice the scarf wrapped around the bracelet.

The purse landed in the trash can. The thief disappeared into the darkness, pulling out a wad of cash and credit cards.

The following day, the garbage trucks collected the can, taking the purse and bracelet to a landfill, where it was buried.

The bracelet was in a bundle of leather and red cloth. The stone slipped into the darkness of earth, the natural marking bright as a blue star.

The Kiowa bundle, still secure in the German safe, remembered how once the pounding hooves of millions of buffaloes had pulverized the earth into dust, obscuring the turquoise sky. A small sigh escaped the bundle, a wisp of powdered red clay.

This was earth. This was West.

3.

It had all started at church. Sally Antonio had been herding her three giggling children down the steps after the service, holding the youngest's hand and carrying the baby in her arms, when a well-dressed young woman had smiled at her, remarking that it was so wonderful to have so many children.

Sally, five months pregnant, laughed and replied that it must be due to her good luck charm. Then she managed to get everyone in the car without too many arguments over who should get a window seat. As she drove away, she wondered where she'd put the coming child. They'd have to get a bus!

Later that night, she got a phone call from the lady she'd spoken to at church, who apologized for bothering Sally, but, well, what did she mean by a good-luck charm? At first, Sally drew a blank, but then remembered. Actually, it was more special than a good-luck charm. Sally regretted being so casual about it. Her Aunt Sophie had given it to her on her wedding night: a kind of doll, only not to be played with, made out of turtle bone and wrapped in red trade cloth. It had no face, just the jut of turtle bone. The doll was Sia; her Aunt Sophie had married a Sia man. They both had chuckled when they gave it to her, saying, "Not that you'll need any help, Sally, we've seen the way you and Charlie look at each other!" Sally had blushed and later put the doll away in her underwear drawer, a most unwise place she now realized as she patted her swollen stomach.

Raven In Eden, detail of collage, by Anita Endrezze

The woman on the phone continued. "My name is Janet Anderson. I've been trying for years to have a baby. This might sound crazy, but, oh could I borrow your good-luck charm?"

Sally hesitated.

"I'm desperate!" the woman begged. "You don't know how much I want to hold my own baby in my arms." The woman began to sob.

"But it's just a piece of bone!" She explained. "Some old Indian stuff." She was slightly embarrassed about the pagan doll.

"I don't care if it's a rabbit's foot! Please!" the woman pleaded.

Between sobs, the woman promised to take good care of it and return it promptly. Sally didn't know what to do, but she was moved. She remembered the first time she had found out she was pregnant, the excitement, the awe, and the anxiety.

She said slowly, "It's a tiny doll, very old, made from a sea turtle."

"But it works," exclaimed the woman. "Do you put it under your pillow when you, uh, you know . . ."

"No," grinned Sally to herself. Her pillow seldom stayed in one place when she and Charlie made love. "You don't do anything with the doll. That's why I don't know if it really works."

"I don't care. If I can just try it?"

"Okay," Sally agreed. "I'll bring it to church next week."

That had been three years ago. Sally had not seen the turtle doll again, although she'd seen the woman, obviously pregnant, and leading a toddler by the hand. Sally spoke to the woman several times at church, asking for the doll back. At first the woman promised to return it next week, then she offered to buy it. Price was no object, she had made that clear. Her husband owned Anderson's Apparells, which was a clothing factory and used poor Asian women and children to sew their clothes. It was doing very well, in spite of the shipping costs.

Sally wanted her Sia doll back. Not that she wanted another baby, but it seemed to call to her, the way one of her children would murmur in her sleep. Sally was angry at the woman. How could she keep something that was not hers?

Sally was part Pima, part White, and part Black. She was by genetic disposition disinclined to possessiveness. She tried to understand her feelings about the turtle doll. It was not that it belonged to her, she decided, but that it belonged *with* her. It had been a gift given in love by her relatives to provide her with the greatest gift of all: her children.

Janet Anderson hadn't been an honorable person. Sally was happy that she had been able to have children and would've let her keep the doll for another few kids, but Janet had been so evasive (even changing churches) that Sally wished she'd never been so generous as to loan out the doll. She imagined it sitting in a display case in Janet Anderson's living room, along with a Japanese fan, a velvet bull from Tijuana, a dusty porcelain shepherdess, and a pair of red candlesticks from Taiwan. Sally knew she was being unfair. But it just wasn't right.

That's where the matter remained until one rainy afternoon when the river flooded. Mrs. Anderson's brick tri-level was in danger of being washed away in spite of the sandbags piled around it. She stood on her back deck and watched the dark clouds churning into the river, the rain blasting the desert so hard that the red soil bounced back up into the sky, forming a low horizon banded by scarlet, dirty air.

She decided it was time to leave when her son's swing set floated away. She grabbed Andy Jr., who was wearing his Toddler tom-tom shoes, from the famous Geronimo shoe line. Every time he walked, small drums concealed in the heels *tha-rumped*. He loved them, stomping his feet energetically. Mrs. Anderson stuffed La Chanson Narcissus Napoleon's Victory III (their pedigree French poodle) into the back seat and drove frantically away.

The turtle doll, which had indeed been part of a collection of items termed "collectibles," with a value only apparent to their owners, smelled the water rising. There were no eyes on the doll, but it could see the red mud flowing into the heart of the river. The waters pumped into the house, reclaiming the ancient channel that had existed many times in the river's long memory. The turtle doll felt the red trade cloth lift slightly in the current. Under the cloth dress was an ancient symbol, like water poured from stars. The turtle bone doll swam into the river, feeling the hard shell of life curve around its bone until there were legs again and strong teeth, and it was whole again, tasting the primitive sea that was there before the desert was born.

In Germany, from inside the medicine bundle, came the soft sound of rain.

This was water. This was South.

4

Buddy Red Buffalo was driving home after the powwow. The drum was in the back seat of his Pinto. Following him, in two other cars, were the other drummers and singers. Buddy was driving carefully due to the drum. He had even rigged up a seat belt for it.

He was fairly new at drumming. He was exhausted. Drumming took a lot of energy and concentration. He wanted to do a good job. He wanted the dancers to feel that the drum had become part of their souls.

Buddy wasn't familiar with the road. There were miles of frozen wheat fields and sage on either side of the road, which wound around the Palouse hills. It was almost dark, the light a soft gray barely distinguishable from the earth. His back ached and his right arm was stiffening. It took a lot of stamina to be a drummer and this had only been Buddy's fourth powwow. He shrugged his shoulders in an attempt to loosen the muscles.

All at once the road seemed to swerve towards the sky and the car started bucking and twisting, skidding on a patch of ice. He remembered later that he could see stars, real stars, not the kind you get with a bump on the head. And, he told his friends, the stars were in a wavy watery symbol, kind of like the one painted on the drum. Ed Yellow Grass's grandmother had dreamed the symbol for the group.

"Then I saw," he hesitated, glancing shyly at his friends, "a door opening in the sky and thousands of animals ran out. Buffalo, deer, antelope, bear, rabbits, birds."

Ed looked at him. "How many fingers do I have, Buddy?"

Buddy squinted. "Four?"

Better lie down again," said Ed. He'd been holding up two fingers.

Jim, a Yakama singer, stood at the edge of the road. Goddam trash everywhere. People were junkin' up the planet. Beer bottles, pizza box, newspaper showing some ad about a trendy shoe, yellowed pages torn from a paperback. His eyes followed the skid marks from Buddy's car. Something strange had happened. He could smell red clay in the air. He thought he heard the drum of hooves, but as he glanced around, he saw the fields were empty. It was weird. He didn't want to be the one to say it, though. He just kept looking at the trash.

But he couldn't help thinking about how the car snorted its way across the field, then rolled the way a horse does when it itches. Finally landing upright, the car shook once and then was still, headlights knocked into a cock-eyed angle. The sound of glass breaking, falling like chunks of stars on to the earth, disturbed their thoughts.

Buddy had been wearing a seat belt, so how in the heck, they all wondered, did he end up in the back seat curled around the drum? All of his life, Buddy'd had bad luck. He was good-hearted, but had no ambition. He took what came his way. Sullen women. Dead-end jobs. Balding—who ever heard of a bald Indian? At last, they thought, the universe did something right for him. It was about time.

They looked at the car. The driver's seat was smashed in, the steering wheel stuck like a burr in the headrest. The front window was cracked in a horseshoe shape. The drum and Buddy were unharmed.

The frozen grass was trampled and broken in a circle around the car. Buddy felt something wet on his cheeks. He touched the skin carefully, thinking it was blood, but it was water—not tears, not salty. Something from a river, where the stones are shaped like sleeping turtles. He knew he couldn't understand what was given to him that night. But he felt stronger, special, standing there alive and aware in the northern night.

All the singers lifted their voices in a song of prayer, the cold air filling their lungs, the night rushing in and out, their warm human breaths flowing over the hills and the dreams of animals.

This was air. This was North.

In Germany, a small crack in the glass box widened. Air spilled in, lifting the bundle gently. The objects within began their transforming journey back to their origins.

Red shadows of buffaloes drifted slowly across the landscape of Herr Trautmann's dreams. He broke out in a rash. The German economy underwent a recession and he lost millions of marks.

Buddy's drum sang about White Painted Woman and her baby, Child Born of Water. He cut a CD that made him famous—in Indian Country—with those who liked a drum solo that lasted fifty-four minutes. Sally traveled to Sonora, Mexico, home of the Sia People, and offered cornmeal to the islands of turtles in the Gulf of California. When she got home she discovered she was pregnant again. Mrs. Anderson choked on a bone and died when her children were too young to remember her later in their lives. Pamela bought a container of Mace and became a very nervous person who avoided traveling. Ms. Winther quit her job at the museum and underwent treatment for Obsessive-Compulsive Disorder.

The Apache line of shoes were copied in Asia and sold in K-Mart for $9.99. Teenagers refused to wear them. Millions were found hanging by their shoelaces from electrical wires spanning the nation's streets. Geronimo sank back into the obscurity of American history, in spite of the popularity of classic western films. Very few knew that Geronimo's real name was Goyathlay, or "One who Yawns."

The medicine bundle in Herr Trautmann's collection vanished, leaving four thin traces of dust.

Into each direction, white horses blinked snow from their eyes, hidden rivers stampeded into mountains, butterfly-shaped bells flooded the air with golden sounds, and crystal skulls burst into laughter.

When the holy symbol had completed its circle, its own song of the four directions, all the Indian people everywhere had the same dream. It lasted just a few seconds, but takes a lifetime of remembering. What you must do is to live your life as if your soul knows the way and is only leading you forward, the way a parent holds a child's hand.

You must remember you are like a medicine bundle, with a drumming heart and a soul that burns forth within and without. There is water and blood. There is air and breath.

There is a dream.

There is memory.   There is a song.

There is life.

ISSN 1066-1883   www.ravenchronicles.org

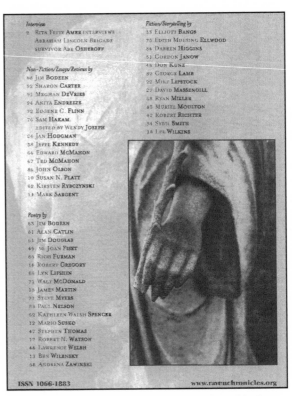

Hand of the Guardian, photograph by Stephanie Shachat

XIV

Volume 11, Number 2, 2004
War Veterans & Peacekeepers

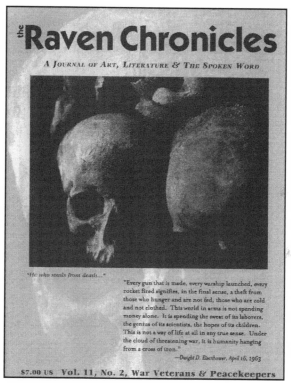

Catacombs I, 2002, photograph by Polly Purvis

A Parade On June 25th

Don Kunz

The first time I heard that old marching tune, "Gary Owen," performed, I was lying on a grassy knoll in Montana watching a parade surrounded by my entire family and all our friends. Emerging from around the crest of a treeless hill to the east, the band stretched out below us in a column two abreast. Its riders were dressed in navy blue; their belt buckles were of brass and glinted like signal mirrors; their boots were long and black and covered with dust kicked up by the hooves of their horses. From the top of the hill we could hear the creak of their saddles, the jingling of bridles. We could see the riders' faces were burnt by the sun and streaked with sweat. They stared straight ahead where the clear waters of the river cut across their route and the early afternoon sun burned in the sky like a white ember. The riders pulled their hat brims down over their foreheads and squinted against the glare. It was painful to look at. But, hey, it isn't like they didn't ask for what they had gotten themselves into. We thought it was entertaining as hell.

We had been waiting for it a very long time. To tell you the truth we had suffered through a patch of rough years. Once we had been rich. But our prosperity had evaporated like the rain that does not reach the ground in summer: We could smell it; we could see it; we could watch it fall, but it never touched us. It just broke into rainbows that teased us with their bright colors. So the grass grew brown and cracked under our feet like glass beads. And the dust rose. We had begun to die. Some broke out in sores that would not heal. Men left and did not return, just disappeared. Sometimes we would find them murdered: Shot, stabbed, skulls caved in like broken ground. For years now life had not gone well for us. But today was different. We would have some excitement. We felt our luck was changing. It had to.

We had been waiting for the parade to start for hours. My family had risen even before first light, and the rest soon followed without being called. Everybody was keyed up. Not a soul needed to be shaken awake, for there was much to do to get ready. The men dressed quickly in what they had laid out carefully the night before. Most of them carried some token—a shining pebble from the river, a colorful piece of cloth, a bent feather from a bird who had spoken to them. The women busied themselves with boiling coffee and heating up leftover stew. There would be time later for painting faces.

We gathered up all our gear and scattered to scout out the best location. Everybody liked the grassy knolls that lined this route, so we set up there and waited quietly. Some dozed. Meadow larks twittered and sang in the grass around us. At mid-morning a golden eagle circled over the river to our west. I watch a family of ants swarm over a dung beetle, roll it onto its back, and kill it. The sun beat on us like a heavy stick, but no one complained. We sucked on pebbles to bring the sweet dew of saliva. We waited.

At midday we felt the rhythm of their horses' hooves in the earth. Gradually we saw them emerge from behind the crest of a hill to the east. Then they were below us. As their horses smelled water, they began to prance. When the riders spied our homes on the other side of the river, the band struck up "Gary Owen," and the whole group broke into a gallop. As the first riders crossed the river they called the Little Big Horn, they felt our arrows on their backs like a hard rain, and raising a shout, we rushed down to join them. 📖

Army Nurses, Vietnam, 1966

Kathleen Walsh Spencer

After the Vietnam Women's Memorial,
Washington, D.C.,
Glenna Goodacre, Sculptor

Too exhausted to swat the flies
that buzz their hair, three nurses
sit back to back on sandbags
to rest, to wait for the wounded
soldier to be choppered out, handed
over to the USS *Sanctuary* floating off Vietnam.

Among the bamboo trees of Phu Non, Vietnam,
one of the nurses holds the flyer,
stretches her arm, reaches her hand
across his chest: a pieta of nurse
and soldier, her limbs wound
around him to contain this awkward package

slipping from her grasp. She opens her bag,
wets her bandanna to shield him from Vietnam
sun, cools his forehead, covers his wounded
eyes until a surgeon can attempt repairs, mid-flight.
There is too much damage, but still she nurses,
grieving the loss of yet another handsome

face. To keep him on her lap, she grasps a handful
of the soldier's shirt. A plastic bag
rustles in his pocket. The nurse
peeks at the photo he carries in this jungle:
a young woman with flowing hair. *Fly High,*
Love You, she wrote with curlicues winding

into hearts. Placing the photo in its flimsy bag,
the nurse seals it, tucks it back, wounded.
The faces of all the Joes, Bobs, Gerrys, and Smittys fly
through her mind, blur with the rows of body bags
that carried them from Vietnam—
last words spoken, spoken to their nurse.

Lifting her chin, rising to full height, the second nurse
turns dark eyes to the sky. Hot wind
stirs the tight curls underneath her cap. In Vietnam,
unarmed, she reaches back to lay a hand
on her comrade's elbow, touching her baggy
sleeve, waiting for rescue, waiting to fly

out. The third nurse kneels, motionless as a butterfly
regaining strength after tearing from its silk cocoon.
The fine red dust of Vietnam coats her helmet, her hands.

Shadow Dance #98, photograph, 1994, by Glenda J. Guilmet

Lifestyles of the Rich and Berserk

John Olson

A m I a warrior? Is there a warrior in me screaming to get out? Do fires and tornadoes imbue my blood? Is war the breast my ancestors suckled?

My ancestors were Vikings. Does this mean there are sagas in me, the howling prodigality of Saxon villages put to the flame, great hordes of Norman treasure dragged to a wooden ship with a dragon on the bow?

Probably not. That is to say, there have been few indications of this kind of behavior in my life. I have never shot, stabbed, punched, skewered, smacked, stomped, sliced, gouged, impaled or bayoneted anyone. This is not to say I haven't, at certain junctures in my life, wanted to shoot, stab, punch, skewer, smack, stomp, slice, gouge, impale or bayonet anyone. There have been numerous opportunities and compelling inducements to garrote various bus drivers and bank tellers, bureaucrats and pedants. But I haven't. I have, in all occasions, demonstrated restraint. But is restraint heroic? Is restraint the stuff of sagas? Did Sigvat the Red use restraint? Did Sigurd Snake-i'-the-eye or Kettle Flatnose use restraint? Did Eric Bloodaxe or Harold Grayfell exercise poise and self-possession in all things?

I have only been in one fight, though it wasn't much of a fight. In fact, it wasn't really a fight at all. It was New Year's Eve, I was eighteen, and my friends and I crashed a party. The party was in a basement. The Christmas tree was still up. That's about all I noticed, because I was extremely drunk. My friends and I appeared to be welcome. I remember sitting on a flight of steps and several people laughing at the things I said. I felt comical and popular. I migrated to a conversation one of my friends was having with a girl. Two young men appeared and I smiled at one of them. A fist hit my face and I found myself crashing into the Christmas tree. I wasn't sure what had happened. I got up. I got slugged again. I was on my hands and knees and people were kicking me in the sides. There was an enormous amount of blood dripping on the linoleum floor. I exited the room very swiftly. Considering my state of intoxication, I was lucky to get out at all. It was an inglorious escape. My ancestors would not have been pleased.

I have often wondered what sort of Viking I would have made, assuming I had been born in, say, Skiringssal in 880 A.D. with my current interests (art and poetry) and earning power (modest to negligible) intact. The first thing I would need is a sword. This would prove a problem.

The Viking sword was a marvel of ingenuity and beauty. It wasn't cheap. Its production was labor-intensive. Medieval sword construction and metallurgy were complex and involved. Fish divulge moonlight dripping with color. The ocean enlightens us with its breath. But the production of steel is a labor of blistering perplexity. Steel is iron with a higher carbon content. Iron is a glutton for heat and carbon. When the temperature in a smelter rises, more and more carbon is absorbed by the iron. Once iron is saturated with carbon it cannot be shaped any further. The optimal amount of carbon is 1%. This results in steel. Too little carbon and one gets wrought iron. Too much and one gets cast iron. Medieval smelting was a courtship, not a routine, a precarious conjugation of elements and heat.

The medieval swordsmith mingled iron with steel in a frenzy of constant hammering. Strips of iron and steel were twisted together and hammer-welded into a single blade. The steel was heated then plunged into a liquid bath of water (or oil or wine or honey or urine or blood) to temper it. A fine balance was needed between hardness on the edge for cutting and softness in the body for flex and durability. The final product was a blaze of death and vindication, a strip of awakened metal enduring as wind.

The cost of such labor and skill was approximately 240 shillings, the equivalent of 24,000 English pounds according to today's exchange rates, or 38,400 dollars, roughly the price of a '95 Lexus with traction control, heated seats, and a telephone. Bartering was encouraged in the middle ages, so one might also purchase such a coveted item for 20 sparrow hawks, twelve pigs, 3500 chickens and an old swarm of bees. One might be able to purchase one sword for two greyhounds and get a helmet for free, or shield and spear for 780 chickens and a pup with unopened eyes.

Once in possession of such a sword, one would be required to use it. To bring it into battle. To inflict damage on it. To bang armor with it. To expose it to the elements. To rust. To saltwater. To chop human limbs off. To flail at human torsos. To swing at human necks. To get it bloody. Would the violence be worth it? Would the exaltation of battle be worth it? Obviously, in the case of the Vikings, the answer would be an emphatic yes. Or am I being presumptuous? I don't think so. Somewhere in my genes lurks the thrill of death and violence.

Georges Bataille refers to war as an aggressive and extravagant exuberance. There is a potential killer in each of us. Mine is a redirected war lust. An energy channeled into revelation and language rather than blows of steel and the joy of holding a steaming human heart in my hand.

Mine is a shadow of fingers stroking the air of Egypt. Mine is a look. Mine is the ache of wonder in the gaze of Lepage's Joan of Arc. Mine is an alloy. Mine is a regenerative furnace splattered on the meat of a book. 📖

America, A True Story

Stephen Thomas

Freed from Castro's jails, a pickpocket,
native Habañero, sweet-tempered Pedro
of the bedroom eyes,
what was he doing here in the gray, wet Pacific winter?
'

And Wen Pu, from the steams of Indo China,
another colonial indigene,
what refuge was there for him under the dull skies of Seattle?

Myself, the disgruntled native, never been anywhere,
never traveled.

Three of us—busboy, kitchen help, waiter—
on the night shift in an Italian Restaurant
owned by an Irish American drunk.

Some things cannot melt.
Experience for one.
And the dream of a common language
remains, therefore, a dream.

Pedro taught me Marti: *Una rosa blanca.*
He coached me in Lorca: *Toronjas*, he said,
and I repeated *toronjas.*

No! No! Esteben. No toronjas. To-ron-jas.

I couldn't hear it. Vowel or trill or nasal.
It boiled like the song of a river.
But still I repeated *toronjas . . .*
toronja, as though I could taste
or learn how to taste

the juice of the noun
and the air of the place whence it came.

Wen Pu mounting the stairs
with a crate of romaine
looked at me strangely.
Toronjas? he asked.

Yes, I replied. *It means some fruit in Spanish.*
Pedro has taught me a poem.

0, he sighed, suddenly elsewhere. *In Laos*
it mean . . . Never mind.

Jerry and the Mick

Mark Sargent

Down my childhood streets of football, flyout, chestnut and water fights—the natural heaving fascism of adolescent males bumping and banging, slapping and spitting, leading and led, climbing over and breaking through, their kicking digging fusion with the earth, their shadowy figures flashing everywhere, I flabby middle-aged walk. Exercise, I need it, especially after intercontinental flight. The neighborhoods haven't changed except that the only kids I see flashing across the lawns are the phantoms of my memory. There aren't any kids on the streets anymore, no, they're all off at activities designed by adults to keep them off the streets. To keep them busy. How do they stand it? It's the middle of August and not one ball is being thrown, not one water balloon.

There's the Grahams' old house where I spent nearly everyday hanging out, shooting hoops, throwing footballs or escaping into the woods. The old uneven driveway leading to the dilapidated garage where the hoop hung. All the same, but no hoop. There on those steps leading to the kitchen we'd rest between games on days like this, talkin' baseball. Often we'd argue the relative merits of our heroes. I favored the *Say Hey Kid*, Willie Mays of the Giants, recently relocated to San Francisco, and John insisted that the premier player in the land played centerfield for the New York Yankees, Mickey Mantle. The Mick had the lineage: Ruth through DiMaggio to this densely powerful Oklahoma bull. He could hit it over buildings from either side of the plate, and could do this, unbeknownst to us, nursing incredible hangovers. And the Yankees, every year it seemed, were in the World Series, playing for the big one with everyone watching, or listening, *listening*, to baseball on the radio. And now he's dead. The Mick and Jerry Garcia go down within days of each other. Oddly, weirdly, heroes to the same generation. The same boys that checked the Mick's stats in the afternoon paper in 1960 were dancing in front of the speakers with a headful of acid in 1970. The same kids who swung for the fences imagining they were at Yankee Stadium, deftly picked Jerry's segue from *Wharf Rat* to *Going Down the Road* on their Fenders of air or actually picked up a guitar. Jerry and the Mick were male heroes with their phallic wands: guitar and bat, with their dark self-destructive demons urging them on, with their casual acceptance of their fans' adoration. No jumping stage gyrations for Jerry, his concentration on the moment of the music, the communal intuition of the Dead, was total; while the Mick might, with a *'aw shucks folks, it was nuthin' grin,'* briefly touch his cap, imperceptively lifting it, while rounding second after another homer. But while barely acknowledging the crowd they took that massed energy and transformed it into superhuman gestures that could yet be experienced by all. That's what a hero does. He transcends and takes everyone who tunes in along for the ride.

A hero is not a role model. Is not an exemplary being. Some forms of heroism are indeed states of possession, akin perhaps to shamanic trance wherein the spirit world communicates to the tribe through a medium. The communal energy focused on the hero has great mass, a frenzied all-or-nothing density, and this weight, the hero's burden, may sometimes be too great to bear, so that after the public ascent there is a private fall, a need to disappear, to reverse the magical transformation. And, certainly, the ego of the hero often tricks him into the myth of invulnerability. So Jerry and the Mick contaminated themselves with their addictions. But at their deaths reactions could hardly have been different. For Jerry, who had made music with all its advantages and cosmic power, there was adoration and acclaim with but bare mention of his twenty years of heroin addiction and how that may indeed have been reflected in his work. But as for the Mick, he was just a drunken old jock with a blown gut. A memory pimp. A man who had flushed the last thirty years of his life down the tubes on a river of booze. His demise did not sound the resonant chord of mortality that Jerry's death played, for we had already left the Mick far behind with our childhood, with all those Summer afternoons with nothing to do. Sport is fleeting, music eternal, nothing new in that. The sports hero is a finite extension of youth, nothing is more fleeting than physical power. And although baseball prides itself as a sport with great tradition, the connection between the Mick and the Babe is faint and tenuous when held up to the continuous development of music, that is, you can clearly hear Bill Monroe in Jerry Garcia, but you need a great deal of imagination to see DiMaggio in Mickey. Generally, the feats of athletes are not as closely built on the efforts of previous genera- tions, while that's mostly what music is. Only by conjuring my youth can I summon the Mick, but Jerry is there for me every time I play a tape, still transmitting from his dark star.

Unhappy the land that is in need of heroes, wrote Brecht. I've always wondered, did he mean that unhappiness sprung from the *need* for heroes or the inability to *produce* heroes. Heroes are products of a collective imagination, of 'nothing to do' time. Who will dream them to life now in frantic cynical America? The land doesn't look capable of heroes anymore. Perhaps children who go to *activities* don't require them. Enough to know how much they make, the stuff they have. And here too, in tired old Greece, maker of heroes, the dream-blood runs thin. My wife asked a group of teenagers, who are the heroes of today? They couldn't come up with anyone, but they all agreed it would be someone with a lot of money. Oh, unhappy the lands so in need of a penniless hero to fashion action outside of commerce. 📖

Urban Life: Parking, photograph, by Manit Chaotragoongit

Letter To Leo Tapia In Kuwait
Near The Iraqi Border

February 28, 2003

Jim Bodeen

I carry your letter in my back pocket,
Lance Corporal, asking for poems.
We're afraid, here, too. Every one of us.
We want you home safe. I read your letter

To my class of Turtle Islanders,
Where you met Maggie. I show them
Your picture on the wall as a Marine.
We're writing poems. I've told them

Poetry is medicine and ammunition.
They know you carry both. When I read
Your letter I hear echoes of the ones
I sent from Viet Nam. For the sake

Of peace, I carry a sign into the street,
Asking to bring you home. It's a poem
About nations, asking for reversal,
And the giving up of guns. It's not a new sign.

It's the sign that brought me
To you, and the *abrecaminos*, a dozen years ago.
This is the path that brought us together
After Maggie died, and you put her

Obituary on the Poetry Pole.
My sign says I want you home.
My sign is the easiest to carry,
Bearing only love, and you.

The All

Mario Susko

as a child I thought eternity
began whenever I stopped to count
the invisible stars in my room
because I ran out of numbers
trying to outpace the squeaking
of iron springs behind the paper wall.

when I kissed my grandmother's cheek,
her skin smelling of churned butter,
I knew she wasn't dead for I too
could lie in my bed with a wooden cross
in my hands and hold my breath forever.

I believed pregnant women were smugglers,
carrying, after the war, sacks of potatoes
or coal under their dress, and I learned
through fear, having seen a horse drop
out of a horse, I hadn't come from an egg.

there was so much unlearning
later on to be done, about the suitcase
full of maps with shortcuts to life
after life, a tree that could hide
its shadow, and words bring salvation
when ripeness starved its fruits to death.

sleeping in a different bed every night
to outguess random targets practitioners,
I came to see the all as a counted nothing.

XV

Volume 11, Number 3, 2004-2005
Speaking In Tongues

Pilgrimage, painting, by Scott Martin

Entre deux langues

Natalie Pascale Boisseau

Une prière pour trouver l'ouverture, l'entrebâillement de la porte, la parfaite auspicieuse fissure, là où on insert un doigt, puis un regard, puis le corps, et la présence.

Une prière pour voir le fil relier les perles, les grenats, les rubis, les améthystes, les quartz aux formes irrégulières.

Une prière au hibou, voyant dans les bois d'ombres.

Le joyeux mélange de savoir et de discernement, de lumière et d'obscurité.

Between Tongues

Natalie Pascale Boisseau

A prayer to find the opening, the crack of the door,
the perfect auspicious interstice, where to insert a
finger, then a peek, then the body, then the presence.

A prayer to see the thread pulling together pearls,
garnets, rubies, amethysts, quartz of irregular
shapes.

A prayer to the owl, seeing in the dark woods.

The merry mix of knowing and insight, of light
and darkness.

Listening Only

Ann Spiers

Being in small town cafes and being alone in vacated houses on the beach, I hear language. I have hiked the Washington beach from the Columbia River to Cape Flattery. Below is an excerpt from my journal.

Going north on the Washington coast, I walk the highway looking for breakfast. In early morning, the road kill is fresh, their identities discernible. Newly dead raccoons, reminiscent of well-hugged stuffed animals, are still cute in spite of bloodied parts. As the day proceeds, the various carcasses are tire flattened beyond recognition. By afternoon, crows have feasted on them, pecking and tearing, dodging the day's traffic. By nightfall, the bodies have vanished.

No tavern hereabouts offers a breakfast special, but a converted house does. This house is sky blue. Its rooms elbow each other awkwardly trying to be restaurant like. Everyone—diners, waitress, and cook—knows each other too well. I am invisible, a dressed-down middle-aged woman ordering two eggs, etc. The assembled diners talk, and the talk gets personal fast. One woman, her back supported by the staircase wall, announces she does not drink. I wonder why she says that, but the guys scattered about at the other tables are beefy dudes with broken faces, swollen and flushed. One guy says a neighbor man has died at thirty. But all in all, he was a lucky guy because he was predicted not to live past twenty. The woman says they should only drink socially. She adds that she jokes about sex because joking about sex is the closest she can get to it. She says, "I never could walk into a tavern."

As they discuss tavern visiting, a *bing* goes off in my head at the phrase "walk into a tavern." Implied in "walking into a tavern" for a woman is that she does so unescorted. During my college days in the mid-sixties, Seattle's University District taverns were the hangouts where we college kids on the fringes of being hip, socialized. We smoked and drank beer, debating whether we got more brew for our buck by buying schooners, or a pitcher, or bottled quarts. Throughout Washington State, tavern decor was determined by defunct laws called "Blue Laws." For the edification and protection of society, tavern windows must not allow passersby a view into the interior. So throughout Washington, taverns were dark and usually seedy places. Better taverns were furnished like home kitchens with wooden tables, straight-backed chairs, windows greased up a mite with deep-frying fumes. Taverns could sell only beer. Cocktail lounges sold hard liquor, up scaled as Manhattans or martinis for the home-come WWII GIs and their wives. These cocktail lounges, although also dark, had a modish ambience defined by deep leather booths that enclosed the drinker. He or she drank protected and encushioned in a finer set of furniture than the sticks at home. Earlier during Prohibition, pool halls were the dens for the looser edges of town life.

"Walking into a tavern" was not something my World War II-era mother would do in her small towns clustered around Grays Harbor. She considered herself a classy broad. However, lacking in small-town niceties, I got so I could walk into a tavern. I could walk into a tavern unescorted. To be able to do so back then was to experience a moment of social defiance, of opening possibilities, of making an entrance, of walking through heavy doors to self reliance. Walking into a tavern allows everyone a moment of drama in the ordinary social landscape. As your eyes adjust to the dim light, you note if someone has noticed you, and you notice the most promising place to sit. Depending on your mood, you stride/shuffle/slink/dance to a booth, a stool, with friends, alone, or close enough to the action to encourage a pickup.

Today here at breakfast, I choose to sit under the lesser staircase, the one up to the back of the house. I down my eggs once-over too-easy. The woman who does not drink and has little sex greets her son as he arrives for breakfast. He is another big ball of a man. She tells us all about the men in her family. Her son and grandson live in the same house. The young man lives in one end of the house and her son lives in the other. Her son has gotten so big that he must walk joist to joist across his home's floor because the floorboards no longer have the capacity to bounce back to their original level under his weight. When she visits, her grandson is asleep in his recliner at the entry end of the house, and her son is asleep in his recliner at his end of the house.

She asks if the two males have "gone in to work lately." "Gone in to work" hits me as another phrase like "walking into a tavern." The determining phrase is "in to." A boss, perhaps because business is off, allows this "going in to work." This pass-through is the minimally required commitment needed to hang onto the job. Maybe all jobs down here along this beach allow "going in to work" as opposed to eight hours a day or the big 24/7. Full employment might put more folks out of work everywhere. It is better to be casual, better to say "going in to work" sometime today, sometime this week, sometime this month. If you don't go to work, the job won't get done. And you—and everyone—will be always employed.

Totally unemployed myself and not intending to go in to work anytime soon, I eat my biscuit, risen to a miraculously lovely level. The group exchanges directions to a nursing home outside of Bellingham off I-5. Someone has gone over the edge, the edge of what they do not reveal. I decide, in spite of the angel biscuit, that yogurt and juice pulled from my backpack and eaten on the beach will do for breakfast during my hike north.

Back on the beach, I move along, mumbling to myself about depressing meals. The tide is receding. The wind bullies me. It is Christmas-week cold. One, two miles go by slowly although I am trucking along. The beach is narrowing. The surf curls a jagged lip. The cut bank grows to three feet high. The southwest wind presses my back, and wet crawls up my ankles, then girdles my waist. As I go north, I near giant, vertical forms on the upper beach. They are ghost trees, branchless, black with salt curing, probably spruce or cedar, not the tweaked trunks of shore pine. They are still rooted in place where the forest floor dropped below high-tide level, perhaps after an earthquake. There is no elevation from which they could slip forward, and no forest of their age or kind grows on the shore. I cannot decipher how they got here.

Battered by wind, I move into the dunes, maneuver through their troughs and along deer trails. The dune grass thickens, and I move to the top of the fore dune, here only a few feet high. Wave overwash frosts the dune grasses with sand. Each of my steps breaks through, making tedious footfall. I seek out another deer path in the trough behind the fore dune. Eerily warming this grey seascape, dormant dune grasses flush red and yellow. Why is there color now in winter? I look west into the cloud-cluttered horizon. The long winter sunset has commenced, and noon was just three hours ago.

In a chair in the dunes, a girl doll, decked out in indestructible ringlets and ruffles, waits here in the rain. She will outwait winter until spring's low tides bring the family back for razor-clam digging. Settled behind the dunes are architecturally kissed houses, very Northwesty, two floors high, cedar-sided, and windows wood-framed. Inside the windows, mirrors reflect beach light into the homes' dim interiors. These houses are vacant for the winter. On their eaved porches and wide verandas, chairs invite a sit-down, a rest-a-spell, a come-take-a-load-off. I do. I dream of Captain Wiley, my grandfather, long ago master at crossing the Grays Harbor bar, now out to sea eternally in a phantom tug. I say to him what he used to say even after he was beached on my parents' front porch over in Seattle. I say as I dare to nap huddled in the someone else's big deck chair, "Wake me when the tide turns." 📖

Ghost Trees, Metolius River Canyon, Central Oregon, 2015,
photograph by Andrew Wesner

For Matthew

Qwo-Li Driskill

"I have died too many deaths
that were not mine."
—Audre Lorde

I have found my body collapsible,
choking on your death
like a small child who seeks to understand
by stuffing pennies and marbles into mouth.

It reverberates across the continent,
fallout from an old, old, story.
How when they found you
at first they thought you were a scarecrow
crucified on a Wyoming fence.

Make no mistake,
the men who killed you meant you
as SYMBOL
as WARNING
as HIDEOUS BIRTH.

I am trying to re-member you
as MOVEMENT THROUGH AIR
as PRESSURE ON EARTH
as WARM LIFE BREATHING.

In Seattle, 1000 lit candles.
(I wanted the city to burn.)

In San Francisco, a rainbow flag hung half-mast
(I wanted earth to split open.)

In DC, the president finally spoke.
(I wanted screams to shatter glass.)

In Laramie, they wore armbands.
(I wanted a revolution.)

Thousands upon thousands say *Never Again,*
        Never Again.
(I don't want to remember you as SYMBOL.)

We have no more time for symbols.
We have no more time for vigils.
WE HAVE NO MORE TIME

because when I started writing
This poem for you, Matthew,
you were still ALIVE.

The Cross/La Crusada

Waverly Fitzgerald

Learning tango one learns a new vocabulary, a vocabulary that is foreign but quickly becomes familiar. What was my first word in my new language? The cross. *La crusada*.

Walk me to the cross. A phrase which means nothing in English but becomes as commonplace as "How's it going?" in tango.

"Walk your partner to the cross." That's what the teacher repeated over and over in the first tango class I attended. It was the seed point from which all the other moves blossomed, the sweeping curves of forward *ochos*, the lively romp of a *molinetta* turn.

Walk me to the cross. It evokes images of Christ hanging crucified, waiting for death. In a sense, the woman waiting in the cross is tortured, as well, waiting for her release, poised on one foot, the other tucked unnaturally behind her, like Christ's feet pinned together with a single nail.

Walk me to the cross. And I will step on my right foot, then bring my left foot in front, crossing it and shift my weight to my left foot, leaving the right one tucked behind. In this position, I am hung up, unable to move, unless my partner releases me, shifting his body to unlock the foot that is behind and then encouraging me to take a step forward or to the side. Without this release, I will stumble and fall, as clumsy as if my shoelaces were tied together.

The only easy way out of the cross is back and sometimes I move too fast, take that backwards step without being led, so eagerly do I anticipate my release from my foot bondage. But if this is not the direction my partner wishes to move, I fly away from him and the beauty of the cross is lost.

For the beauty of the cross is all in the yielding. It is the emblematic position of tango, combining all the longing, all the yearning the dance permits me, encourages me to express.

Walk me to the cross. It's a subtle move, one probably not even noticed by an observer who has not learned tango. My partner, holding me in his arms, drifts slightly away from me. Wishing to stay connected with him, I elongate my backward steps, trying to keep in front of him. At the last moment, when we are about to lose each other, he turns back to me, a move so small that it might be a millimeter of difference but it's enough. I swivel to match him, my one foot tucked behind the other, so that I am fully in his arms again and my body leans towards his. Once more, heart to heart.

Walk me to the cross. It's an odd maneuver, not found in any other dance. I was told that I always crossed when my partner took two steps to the outside on the left side. I was constantly on the lookout. "Were those outside steps? Was that a second step? Am I supposed to cross now?" It made me cross, all that counting and worry. I still missed the cross more than I achieved it. Then my partner would look at me, as frustrated as I was. "You are supposed to be in the cross," he would say crossly. As if the cross was a place, a position of humility, a posture of submission.

I kept asking my teachers: "how do I know when to cross?" "Don't worry," they'd reply. Soon you will do it automatically. It will be natural." Right. Like I would cross my feet at my ankles and then stand on my forward foot for fun. Now I find myself doing this all the time, while waiting for the bus at the bus stop, while standing in line at the grocery store. I like the way it makes me feel like a bird, poised on one long leg, ready to take flight.

Walk me to the cross. I never think about it anymore. My body goes without thought, moved by desire and rhythm. Walk me to the cross. I go there willingly. Surrender is different from submission. Walk me to the cross. 📖

Wah!, 2015, Graphite Sketch, by Anita K. Boyle

Called

Marion Kimes

the work. the work. the calling/the work.
Natalia Ginzburg's *vigilant, radiant eye.* *
essays her craft. poetry mine.
words. gradual dawn or lightning.
magnetic. electric. essential.
words. lines. ideas. spattered on paper
picking them up, putting them down,
move them around. & the work of the beat.
syllables charm, they dazzle.
hypnotic. percussive. you know, even
if we drum *on the nipple of a gunlock.* **
songs seized & sung printed or tongued
with *a vigilant, radiant eye.*
a vigilant, radiant eye.

* Natalia Ginzburg, *A Place To Live and Other Selected Essays,* choisi et traduit de l'italien par Lynne Sharon Schwartz.

** Oxford Pocket Dictionary: in the definition of percussion, percussive (dans la definition de percussion, fusil á percussion).

Interpellée

Traduction de Martha Linehan

le travail. le travail. l' appel/le travail.
Natalia Ginzburg, *son œil vigilant, rayonnant.* *
son métier, les essais. la poésie, mienne.
les paroles. une aube douce ou la foudre
magnétiques. électriques. essentielles.
les paroles. les lignes. les idées. éclaboussées sur le papier
les ramasser, les reposer,
les bouger. & le travail du rythme.
les syllabes charment, elles éblouissent.
hypnotiques. percutantes. tu sais, même
si on tambourine *au téton du chien d'un fusil* **
des chants saisis et chantés, imprimés ou parlés
d'un œil vigilant, rayonnant.
un œil vigilant, rayonnant.

Un Réquiem Furioso

Laura Anna Stortoni

Para Sylvia Plath, Anne Sexton, Alfonsina Storni,
Antonia Pozzi, Marina Tsvetayeva,
Virginia Woolf, y Ingrid Jonker

Si las mejores de nosotras
queremos sólo morir
y acabar nuestras vidas
añorando
el abrazo de la tierra
tan caluroso y húmedo
como nuestros vientres

Entonces
¿quién va a quedar
para cargar con el Dolor
en hombros musculosos
para las hermanas que están ahora
todavía en la cuna?

Pensamos a veces—
cuando la Soledad nos muerde el hígado
con su pico filudo—
que sería fácil
flotar hacia el más allá, nuevas Ofelias
en orillas colmadas de nenífares
o entregarnos a un convento
donde el Dolor es arrullado
por la anestesia de Dios y la Virgen Bendita.

Pero entonces
¿quién va a quedar
para las no-vírgenes de mañana, para las menos
valientes de hoy?

No te permitas
flotar hacia el mas allá. Aférrate a la rocosa orilla.

An Angry Requiem

Traduction de Camincha Benvenutto

To Sylvia Plath, Anne Sexton, Alfonsina Storni,
Antonia Pozzi, Marina Tsvetayeva,
Virginia Woolf, and Ingrid Jonker

If the best of us
want only to die,
and take their lives
yearning
for the embrace of the earth
as warm and moist
as our wombs

Then
who will be left
to carry the Pain
on muscular shoulders
for the sisters who are now
in the cradle?

We think sometimes—
when Loneliness bites our liver
with its sharp beak—
that it would be easy
to float away, new Ophelias
on a streaming bed of water lilies
or to get ourselves to a nunnery
where Pain is lulled
by the anesthesia of God and the Blessed Virgin.

But then
who would be left
for the non-virgins of tomorrow, for the less
courageous of today?

Don't let yourself
float away. Get thee to the rocky shore.

Kitchen, photograph, by Manit Chaotragoongit

I Open My Mouth But No Words Come Out

A First Generation American Encounters the Language Issue

Pat Duggan

From 1999-2000, Pat Duggan and her two school-age children spent almost a year living in Ireland, where she earned a Masters degree at the Poet's House in Falcarragh, County Donegal. Part of the thesis requirements involved translating Irish poetry into English, a task that should have been less daunting than it was, given that all four grandparents and her father grew up in this remote Gaeltacht (bilingual) region of the country. This is her personal account of discovering and reclaiming a language and the larger ramifications for all of us when minority tongues face possible extinction.

It is the last day of January 2000, and I am attending my first Irish wake. This is not part of the lesson plan. The gathering takes place in Cnoc Fola (pronounced Knock Foe-lah) or the Bloody Foreland area on the rugged Donegal coast. As soon as we drive up to the house, it occurs to me that I've been here before. Once inside, I notice a large photograph of a smiling couple. I know the photograph well. I should. I was the photographer. The image had been captured on film almost sixteen years earlier.

In a way, my memories of that prior time are more like a series of individual snapshots, rather than a continuous movie clip, perhaps because the experience had such a whirlwind feel. It was difficult to keep track of all the players. If we weren't visiting one in a long succession of living relatives, we spent time being introduced to those in residence at local graveyards. Scenery was enjoyed catch-can between Point A and Point B—not exactly the "bus tour approach."

One thing I do remember vividly is that Cnoc Fola was my first real exposure to an Irish-speaking populace. That was the summer of 1984. The bond of language gave this community a sense of secrecy, unlike the more open friendliness of neighboring Falcarragh, which had evolved as a market town.

Sixteen years later, sitting in this crowded living room, where basketfuls of loose cigarettes and hard candies are being passed around to all the guests, a Falcarragh-based cousin leans over to me and remarks, "Listen how they're all speaking in Irish."

They were, of course. And the thing that struck me, which I hadn't noticed on the previous visit, is that the Irish accent while speaking Irish doesn't sound at all like the Irish accent used in speaking English. The effect is more guttural than lilt. Yet, when Irish-language poetry is read aloud, the more musical tones dominate, as if these are two distinct languages.

My suspicions will later be confirmed by the poet Gréagóir Ó Dúill, who tells me there are actually three separate dialects of Irish. "Munster," he says, "has long vowels and cadences influenced by Norman French which are (to many ears) attractive. Ulster has a clipped rush like a mountain stream. Connaught is somewhere in between."

Legacy

By rights, I should have known at least a little of the language. I didn't. Being one generation removed from Ireland was enough to break this fragile link. I am not alone.

When Irish-speakers emigrated to the United States in the first half of the last century, most wanted to prove their worthiness as citizens of a new country by leaving behind their old ways. That included abandoning their native language.

In 1978, my maternal grandmother was interviewed by a newspaper reporter and asked whether the Irish were passing on their traditions to subsequent generations. She replied that, although her children felt a connection to Ireland, America had become her country now. "We owe allegiance to this nation and I've tried to pass that idea to them." [1]

For her, Irish was more a spoken language than a written one, much the same way as she approached cooking. The recipes were all filed away in her head. Never did she bother with such nuisances as standardized measuring cups and spoons. The process of making raspberry jam was simple and unfussy: a bowl of berries, a bowl of sugar, a blessing of pectin. Boil it down, skim off the scum, ladle into sterilized jars, cool, then seal with wax. Done.

Try finding that in any cookbook. Above all, it was the practical approach and the standard she applied to everything, including her native tongue. In her new life in America, "Gaeilge" no longer had a useful purpose, other than serving as a secret code between adults who didn't want their children eavesdropping on certain conversations.

Immersion

There is something organic, almost magical about the immersion experience as a learning tool, much like singing along with the radio. Both serve as a kind of coach or prod. Without cues, it's easy to get lost. With them, learning occurs almost effortlessly.

That was my experience living in Falcarragh. Because many of the signs are bilingual, absorbing the language becomes almost subliminal. No textbook has that kind of power.

Shop registers as shop/*siopa*. A bank shares equal billing with *banc*, and so on. Even the Irish-only signs begin to permeate. There is no mistaking *An Fal Carrach*. The term *go mall* [2] is a bit more mysterious, but obviously, in this remote area, has nothing to do with promoting a shopping center. When in doubt, just ask almost anyone. (With the exception of a fellow American, that is!)

Poet John Montague is right. Growing up in Ireland, particularly in a Gaeltacht (Irish speaking) area tends to rub off on a person. [3] Even limited exposure has an effect. Both my children picked up a slight Irish accent, the younger child more than the older one. That's to be expected.

Being in the minority also meant increased social pressure to adapt to local ways. As I told Jon and Keely when we first moved abroad, "Remember that in Ireland, you're the ones who talk funny, not the other way around."

If my eight-year-old daughter wanted to learn Irish step-dancing, as was her passion, she also must learn the language since the teacher's staccato-like instructions defaulted to Irish, more often than not. Necessity is a powerful motivator.

Nevertheless, Irish has always had a reputation for being a difficult language. Not only do the spellings of words give little clue to pronunciation, but even a person's name becomes chameleon-like, depending on how it's used. Seán, for example, transforms to a Sheáin in certain cases.

While this built-in confusion has certainly proved beneficial in spotting outsiders (myself included), it hasn't helped in keeping the language alive. [4] Case in point: even though the study of Ireland's mother tongue is mandatory in schools, Irish newspapers in autumn, 1999, spoke of declining test scores, a lack of interest. Does this mean that, after being revived from near death, the Irish language is again facing its own mortality, this time due more to apathy than oppression? If so, why do Irish poets persist in writing in a language that is, if not dead, then perhaps terminally ill?

The argument could be made that so do Japanese poets, so do Czech poets, so do other poets whose first language is not English. Still, they write with the hope of reaching a larger audience. Unlike those other languages, however, translation from Irish to English is not exactly a two-way street, more like a one-way gravel road with a bicycle path running alongside it.

With the exception of Seamus Heaney, Irish poets writing in English tend not to be translated into the ancestral tongue. Even Heaney, through the pen of poet Gabriel Rosenstock, ends up speaking in Munster Irish and not his native Ulster voice. As an American, I confess that it's all Greek to me, but I suppose it would be much like our own New Englander Robert Frost being read aloud with a Cajun accent. While still qualifying as American English, it somehow becomes jarring to the ear.

While there are Irish poets, such as the late Michael Harnett, who have produced poems in both languages, that practice seems to be the exception, not the rule. Furthermore, even though Harnett wrote exclusively in Irish from 1975-85, critics still consider his best work to be in English. [5] That too, of course, is open to debate.

In some ways, the Irish language poets remind me of the monks of an earlier time, fiercely guarding the written tradition in an almost secret society, where the password is not a single word or phrase, but an entire language.

I am not suggesting that this is how insiders view the situation, but an outsider can easily get that impression, perhaps misreading the passion Irish poets attach to the language.

Irish is, after all, as poet Cathal Ó Searcaigh calls it, his "emotional" language. How could the heart not be involved?

Outsider vs. Insider

February, 2000. Irish language poet Gréagóir Ó Dúill is putting the final touches on a millennium anthology of Irish language poetry due out on St. Patrick's Day. An English companion volume has been on bookstore shelves since January.

One gaping difference: Ó Dúill's book will not contain anything by William Butler Yeats, considered to be the Mt. Everest of Irish poets. Why won't W.B. be included? For the simple reason, he wrote nothing in Irish. Or, as Yeats himself puts it, "Gaelic is my national language, but it is not my mother tongue." [6]

Montague understands the dilemma well. "After living abroad for over a decade, I came to the conclusion that, unlike prose writers, it is impossible for a poet to change languages." [7]

Ó Dúill would disagree, arguing that most of today's Irish language poets, himself included, have learned the language, rather than absorbed it from the cradle. Perhaps the most notable exception is Donegal-born Cathal Ó Searcaigh, whose first words were in Irish, and who still considers it his first language. He also grew up without a clock in the house.

Ó Searcaigh was born in 1956, which makes his circumstances all the more unusual, even by Irish standards. Until recently, he still qualified, in the language specialty, as a "young poet" which, according to Ó Dúill, puts the ceiling at about forty-five years of age. Conversely, the English language poet in Ireland passes this imaginary mark at about age twenty-seven, the age requirements having more to do with how big a group is waiting in the wings.

Decoding the Message

Like any other language, Irish does not always convert directly to English. Rather than relying on translations, I find transliterations far more revealing, even though they don't always seem to make sense to an English-speaking world. However, what they do manage quite well is to provide a window into the mind-set of a people. Until one understands that mind-set, one cannot really understand the language, never mind the poetry.

For instance, in English, the phrase *I am hungry*, in Irish becomes, *Tá ocras orm*, or *I have hunger on me*, a very subtle, but significant shift in perspective. Leave it to the English and Americans, in particular, to personify the thing, to *become* hunger. Other cultures, such as the French, take a step back with *J'ai faim*, or *I have hunger*. Then the Irish come along and assume the condition as a personal burden.

Published Translations

To the uninitiated, even more confusion abounds when comparing various translations of the same Irish language poem. In some cases, they share only a fleeting resemblance. Consider these two very different interpretations of Ó Searcaigh's *Dúil*:

Lust (Translated by Gabriel Rosenstock)

You bar boy—yes any time,
your glowing heart is mine.

When you speak, flames flicker and glow,
passionate poetry in your eyes of sloe.

Your laughter smolders, is bright surf,
is blue flame from dry turf.

You ignite me with your gaze,
lust encompasses all my days.

Take me to your bed.
Who needs Nefertiti? She's dead.

Passion (Translated by Frank Sewell)

I'd rather have the boy behind the bar
whose heart warms to love's occasion,

who speaks in flames
about disappointments and poems,

his laugh as consuming
as the slit in broken turf,

his eyes firing sparks
that light my tinder passion,

than Nefertiti herself plastered on my bed
and the wonders of the Pharaohs about the house.

Still, even poor translations offer what the poetry of Seán Ó Ríordáin, Biddy Jenkinson, and others do not: access for an English-speaking world. Ó Ríordáin's estate will only permit a few of his poems to be translated. Much of his legendary diaries also remain unpublished.

In recent times, Jenkinson has become one of the most outspoken critics of translations. "It is a small, rude gesture to think that everything can be harvested and stored without loss in an English-speaking Ireland."[8]

Why such unwavering resolve? Ó Dúill offers a partial explanation. "When we are writing in Irish, we are reasonably sure we are writing to ourselves."

At the same time, this elite group is steadily shrinking, almost alarmingly so. In their crusade to save Irish poetry, the purists may be unwittingly contributing to its downfall. Even Ó Ríordáin was criticized in his day for taking improper liberties:

The publication in 1952 of Ó Ríordáin's first collection, Eireaball Spideoige, had resulted in some critics accusing him of doing unpardonable injury to the prosodic, stylistic and linguistic norms of traditional Irish verse. [9]

Ó Ríordáin himself makes a sly reference to this in one of his poems, when he mentions "riordanizing" the language and, more recently, Ó Searcaigh has been known to do a bit of improvising. Rather than polluting the language, as some would claim, this allows it to evolve, to be alive.

That's the reason the poet Nuala Ní Dhomhnaill gives for leaving the translating to others. When writing, she wants to be able to think only in Irish. Ní Dhomhnaill, who counts herself among the Innti Poets [10] has also been called "a law unto herself." [11]

Years ago, I saw her give a reading at the Broadway Performance Center in Seattle. Besides that flaming blowtorch of a mane and self-deprecating wit, what impressed me was Ní Dhomhnaill's insistence on working solely in Irish. At the time, I didn't even realize poets were still writing in the language, never mind exclusively so.

She has a lovely poem which sums up this philosophy, entitled, appropriately enough, "The Language Issue," and translated by Pulitzer Prize winner, Paul Muldoon.

The Language Issue

I place my hope on the water
in this little boat
of the language, the way a body might put
an infant

in a basket of intertwined
iris leaves
its underside proofed
with bitumen and pitch,

then set the whole thing down amidst
the sedge
and bulrushes by the edge
of a river

only to have it borne hither and thither,
not knowing where it might end up;
in the lap, perhaps,
of some Pharaoh's daughter.

This approach is not without its downside. Who knows where that basket will end up? As Ní Dhomhnaill herself found out, critics are not as benevolent as Pharaoh's daughters. Ironically, the reviews to which she refers below were of the Pharaoh's Daughter, the very book in which the preceding poem appears. Not only does Ní Dhomhnaill find herself contending with the language business, but also with the issue of being a "woman poet:"

Immediately the critics hailed me in terms of being a kind of Muse. Now let's get one thing quite clear. I was not their Muse. They were my translators. As it so happens, many of them were also translating other Irish-language poets, such as Michael Davitt, Liam Ó Muithile and Cathal Ó Searcaigh, but did anyone have the temerity to suggest that Michael or Liam or Cathal was anybody's Muse? You bet your sweet life they didn't. [12]

And so the little basket occasionally gets caught up in the bulrushes, but remains afloat. Yet, the metaphor really doesn't end or even begin there. In his book, *Anam Cara, A Book of Celtic Wisdom*, author John O'Donohue speaks to the much larger legacy:

The attempt to destroy Gaelic was one of the most destructive acts of violence in the colonization of Ireland by England. Gaelic is such a poetic and powerful language, it carries the Irish memory. When you steal a people's language, you leave their soul bewildered. [13]

As both a first and second generation American, I offer my own interpretation:

Tongue Tied

My mother's mother knew it well;
Irish was her mother tongue
Until she grew another
That choked the language out.

My father called upon it, too,
As litany which allowed him
To say aloud
What could not be said.

Every generation before mine
Has handed down
The china and crystal of names,
The linen of knowing

Weaves its way in under the skin
A place deeper than blood and doubt;
Yet, when I open my mouth,
The words won't come out.

When I first came to Ireland, people asked if I was there seeking out my ancestral roots. Unlike many Americans, I don't have to go very far—just down the street to my uncle's house. As one of my classmates observed, "Is there anyone you aren't related to around here?"

Instead of needing to trace the branches of the family tree—the Donegal phone book will do—my goal was to examine more closely the roots of my ancestral language, the "mother tongue." In a way, my approach mirrors that of an adopted child seeking out a birth mother. To alleviate some of the initial awkwardness, I brought along the grandchildren, thinking that she'd be more receptive to meeting them than me.

As it turned out, my instincts were right.

Works Cited:

1. Lillian Beloin. "Despite Violence at Home, Irish Eyes Smile in America." (Catholic) *Progress*, 10 March 1978:8-9.
2. *Go Mall* means "drive slowly."
3. "What I am trying to say is that the Irish landscape is a kind of primal Gaeltacht and that anyone brought up in it has already absorbed a great deal of the language." John Montague. *The Figure in the Cave and Other Essays*. Ed. Antoinette Quinn. Dublin: Lilliput Press LTD, 1989:44.
4. The *Irish Studies* textbook reports that there were more than 1.5 million Gaelic speakers in 1851, compared to an estimated 25,0000-30,0000 today. "In the space of a few generations, the Gaelic language has disappeared from most of Ireland like 'snow from the ditches.'"
5. Patrick Crotty, ed., *Modern Irish Poetry, An Anthology*, Belfast Press Limited, 1995:235.
6. Eavan Boland. "Gods Make Their Own Importance: On the Authority of the Poet in Our Time," The Ronald Duncan Lecture, October 1994 (The Poetry Book Society).
7. Montague. 109.
8. Crotty. 327.
9. Caiomhím Mac Giolla Léith. "Modern Poetry in Irish, 1940-1970." *Irish Poetry Since Kavanagh*. Ed. Theo Dorgan, Dublin:Four Courts Press, 1996:43.
10. After a magazine launched in the 1970s by students at the University of Cork. The name identifies a new movement in Irish language poetry, one less given to the solemnity of the past.
11. Alan Titley. "Innti and Onward: The New Poetry in Irish." *Irish Poetry Since Kavanagh*. 88.
12. Nuala Ní Dhomhnaill. "The Hidden Ireland: Women's Inheritance." *Irish Poetry Since Kavanagh*. 115.
13. John O'Donohue. *Anam Cara, A Book of Celtic Wisdom*. New York: Harper Collins/Cliff Street Books, 1997. 67. 📖

Jackpot Mexican

Stephen D. Gutierrez

Come right up and try. Give the guy a ride. Punch the keys and test his side. Ghostly barker stands by a booth. Behind a dark curtain, aficionados engage, spend their last earnings on what they know is fruitless. But they try, anyway, to reach the end. When they do, they'll have it all, all; they'll become complete. Until then, they only know struggle. One stumble in the real world and you're hooked. Nobody lets you off easy. Jackpot Mexican demands a lot.

Sees everything, knows everything. Your thoughts, privy to Jack, become your entrapment. They lure you in. They are your own undoing.

Jackpot Mexican demands restitution, justice, a righting. He grins and his eyes light up, his ears smoking, dazzlingly chagrined. When he's happy, his red nose buzzes, tongue darts out, coins spill into your hand.

Jackpot Mexican loves you, says, *Play the game.*

Plug in. Adapt. Write

At the Fair:

My mom and aunt visited from L.A. They came up often, on the train, disembarking at the charming station in downtown Fresno. I met them there, greeting them on the platform and driving them home, my mom saying, "Yoo-hoo," waving me down, and my aunt lugging a bag behind her, complaining all the way.

"Get in the car, Stephen," my mother said. "Hay cholos around here."

"Ay, don't be so prejudiced," my aunt said. "It's just like home, L.A."

"It is, isn't it?" I asked, stopped in front of a taqueria. Brown buildings blended into the landscape. In L.A., the working poor toiled in factories, not fields. Otherwise, the two cities shared a lot. I liked them both, places where lower-middle-class Mexicans, like us, could feel good in.

"Americans," my mother reminded me, taking it in. "Mira nomas, look at how Mexican it is."

But my aunt checked her. "See, Jo, it's Mexican this, Mexican that. But everywhere you go, you want to see where the Mexicans live."

"It's true. I love my people," she said, staring out the window. "But they're so poor. I feel sorry for them."

"Don't be so condescending," I said. "We're no better."

Then she agreed. "We're not, are we? Just poor Mexicans, too."

My aunt said nothing. She was the younger one. The sister who had been a "career girl" into her late twenties, daring the barrio to call her an old maid, working as a secretary for a corporation and saving enough money to travel. She went to Mexico. She went to Hawaii.

She got married and slipped into the life of us, giving birth to three boys and living in a nice house in San Gabriel. She tagged along with my mom everywhere. They visited me because they liked Fresno.

She was the hip one. She nudged me all the time.

We rolled into the driveway. My wife came out and helped with the bags. Then we made dinner and sat around talking. My kid toddled around. Those were good days, everybody happy, everybody content. Those trips were fun.

Fall stung the air. The scent of fields drifted into our living room. If it wasn't true, you could imagine it, campesinos working the rows and rich, ripe fruit piling up on the ground. Fresno was enchanted and great.

We loved Fresno. Nobody complained, really.

On the third day of their vacation, my mom said, "Let's go to the fair!" She spotted the ad in the newspaper. A bunch of grapes hung under a trellis that spelled out FRESNO. We prepared to go, my wife staying home because she taught a class at the university that night, and my son buckled in, strapped into his car seat, secured in the back. We took off. We drove the streets to the Big Fresno Fair.

The fairgrounds are on the southeast side of town, a neighborhood of its own, tough and proud. The streets are dark, the houses pleasant, not-too-shabby tract homes with additions and nicely tended lawns. Sometimes an eyesore blights the block.

"I think Joe lives here," my mom said, referring to a relative of ours who lived in town. I didn't know him.

"Around here, somewhere."

"He does, doesn't he?" my aunt said. We stopped in the middle of the block. It looked like any number of streets in L.A.—in Rosemead, Montebello, Alhambra, Pico Rivera; it looked like my neighborhood back home, with an extra sadness. It seemed a little older.

"The ferris wheel, how pretty," my mom said. The ferris wheel circled in the night, brightly lit, neon streaks staying. I like the sights of fairs; I like the sounds of people, of rides, of games. I liked it all, walking around with my aunt and mom, Ben strapped in the stroller, wide-eyed and amazed.

We ate fair food and then fair dessert and kept walking around. We explored the big buildings with the gems and flowers and the livestock in the pens. We gazed into the eyes of the cows, waiting for answers. When they gave none, we laughed. My kid pointed to a ride, and we put him in a big orange fish, watching him go round. He shrieked with glee. His balled up fists shook.

Then it was time to go home. We decided to call it a night. We stood on the concourse, watching the people. On the midway, la gente del valle had fascinated, farmworkers spending their money on crazy games to impress girlfriends, who hooked onto their tooled leather belts. Whole families carted stuffed animals bigger than any of them and beamed. When I bumped into a man in charge of a brood, I apologized; he gave me a smile. The fair atmosphere worked on us all.

Cholos, coupled with fine broads, skirted the aisles, but dove into a game on the sudden, pulling out wads of cash from baggy pockets. They acted cool with each other; bikers strolled the lanes, impressing their ladies with their own acumen. Blacks from the maligned west side blended in. Nobody warred.

The Big Fresno Fair calmed. Peace entered into the night,

and anybody caught stupid would be thrown out. Cops patrolled the grounds. On walkie talkies, security kept in constant touch. A recent stabbing in Fresno wouldn't ruin it.

It was time to go home. Then they started pouring in, kids from a different group, streaming through the turnstiles onto the concourse. They came in a horde, the hip-hop generation in numbers, kid after kid looking so severely disconnected they scared you, stepping in through the gate after the pat-down, scowling on the concrete expanse, waiting to hook up with partners. Chicks, clumped together, swaggeringly bitched about the fucking looks somebody had given them.

Old-time cholos stepped aside, gathering their families. The tired and beaten didn't have the energy to confront them. They didn't want to save face. They wanted to get out of there.

"Let's get the hell out of here," my mother said. "This is too much, this place."

"Yeah, Steve, it's a little rowdy now," my aunt said.

We stood by the bathroom watching the kids come in. Cops followed them with their eyes. Tough, mean kids taking over the fair, spreading and talking.

"Fuck him."

"That bitch don't know . . ."

Syllables, out of every mouth, canned and predictable; hardly an expression of life in the eyes. A language dead-ended in the throat, expelled out the lips and left to linger in the air, stale and rotten.

"Hey, look at those two kids," my mom said, "they're nerds."

Against the wall of the bathroom, hanging out with themselves in their own style, stood two nerds, white and brown, wearing the right clothes the wrong way. They reminded me of me.

"What are they doing?"

"Trying to be cool," I said.

"Good luck," my aunt said, and we all laughed.

"Hey, man," one said to the other, unaccented, "what are we going to do tonight?"

"Nothing, hang out." They spoke clearly, forcefully, unambiguously. You expected poetry to come tumbling out of their mouths. They were different enough.

They were the nation's leaders, and everybody knew it. They hated them for it.

Tomorrows leaders. We passed them.

"Stephen, let's go now," my mother said, making her way out, and my aunt followed in agreement, both of them muttering. This place was too much for them, this world too new.

Jackpot Mexican balks, freaks out, goes berserk. Spits at me: *unaccented? unaccented? unaccented?* In triple insistence, questions my every move, my every choice.

I punch in new words, say, instead: *"Hey, man," one said to the other,"* harmlessly, *"what are we going to do tonight?"* That should get Jack off my back.

Ack! Jackpot Mexican flares and thunders: *Give me an answer! Where do you stand? Are you an elitist bastard? A lower middle-class critic of those beneath you, a social snob?*

No! But I punch in my answer just as quickly. I'm writing furiously.

I'm out-Jacking Jack. I'll beat this game.

I'll be a writer. Damn the odds.

Right words wrong truths?

One slant only, mine yours?

Get a hold of myself.

The hip-hop generation left me wanting more. They failed in language, which is life. They were obscure and commercial. They wore logos. They mouthed cheap slogans.

They strutted into corporate America unawares. They were pathetic. They made me laugh.

Jackpot Mexican fades. A coded message asks for more, says: *Feed the machine and live. Miss and die. Do something unique. Don't sell your soul. Find your own, too. You only have this time to do it in.* 📖

XVI

Raven Notes

Corvid, Seattle, Washington, photograph by Alfredo Arreguín

BIOGRAPHICAL NOTES
WRITERS
(PAGE NUMBERS INDICATE WHERE WORK APPEARS)

Kathleen Alcalá (p.128) was born in Compton, California, to Mexican parents, and grew up in San Bernardino. Both a graduate of and instructor in the Clarion West Science Fiction and Fantasy Program, her work embraces both traditional and innovative storytelling techniques. She is the author of six award-winning books that include a collection of stories, three novels, a book of essays, and *The Deepest Roots: Finding Food and Community on a Pacific Northwest Island*. With Norma E. Cantú, Kathleen is the co-editor of *Weeping Women: La Llorona's Presence in Modern Latinx and Chicanx Lore*. A member of the Ópata Nation, Kathleen makes her home on Suquamish territory.

Bobby Anderson (p.98) lived and worked in Seattle in the 1980s and 90s. His work appeared in *The Kenyon Review, Ploughshares, Michigan Quarterly Review, Threepenny Review, Seattle Review*, and *The Seattle Weekly*. "Writing A Place in the City" was presented at Richard Hugo House, in October 1998, at the "Power of Place" symposium.

Amontaine Aurore (p.277) is a writer, playwright, actor, producer, director, and performance artist. She has a BA in Liberal Arts with an Emphasis in Writing from Antioch University. Her plays have been produced in Seattle, New York, and abroad. Amontaine is the recipient of several artist grants from Artist Trust, Seattle Office of Arts and Culture, 4Culture, and the Puffin Foundation. Her plays were named finalists in the Bay Area Playwrights Festival and Seattle Public Theater's Emerald Prize in Playwriting. She was a writer in residence at the Hedgebrook Writers' Retreat on Whidbey Island. A filmed version of her play, *When a Tree Falls*, premiered at SIFF Cinema in 2022.

Anna Bálint (p.263) is a London-born, Seattle-based poet, writer, editor and cultural activist of East European descent. Her many years of editorial work for Raven Chronicles Press include *Take a Stand, Art Against Hate* anthology, and *Words From the Café*, an anthology of writing by people in recovery. Her short fiction collection, *Horse Thief* (Curbstone Press, 2004), spans cultures and continents and was a finalist for the Pacific Northwest Book Award. Anna currently teaches adults in recovery from trauma, addiction, mental illness, and homelessness at Seattle's Recovery Cáfe, where she founded Safe Place Writing Circle.

Camincha Benvenutto (p.356) is from Miraflores, Lima, Peru. She was the 2017-2020 Poet Laureate of Pacifica, California. She was selected by KDTV for their segment "One of Ours" to honor her contributions to the Latin American community. Her novella, *As Time Goes By*, was published by iUniverse. She self-published her novel, *Con el Pasar del Tiempo*. The San Francisco Bay Guardian said: "Camincha frames the ordinary in a way that makes it extraordinary, and that is real talent." She served as an interpreter at the San Francisco Superior Court.

Jim Bodeen (p.336) is the caretaker of 30+ trees surrounding 2010 house in Yakima where he cooks and keeps house for Karen, his wife and partner since 1968. He is a walker, and his practice includes prayer and watchfulness. He says Storypath/Cuentocamino arrived as a gift. He is a non-uniformed rover for the Celestial All-Stars.

Natalie Pascale Boisseau (p.340, 341) is a French Canadian writer from Montreal living in Washington State. She is currently writing her memoir "Migrations, the Long Return Home," on living in the long wake of maternal suicide. Recently, her stories have been published in *Isele Magazine*, *Raven Chronicles*, and *Crab Creek Review*. Her life's work includes working for Cirque du Soleil, being a copyright attorney for artists, and saving a forest near her home in Lake Forest Park.

Margot F. Boyer (p.156) was a poet and teacher, but has turned her hands to fiber art: she quilts novels and knits poems on an island in Puget Sound.

Matt Briggs (p.179) is the author of eight works of fiction, including *The Remains of River Names* and *The Strong Man*. A collection of very short stories is forthcoming from Dr. Cicero Books. His fiction has appeared in the *Northwest Review*, *Chicago Review*, *Word Riot*, *ZYZZYVA*, and elsewhere. Briggs's fiction has been awarded The Stranger Genius Award, The Nelson Bentley Prize in Fiction from *The Seattle Review*, and The American Book Award for his novel *Shoot the Buffalo*. He has an MA in Fiction from The Writing Seminars at Johns Hopkins University, and lives near Seattle.

Ronda Piszk Broatch (p.254) is the author of *Chaos Theory for Beginners* (MoonPath Press, 2023) and *Lake of Fallen Constellations* (MoonPath, 2015). She is the recipient of an Artist Trust GAP Grant. Ronda's journal publications include *Fugue* (2019), *Blackbird, 2River, Sycamore Review, Missouri Review, Palette Poetry*, and NPR News / KUOW's *All Things Considered*. She is a graduate student working toward her MFA at Pacific Lutheran University's Rainier Writing Workshop.

Rebecca Brown (p.71) is a novelist, essayist, playwright, artist, and teacher. She was the first writer in residence at Richard Hugo House, co-founder of the Jack Straw Writers Program, and served as the Creative Director of Literature at Centrum in Port Townsend, Washington, from 2005 to 2009. She is the author of many books, including *The Gifts of the Body*, which won a Lambda Literary Award in 1994, *Not Heaven, Somewhere Else, The Dogs: A Modern Bestiary, The Terrible Girls*, and *You Tell the Stories You Need to Believe*. She lives in Seattle.

Polly Buckingham's (p.226) books include *The River People* (Lost Horse Press, 2020), *The Expense of a View* (Katherine Anne Porter Prize, 2016), and *A Year of Silence* (Jeanne Leiby Memorial Chapbook Award, 2015). Her work appears in *The Gettysburg Review, The Threepenny Review, The Poetry Review, Alaska Quarterly Review, Sugar House Review, North American Review, The Moth, Hanging Loose*, and elsewhere. She was the recipient of a Washington Artist's Trust Fellowship and is the founding editor of *StringTown* magazine. Polly teaches creative writing at Eastern Washington University where she is the editor of *Willow Springs* magazine. She is also Series Editor for The Katherine Anne Porter Award.

Eric Lee Christensen (p.35) attended Stanford Law School and works as an Energy and Regulatory Attorney at Beveridge & Diamond PC in Seattle. He is on the Board of Directors for NatureBridge, Olympic National Park's environmental education center, and is Co-Chair of the Sustainability Committee for Seattle Rotary Club No. 4.

Glenna Elizabeth Cook (p.56) is the author of two poetry collections: *Thresholds*, a finalist for the Washington State Book Award for Poetry in 2018, and *Shapes of Time*, published in 2022, both from MoonPath Press. She has spent most of her life in Tacoma, and now, a widow in her

80s, lives in an independent apartment in a senior housing community in Puyallup, Washington. She continues to write.

Victor Hernández Cruz (p.106) was born in 1949 in Aguas Buenas, Puerto Rico. He is the author of numerous collections of poetry, including *Beneath the Spanish* (Coffee House Press, 2017); *Maraca: New and Selected Poems, 1965-2000* (Coffee House Press, 2001). Cruz is one of the founders of the Before Columbus Foundation, a nonprofit organization that promotes the recognition of multicultural writers.

Michael Daley (p.195) published three full-length books in 2022: *Reinhabited: New & Selected Poems* (Dos Madres, Ohio); *Telemachus*, a novel (Pleasure Boat Studio, Seattle); and *True Heresies* (Cervena Barva, Massachusetts); as well as a chapbook, *Romance with the Unexpected* (Empty Bowl, Anacortes, Washington); and two issues of his anthology, *The Madrona Project* (Empty Bowl, Chimacum).

Suzannah Dalzell (p.267) lives on Whidbey Island north of Seattle, Washington, where she divides her time more or less equally between writing and mucking about in wetlands. In addition to *Raven Chronicles*, her work has appeared in *Pilgrimage Magazine, Flyway, Adanna, Minerva Rising, Crosswinds*, and *About Place*. She is currently working on a collection that explores the places where her ancestry intersects with race, class, and environmental damage.

Pamela Moore Dionne's (p.33) work has appeared in several journals, including *Raven Chronicles, Shenandoah*, and *Crab Creek Review*. She was a Jack Straw Writer who earned their Artist Support Grant to record a CD of her *Sabina Spielrein Ghazals*. Dionne also earned a Centrum residency and an Artist Trust Gap Grant. Her visual art has been published in journals and presented in one-woman shows. Other credits include founding and managing the online art & literature journal *Literary Salt*. She received her MFA in Creative Writing from Goddard College.

Qwo-Li Driskill: (p.347) Unenrolled Cherokee poet, scholar, and activist, s/he grew up in rural Colorado. Driskill earned a BA from the University of Northern Colorado, an MA from Antioch University Seattle, and a PhD from Michigan State University. Driskill's poetry engages themes of inheritance and healing, and is rooted in personal Cherokee Two-Spirit, queer, and mixed-race experience. *Walking with Ghosts* (2005), Driskill's first poetry collection, was named Book of the Month by *Sable: The LitMag for New Writing*, and was nominated for the Griffin Poetry Prize. S/he is the Director of Graduate Studies and the Queer Studies Curriculum Organizer in Women, Gender, and Sexuality Studies at Oregon State University.

Pat Duggan (p.359) has a MA in Creative Writing from Lancaster University through its branch campus in County Donegal, Ireland, where she and her two children spent the 1999-2000 school year. Her poems have appeared in *Poetry Ireland Review, New Writer* (UK), *Seam* (UK), *Poets West*, and the *Poets Table Anthology*. She was a Senior Media Consultant, freelance video producer, and medical researcher for *CBS News, Evening News*, King-TV, and other news organizations, from 1975-2016. She was awarded a regional Emmy, National Women in Communications Clarion Awards, and a New York Times Fellow Award.

Taha Ebrahimi's (p.185) writing has appeared in *Creative Nonfiction* and several other anthologies, earning awards from the Pacific Northwest Writers Association, the *Bellingham Review*, Hedgebrook Writers Colony, and the Thomas J. Watson Foundation. A Seattle native, she taught creative writing at the University of Pittsburgh and began her career as a journalist at *The Seattle Times*.

Keith Egawa (p.282) is a member of the Lummi Indian Nation, a graduate of the University of Washington's Creative Writing Program, and author of the novel *Madchild Running* (Red Crane Books Inc., 1999). Keith's extensive work experience in the fields of Child and Family Services and Indian Education Reform has provided him with both inspiration and insight into his subject matter. Keith has been awarded several artists grants, in addition to conducting literary readings and presentations in public schools and writing workshops for Native Youth. He has collaborated with his sister Chenoa Egawa on young readers books, *The Whale Child* (North Atlantic Books, 2020) and *Tani's Search for The Heart* (2013).

Anita Endrezze (p.304) is an author and artist. Her short story collection, *Butterfly Moon*, was published in 2012 by the University of Arizona Press. Anita's Red Bird Press Chapbooks include *Breaking Edges* (2012), and *A Thousand Branches* (2014). She won the Bumbershoot/Weyerhaeuser Award, a Washington State Governor's Writing Award, and a GAP Award for her poetry. She collaborates on art projects with a small group of women, and her altered book project on the value of art in Latin America is archived at the Smithsonian. She is half-European (Slovenian, German, and Italian), and half Yaqui (a nation native to Mexico). She has MS and is housebound.

Joan Fitzgerald (p.291) is a poet, an author, and an artist. She has had two poetry chapbooks and *A Collection: Poems by Joan Fitzgerald*, published. Additionally, her four children's books were followed by four young adult novels and three crime novels. She is an award-winning abstract artist whose work has been shown in national and international exhibitions.

Waverly Fitzgerald (p.349) (September 4, 1951–December 13, 2019) was a beloved friend, teacher, reader, student, author, publisher, and urban naturalist. She collaborated with her friend, Curt Colbert, on a series of humorous mystery novels about a talking Chihuahua. In 2007, Waverly published *Slow Time: Reclaiming the Natural Rhythms of Life*, which helps readers shift their relationship with time. *Hard Rain, a Rachel Stern Mystery*, was published in 2020. She taught writing classes online for Creative Nonfiction and for organizations like Richard Hugo House.

Avital Gad-Cykman (p.238) is the author of *Light Reflection Over Blues* (Ravenna Press, 2022) and *Life In, Life Out* (Matter Press). She is a past winner of the Margaret Atwood Studies Magazine Prize and The Hawthorne Citation Short Story Contest; she was twice a finalist for the Iowa Fiction Award and a six-time nominee for the Pushcart. Her stories have appeared in *The Dr. Eckleburg Review, Iron Horse, Prairie Schooner, Ambit, McSweeney's Quarterly* and *Michigan Quarterly*, and anthologized in W. W. Norton's *Flash Fiction International Anthology, Best Short Fictions*. She grew up in Israel and lives in Brazil.

Murray Gordon (p.95) (October 30, 1937–December 23, 2021): Born in Scranton, PA. Anthracite coal. Smoldering slag heaps. To Philly. Saw swastikas flying from rowhouses pre-Pearl Harbor. To the Beat Generation. Poetry. Jazz. To crossing the country. To Seattle. To write. Right here. Right now. Published in *Poets West, Community Connection, Raven Chronicles, Point No Point, Drash: Northwest Mosaic*, and *Poets Table Anthology: A Collection of Poetry by Northwest Poets* (2002).

Robert Gregory (p.276) (1947–2018) was an Omaha native, a Marine Corps veteran, a UC Irvine-trained deconstructionist, a musician who played the guitar and mandolin in several bands, one of them called New Standard Rain, a "semi-bluegrass band" (his description). He was the author of numerous books of poetry, including *Interferences* (1987), *Boy Picked Up By the Wind* (1992), *The Skinny Man* (2003), *The Beautiful City of Weeds* (2005), and *You Won't Need That* (2013). Madeline DeFrees said of the poems collected in *Boy Picked Up By the Wind*, winner of the Bluestem Poetry Award: "Here is a sensibility so limber that it requires the reader to reinvent imagination."

Stephen D. Gutierrez's (p.370) essays and stories recreate the Mexican-American culture of Fresno and the working-class East LA of his youth in the 1970s, offering memories as both poignant and sharp, painful and funny. *The Mexican Man in His Backyard: Stories & Essays* is the third and culminating volume in Gutierrez's trilogy of essays and stories, which also includes *Elements* (winner of the Nilon Award), and *Live from Fresno y Los* (winner of an American Book Award sponsored by the Before Columbus Foundation). He lives in the San Francisco Bay area, and plays Jackpot Mexican continually.

Paul r. Harding: (p.221) At the outbreak of the pandemic Paul recorded his original Spoken Music with his band, Juju Seahorse (pending release). Paul's published work includes a full-length book of poetry, *Hot Mustard & Lay Me Down* (En Theos Press, 2003), and collections of verse, fiction, and interviews in *Arte Noir, Black Renaissance Noire, Konch, Transition 112, Coon Bidness, Berkeley Poetry Review, Raven Chronicles, Earshot Jazz*, and various anthologies. Manuscripts of his early poetry are housed in both the Gwendolyn Brooks Papers at the Bancroft Library, University of California, Berkeley, and the Derek Walcott Collection at the Alma Jordan Library, University of West

Indies. He was awarded a Philip Whalen Memorial Grant for poetry and the Edith K. Draham Scholarship for fiction.

Sharon Hashimoto's (p.26) first book of poetry, *The Crane Wife* (co-winner of the 2003 Nicholas Roerich Prize and published by Story Line Press), has recently been reprinted by Red Hen Press. Her work has appeared in *American Fiction, The American Scholar, Barrow Street, Louisiana Literature, North American Review, Poetry, Prairie Schooner, River Styx, Shenandoah,* and other literary publications. Her second book, *MORE AMERICAN* (Off the Grid Press, 2021), won the 2021 Off the Grid Poetry Prize and the 2022 Washington State Book Award for Poetry. Recently retired from Highline College in Washington State after twenty-nine years of teaching, she writes poetry, short stories, and is currently at work on a novel.

Paul Hunter's (p.139, 140) poems have appeared in numerous journals, as well as nine full-length books and four chapbooks. His first collection of farming poems, *Breaking Ground* (2004, Silverfish Review Press) was reviewed in *The New York Times* and received the 2004 Washington State Book Award. A second farming volume, *Ripening,* appeared in 2007, a third volume, *Come the Harvest,* followed in 2008, and the fourth, from the same publisher, *Stubble Field,* appeared in 2012. He has been a featured poet on *The News Hour,* and has a prose book on small-scale, sustainable farming, *One Seed to Another,* from the *Small Farmer's Journal.* An autobiography in prose poetry, *Clownery,* appeared in 2017, and two western novels, *Sit a Tall Horse* and *Mr. Brick & the Boys,* were published in 2020 and 2022, from Davila Art & Books, in Sisters, Oregon.

Marion Kimes: (p.248, 352) (1930–2014) Poet Belle Randall: "In the Northwest where she was a vital presence for over thirty years, friends and admirers of the poet Marion Kimes know her to possess a cheek as hollow and a beauty as severe as Samuel Beckett's, coupled with a voice as clanging as the pots and pans one bangs on New Year's eve … Poet and publisher Paul Hunter once told me of a steel banjo that he prized because it had the same sound. 'Words must churn … to keep us from flying out the window on an updraft,' says Kimes—a danger that would seem merely whimsical coming from another poet, yet seems a distinct possibility for Kimes—who, in her physical presence, possesses the steely fragility of a sparrow coupled with a voice that recalls the admonishment of 13th century poet Yang Tsai: 'You should have the sound of stone and metal in your use of words.'"

Don Kunz (p.322) was born in Kansas City, Missouri, in 1941, married Sandra Steele in 1965, and their son, Erik, was born in 1969. Don earned the following degrees: BA (Kansas State University, 1964), MA (University of Texas, Austin, 1965), PhD (University of Washington, Seattle, 1968). He taught literature, creative writing, and film studies at the University of Rhode Island from 1968 until his retirement in 2004, and now holds the rank of Professor Emeritus. His essays, poems, and short stories have been published in over sixty literary journals, and he was nominated for a Pushcart Prize in 2004. Don and his wife currently reside in Bend, Oregon, where he continues to write fiction and poetry; volunteer with Habitat for Humanity; hike, mountain bike, and XC ski.

Susan Landgraf (p.162) was awarded an Academy of American Poets' Laureate Award in 2020 to produce a book of Muckleshoot poetry. Her books include *Crossings*, just released by Ravenna Press in *Triple No. 17* in its Chapbook Triple Series. Others include *The Inspired Poet*, a writing exercise book, from Two Sylvias Press (2019); *What We Bury Changes the Ground*; and a chapbook *Other Voices*. More than 400 poems have appeared in *Prairie Schooner, Poet Lore, Margie, Nimrod, The Meadow, Rattle,* and *Calyx*. She served as Poet Laureate of Auburn, Washington, from 2018 to 2020.

Larry Laurence's (p.206) books include a full-length volume of poems, *Life Of The Bones To Come* (Black Heron Press); a chapbook, *Scenes Beginning With The Footbridge At The Lake* (Brooding Heron Press, Waldron Island, Washington); and an e-chapbook, *Successions Of Words Are So* (E-Ratio Editions, New York). His poems have appeared in the anthologies *How Much Earth: The Fresno Poets* (Roundhouse Press, Berkeley), and *Jack Straw Writers Anthology* (Jack Straw Productions, Seattle); and in journals including *CutBank, Floating Bridge Review, Poetry Northwest, POOL, Raven Chronicles,* and *Southern Poetry Review*. Larry earned an MA in English at California State University, Fresno, studying poetry under Philip Levine.

Mercedes Lawry (p.237) is the author of three chapbooks, the latest, *In the Early Garden with Reason*, was selected by Molly Peacock for the 2018 WaterSedge Chapbook Contest. Her poetry has appeared in such journals as *Poetry*, *Nimrod*, and *Prairie Schooner*, and she's been nominated seven times for a Pushcart Prize. She's frequently published short fiction and was a semi-finalist in *The Best Small Fictions 2016*. Her poetry book, *Vestiges*, will be published in 2023 by Kelsay Press.

James R. Lee's (p.215) work has appeared in *Drumming Between Us*, *The Arkansas Review*, *The Washington Review*, *Drumvoices Revue*, *The Journal of African Travel Writing*, *Abbey*, *Cricket*, *Fodderwing*, and in the anthology, *Beyond the Frontier*, *African American Poetry for the 21st Century*, edited by Ethelbert Miller (Black Classic Press, 2002). He attended Howard and American Universities, and graduated from Lincoln University in Pennsylvania.

Stacey Levine (p.90) lives in Seattle, and her story collection *The Girl With Brown Fur* was longlisted for The Story Prize and the Washington State Book Award. Her novel *Frances Johnson* was a finalist for the Washington State Book Award, and her first collection, *My Horse And Other Stories*, won a PEN/West Fiction Award. Recipient of a Stranger Genius Award for Literature, her fiction has appeared in *Tin House*, *Fence*, *Yeti*, *The Fairy Tale Review*, *The Iowa Review*, *Your Impossible Voice*, *Golden Handcuffs*, *Seattle Magazine*, and other venues. Her short fiction has been translated for Japanese and Danish publications. Her novel *Mice 1961* will be published in 2023.

Martha Linehan (p.353) is a poet, art maker, Chemical Dependency Professional (CDP/SUDP), and Integrated Movement Therapist (IMT). She has worked as a counselor in the Seattle area for over twenty-five years with homeless and foster care youth, and with survivors of commercial sexual exploitation (CSE). Martha co-founded Word UP SHOT, a photography and writing program for young women in early recovery, with her sister Jennie Linehan—which was later adapted to specifically serve commercially exploited girls. She started the art program at Seattle's Organization for Prostitution Survivors (OPS) with co-founder Peter Qualliotine, and replicated the Art Workshop in King County Jail in 2018.

Jeanne Ruth Lohmann (p.58) (1923–2016) was born in Arcanum, Ohio. She attended Otterbein College for a year on a scholarship in French, and graduated from Ohio State University in 1945 with a degree in the social sciences. She earned an MA in Creative Writing from San Francisco State College in her mid-fifties. She was a Quaker and a generous listener—committed to the craft of poetry until her death. Jeanne's published work comprises ten collections of poetry, including *Calls from a Lighted House* (Fithian Press, 2007), and *Autumn in the Fields of Language* (2016). Six of her poems can be found in the woods and walkways at Providence St. Peter Hospital in Olympia. The annual Jeanne Lohmann Poetry Awards, established by her San Francisco writer's community in honor of her 80th birthday, were given each spring under the auspices of the Olympia Poetry Network. Garrison Keillor read three of her poems on *Writer's Almanac*, in 2007 and 2016.

Priscilla Long (p.293) is a Seattle-based author and an independent teacher of writing. Her latest book is *Dancing with the Muse in Old Age* (Coffeetown Press). Her two books of poems are *Holy Magic* (MoonPath Press, 2020, winner of the Sally Albiso Award) and *Crossing Over* (University of New Mexico Press). Her other books include *The Writer's Portable Mentor, 2nd edition*; a collection of linked creative nonfictions titled *Fire and Stone*; and *Minding the Muse: A Handbook for Painters, Composers, Writers, and Other Creators*. Her awards include a National Magazine Award

Peter Ludwin (p.42) is the recipient of a Literary Fellowship from Artist Trust and the 2016 winner of the Muriel Craft Bailey Memorial Award from *The Comstock Review*, judged by Marge Piercy. He has three published books of poetry, another manuscript seeking a publisher, and is currently working on a memoir. His work has appeared in many journals, including *Atlanta Review, The Bitter Oleander, The Comstock Review, Crab Orchard Review, Nimrod, North American Review* and *Prairie Schooner*. He works in a greenhouse in Auburn, Washington.

Kevin Miller: (p.61) MoonPath Press published Miller's *Spring Meditation* in 2022. In 2019, his collection *Vanish* won the Wandering Aengus Publication Prize. Pleasure Boat Studio and Blue Begonia Press published earlier collections. Miller divides his time between Tacoma and the midwest of Whidbey Island.

Deborah A. Miranda (p.63) is an enrolled member of the Ohlone-Costanoan Esselen Nation of California. Born in Los Angeles, she grew up in Washington State, earned a BS from Wheelock College in 1983, and an MA and PhD in English from the University of Washington. Miranda's collections of poetry include *Raised by Humans* (2015); *Indian Cartography: Poems* (1999), winner of the Diane Decorah Memorial First Book Award from the Native Writers' Circle of the Americas; and *The Zen of La Llorona* (2005), nominated for a Lambda Literary Award. Her mixed-genre collection, *Bad Indians: A Tribal Memoir* (Heyday Books, 2013), won a Gold Medal from the Independent Publisher's Association and the PEN Oakland Josephine Miles Literary Award.

Anna Mockler's (p.73) novel, *The Rat Hunt Boys*, was published in 2016 (Unbearables/Autonomedia). Her story collection, *Burning Salt* (StringTown Press) appeared in 2004. Her fiction has appeared in *Brooklyn Rail, Sensitive Skin, Exquisite Corpse, Crab Creek Review, Raven Chronicles, Dial, Smoking Poet, Oxygen, Point No Point*, etc. Other fiction was included in *The Big Book of Sex* (2011, Unbearables/Autonomedia), *The Worst Book I Ever Read* (2009 ibid.), *Wreckage of Reason: Anthology of Contemporary Xxperimental Prose by Women Writers* (Vol. I 2008; Vol. II 2014, Spuyten Duyvil), and *Dogs Cats Crows* (2001, Black Heron Press). She lives in Bremerton, Washington, where she sits on the City Council.

Jo Nelson (p.125) taught creative writing at Tacoma Community College, in Washington State, and was a writer in residence for the Washington State Arts Commission. Her poems, articles, and short stories have been published in numerous national anthologies and magazines, including *Blueline, Chachalaca,* the *Chariton Review, Confluence, Comstock Review, Harrisburg Review, Pacific Coast Journal, Plainsongs, Pleiades, Portland Review, Poetry Seattle, Switched on Gutenberg,* and *Willow Creek Journal*. Her poem "Tuning the Interior" was used in an original composition for German radio by Johannes Schmidt-Sistermanns. Jo passed away in January of 2001, of natural causes.

Paul E. Nelson (p.103) founded The Cascadia Poetics Lab & the Cascadia Poetry Festival. Author of a serial poem re-enacting history, *A Time Before Slaughter* (shortlisted for a 2010 Genius Award from

The Stranger); and a second edition including the poems *Pig War: & Other Songs of Cascadia,* as well as *American Sentences.* Co-editor of *Make It True: Poetry from Cascadia,* he's interviewed Allen Ginsberg, Michael McClure, Anne Waldman, Sam Hamill, Robin Blaser, Nate Mackey, Eileen Myles, Brenda Hillman, among others; has had work translated into Spanish, Chinese and Portuguese; and writes an American Sentence daily.

Doug Nufer (p.145) is the author of various novels and poetry collections, including *Rotalever Revelator* (Sagging Meniscus, 2020), *The Me Theme* (Sagging Meniscus, 2016), *Lifeline Rule* (Spuyten Duyvil, 2015), *Lounge Acts* (Insert Blanc, 2013), *By Kelman Out of Pessoa* (Les Figues, 2011), *We Were Werewolves* (Make Now, 2008), *The Mud-flat Man / The River Boys* (soultheft records, 2006), *On the Roast* (Chiasmus, 2004), *Negativeland* (Autonomedia, 2004), and *Never Again* (Black Square, 2004). He sells wine in Seattle.

John Olson (p.327) is the author of numerous books of poetry and prose poetry, including *Echo Regime, Free Stream Velocity, Backscatter: New and Selected Poems, Larynx Galaxy, Dada Budapest,* and *Weave of the Dream King.* He was the recipient of the The Stranger's 2004 Literature Genius Award, and in 2012 was one of eight finalists for the Washington State Arts Innovator Award. He has also published four novels, including *Souls of Wind* (shortlisted for The Believer Book Award, 2008), *The Nothing That Is, The Seeing Machine, In Advance of the Broken Justy,* and *Mingled Yarn,* an autofiction. *You Know There's Something,* a recently completed novel, is forthcoming from Grand Iota Press in England.

Sue Pace (p.166) has had over 250 pieces of prose, poetry, and personal essays published in Australia, the UK, and the USA. In the beginning, she would tell publishers, "Writing is the most selfish thing I do." Over the years, that quote hasn't changed. She is grateful to *Raven Chronicles* for being one of the first journals to support her writing.

Deborah Parks-Satterfield (p.81) is an actor, playwright, and educator. In 1998 she wrote: "as a large African-American, middle-aged lesbian I am under-represented in all aspects of the media. I write to see myself, my culture, and my subculture reflected on stage. I write in a language that is purely my own . . . not interpreted by someone else or seen through someone else's lens." Her work was included in *The Queerest Art: Essays on Lesbian and Gay Theater* (Sexual Cultures, Series #48, 2002), and in "Out across America: playing from P.S. 122 to Peoria, a conversation."

Whitney Pastorek (p.257, 259) is a writer, neighborhood activist, and middle-aged lifeguard who lives in East Nashville with her supermutt, Wally. She is currently trying to figure out what comes next.

David Warren Paul (p.273) (June 30, 1944–May 2, 2013) was born in Cherokee, Iowa. He was a Seattle-based writer and editorial consultant; a former political scientist who taught at Princeton and the University of Washington. He authored or co-authored six books and many articles ranging from politics and history to film criticism, the Internet, and poetry translations. As a technical writer and editor, he worked on contract with Microsoft, Adobe, Boeing, and other companies in the Puget Sound area. His recognitions include awards from the Pacific Northwest Writers Association and the Seattle Arts Commission. He was a National Endowment for the Humanities Fellow, a Fulbright-Hays Fellow, and a scholar-in-residence for the Washington Commission for the Humanities and the Washington State Arts Commission. His novel, *Fantasy on the Theme B-A-C-H*, was published in 2014. He co-authored, with Craig Rennebohm, *Souls in the Hands of a Tender God* (Beacon Press, 2009).

Peter Pereira (p.151) is a family physician in Seattle and the founder of Seattle's Floating Bridge Press. His poetry collections include *Saying the World* (2003) and *What's Written on the Body* (2007), both from Copper Canyon Press. He also has a chapbook, *The Lost Twin*, from Grey Spider Press (2000). Pereira's work has appeared in numerous publications, including *Poetry, the Virginia Quarterly Review*, and several anthologies, including *Best American Poetry* and *To Come to Light: Perspectives on Chronic Illness in Modern Literature*. He has received the "Discovery"/The Nation and Hayden Carruth prizes, and has been a finalist for a Lambda Literary Award. He lives in Seattle, Washington.

Cynthia R. Pratt (p.122) is a founding member of the Olympia Poetry Network's over thirty-year-old board. Her poems have appeared in numerous journals, and in anthologies *Godiva Speaks* (2011), *Dancing on the Edges* (2017), and *Garden of the Covid Museum* (2021). One of her poems was accepted for display at the Seattle Salmon Strategy Summit 2005. Her manuscript, *Celestial Drift*, was published in 2017. She is a former Lacey Councilmember, Deputy Mayor of the City of Lacey for twelve years, and the first Poet Laureate of Lacey, as of 2022.

Jan Priddy (p.249) earned an Oregon Literary Arts Fellowship, Arts & Letters Fellowship, Pushcart nomination, and publication in numerous journals such as *CALYX*, *Liminal Stories*, *The Humanist*, and *North American Review*. She is an MFA graduate from Pacific University and lives in the northwest corner of her home state of Oregon. She occasionally blogs at IMPERFECT PATIENCE: *https://janpriddyoregon.wordpress.com*. [Note: In her story, "The Scar Map," the names and some aspects of the story are from her family.]

Lisa Purdy (p.66) is a former editor of *The Raven Chronicles*. In the early 2000s, she switched from writing poetry to songs, and now writes music and plays with synthesizers when she's not hanging out with her family in Des Moines, Washington.

Lois J. Red Elk-Reed (p.118) is an enrolled member of the Ft. Peck Sioux in Montana, with roots from the Isanti on her mother's side, and the Hunkpapa and Ihanktonwa from her father, who is descended from the Sitting Bull family. Raised in her traditional culture, she is a quill and bead worker, a traditional dancer, and an advocate for cultural preservation and practice. Her poems, prose, and children's stories have been published in many magazines and anthologies. Her first book, *Our Blood Remembers* (Many Voices Press, 2011) won the Best Non-Fiction award from the Wordcraft Circle of Native Writers and Storytellers. A recent book is *Dragonfly Weather* (Lost Horse Press, 2013). She has been a member of Screen Actors Guild and the American Federation of Television and Radio Artists for 40 years.

Nancy Redwine (p.45) (1959–2009) decided to become a writer in 5th Grade and never wavered. She wrote poetry, short fiction, novels, and journalism in the US and in Mexico. Defining passions were social justice, healthcare equity, gardening, the ocean, deep personal friendships, and her kitties. She worked in an AIDS hospice in

Seattle. She died at home in Santa Cruz, California, surrounded by her community.

Judith Roche (p.133) (1941–2019) was a longtime pillar of the Puget Sound literary community. She published four books of poetry including *Wisdom of the Body* (2007 American Book Award); she was Literary Arts Director for Bumbershoot (1986—2005); she co-edited *First Fish, First People* (1998 American Book Award); and had poems installed on many Seattle-area public art projects. Judith influenced numerus generations of Northwest-area writers, poets, artists and students. She was a mentor to many through her co-founding of Red Sky Poetry Theater and as a poetry teacher at Seattle University, Cornish College, in state prisons, and at the Richard Hugo House.

Danny Romero (p.212) earned a BA from the University of California at Berkeley and an MA from Temple University in Philadelphia, where he taught writing for many years. Romero's poems and short stories have been published in a variety of journals including *Bilingual Review, Colorado Review, Drumvoices Revue, Paterson Literary Review, Ploughshares, The Raven Chronicles,* and *Solo.* His work is also in many anthologies: *West of the West: Imagining California, Pieces of the Heart: New Chicano Fiction, Los Vasos Communicantes: Antologia de Poesía Chicana* (Spain), and *Latinos in Lotusland: An Anthology of Contemporary Southern California Literature.* He is the author of the novel *Calle 10* (Mercury House, 1996), and *Traces: A Book of Poetry* (Bilingual Press/Editorial Bilingüe, 2012).

Cat Ruiz (p.120, 123) was born in Seattle. She is the author of three poetry books: *Beach Notes* (TwoNewfs Publishing, 2020), *At the Town Café* (Goldfish Press, 2016), and *Stirring up the Water* (Salt Publishing Ltd, 2008). Her fourth poetry book, *Glimpses,* is in process. Her poetry has appeared in many journals, including The Jung Institute of Los Angeles' *Psychological Perspectives.* She taught English and Humanities for two decades to college students in Seattle and Northern California. She currently lives in the Seattle area, Washington State, USA. (https://www.facebook.com/authorcatruiz)

Mary Lou Sanelli: (p.158) author, speaker, and master dance teacher, she has published six books of poetry and four works of non-fiction.

Her latest collection of essays, *Every Little Thing*, has been nominated for a PNBA and a 2022 Washington State Book Award. Her first novel, *The Star Struck Dance Studio of Yucca Springs*, was released in 2019, and her first children's book, *Bella Likes To Try*, was published in October 2022 (Chatwin Books). She contributes to *The Seattle Times Opinion Page*, and her regular columns appear in Pacific Publishing newspapers.

Mark Sargent: (p.217, 332) Born long ago in Olympia, Washington, into a typical white, middle-class family. Studied art at Mt. Angel College, Buddhist Poetics at Jack Kerouac School of Disembodied Poetics; in Portland, Oregon, 1975 to 1990, worked as a carpenter, snake-oil salesman, street saxophone and combo honk, and bartender. While in Portland he co-founded the Impossibilist Collective and jazz/poetry band Defenestration. In 1990 he moved with family to a small village in the mountains of Southern Greece, where he remains. Work includes, films: *Ellada; Fire; Behold;* and *Wall*. Recent fiction: *Fool on the Hill; Serbia by Night; Ova the Moon;* and *OXI AKOMA*. Most recent book of poetry: *Pagan Favors*.

Janet Sekijima (p.131) is a native of Seattle who is enjoying her retirement years by writing, traveling to places near and far, and learning to oil paint. She is a member of the Cloud Gazing Society of Washington State and has two sweet Society Finches named Dubdub and Hiroshi.

Martha Silano (p.192) is the author of five full-length poetry collections, including *Gravity Assist* (Saturnalia Books, 2019), *What the Truth Tastes Like* (Two Sylvias Press, 2015), *Reckless Lovely* (Saturnalia Books, 2014), and *The Little Office of the Immaculate Conception*, winner of the 2010 Saturnalia Books Poetry Prize. She also co-edited, with Kelli Russell Agodon, *The Daily Poet: Day-By-Day Prompts For Your Writing Practice* (Two Sylvias Press, 2013). Martha's poems have appeared in *Paris Review, Poetry, American Poetry Review, New England Review, Kenyon Review Online,* and *North American Review*, where she was awarded the 2014 James Hearst Poetry Prize; and in many anthologies, including *American Poetry: The Next Generation* and *The Best American Poetry* series. She teaches at Bellevue College.

Kathleen Walsh Spencer (p.324) is a nurse educator living and teaching in Michigan. She has been published in the *Red Cedar Review, Red Rock Review, Rosebud, Rattle, Ekphrasis, Clackamas Literary Review, U.S. Catholic,* and many other journals and publications. She contributed a chapter for *The Poetry of Nursing: Poems and Commentaries of Leading Nurse-Poets* (Kent State University Press, 2006).

Ann Spiers (p.342) is completing a manuscript about her hike from the Columbia River to Cape Flattery. Its first draft was completed in Oysterville, Washington, during a residency provided by the Willard R. Espy Literary Foundation. She lives on Vashon Island where she served as its first poet laureate and stewards its Poetry Post. Ann's poems appear widely in journals, anthologies, and online. Her 2021 publications include *Rain Violent* (Empty Bowl Press) and *Back Cut* (Black Heron). In 2022, Ravenna Press published *Harpoon, No. 16* in its Chapbook Triple Series. She was included in Empty Bowl's women's anthology *Keep a Green Bough: Voices from the Heart of Cascadia, The Madrona Project #2.* (See www.annspiers.com.)

Virgil Suárez (p.69) was born in Havana, Cuba in 1962. He received an MFA from Louisiana State University in 1987. He is the author of eight collections of poetry, most recently *90 Miles: Selected and New Poems* (University of Pittsburgh Press, 2005). His work has appeared in a multitude of magazines and journals internationally. He has been taking photographs on the road for the last three decades. When he is not writing, he is out riding his motorcycle up and down the Blue Highways of the Southeast, photographing disappearing urban and rural landscapes. His tenth volume of poetry, *The Painted Bunting's Last Molt,* was published by the University of Pittsburgh Press in 2020.

Laura Anna Stortoni (p.354) was born in Italy and received higher education degrees at the University of California at Berkeley. She has co-authored, with Mary Prentice Lilli, two books of verse translation of Italian Renaissance women poets, *Gaspara Stampa: Selected Poems* and *Courtly Ladies and Courtesans of the Italian Renaissance.* She recently completed a translation of Maria Luisa Spaziani's book of poetry, *Torri di vedatta,* entitled *Sentry Towers.*

Mario Susko (p.337) is the recipient of numerous awards and international recognition. In 2012, The Walt Whitman Birthplace Association named him Poet Of The Year. That year he was also elected into the Croatian Academy of Sciences and Arts. In 2013 he was named The Poet Laureate of Long Island. He was awarded The Goran's Wreath award, in 2015, given to poets for their overall contribution to poetry. Susko is a translator of Saul Bellow, William Styron, Kurt Vonnegut, James Baldwin, Walt Whitman, and others. With Branko Cegec, he is the co-editor of *Surfacing: Contemporary Croatian Poetry*.

Mark Svenvold (p.101, 102) received his MFA from the University of Iowa Writers' Workshop. He is an associate professor at Seton Hall University, with an area of specialty in creative writing. He has published two books of poetry, and is currently working on a third book entitled *Orpheus, Incorporated*. His poems have been published widely in places like *Orion*, *Crazyhorse*, *Agni Review*, *The Literary Review*, *The North American Review*, and *The New Yorker*. Recent poetry awards include the 2018 Spoon River Editor's Choice Award, selected by Li-Young Lee, and the 2018 Beyond Baroque Poetry Prize, selected by Matthew Zapruder. His nonfiction books are *Big Weather* (Henry Holt & Co.) and *Elmer McCurdy: The Misadventures in Life and Afterlife of an American Outlaw* (Basic Books).

Joan Swift (p.163) (Nov. 2, 1926–March 13, 2017) was originally from Rochester, New York. Swift was among the first poets published in Seattle's *Poetry Northwest Magazine* (in the fall issue of 1959). She published four full-length books of poems and two were winners of the Washington State Governor's Award. She is the recipient of three National Endowment for the Arts Creative Writing Fellowships, as well as grants from the Washington State Arts Commission, an award from The Poetry Society of America, a Pushcart Prize, and residencies at Yaddo and The Virginia Center for the Creative Arts. She had a long and notable career as a writer, drawing extensively from her life and experiences in the Pacific Northwest. She died in Edmonds, Washington, at the age of 90.

Stephen Thomas (p.330) played his role in Seattle's poetry scene of the 80s, 90s and early 2000s. He performed often at Red Sky Poetry Theater, at Bumbershoot, and many other regional venues, as well as farther afield. In 1984, he founded and built The Cabaret Hegel, where now an off-ramp leads I-5 traffic into the Industrial Flats. There Stephen presented and performed with many other Northwest writers and musicians, including Jesse Bernstein. He has published his work in many ephemeral magazines, as well as in *Exquisite Corpse, Poetry Northwest, The Malahat Review, Windfall, Malpais Review*, and others. His book, *Journeyman*, was published by Charles Potts' Tsunami Inc. He currently lives in Germany, where he helped found Gemeinschaft Sonnenwald: a sustainable, regenerative, agriculture community.

Gail E. Tremblay (p.55) is descended from Onondaga, Kanien'kehá ka, and Mi'Kmaq peoples in her father's family, as well as Welsh and English people in her mother's family. She earned a BA in drama from the University of New Hampshire, and an MFA in Creative Writing from the University of Oregon. She is a faculty emerita at The Evergreen State College in Washington State, where she taught from 1979 to 2014. She is the author of four books of poetry, among them *Indian Singing in Twentieth Century America* (Calyx Books, 1990), revised as *Indian Singing* in 1998, and *Farther From and Too Close to Home* (Lone Willow Press, 2014). Tremblay's art and writing explores modern Indigenous experience and the ways in which the pressures of colonial policies have affected her life and the lives of her ancestors and indigenous friends. She is currently working on a new book of poems.

Suzanne A. Villegas, (p.152) akin to her ancestors since 1855, was raised Tejana, but feels she grew up a huevo (with balls) while living across the USA. She was a Jack Straw Writer, featured on NPR multiple times, and published in *The Raven Chronicles, La Voz*, and various other publications. In describing her fiction/memoir and abuse of poetry, she says she likes to get technical in English and emotional in Spanish, it's the best of both worlds. By day Suzanne is faster than a speeding email, more powerful than a scathing policy able to leap tall file cabinets in a single bound as a career Human Resources professional. Most weekends find her on a river as whitewater kayaker.

Connie K. Walle (p.59) is the founder and past President of Puget Sound Poetry Connection. She also founded Our Own Words, a teen writing contest in conjunction with Pierce County Library. A widely-published poet, she was awarded the Amocat Award for her influence and efforts to promote the arts in Tacoma, Washington. Her first poetry collection, *What's Left*, was published in 2018 by MoonPath Press.

Diane Westergaard (p.210) grew up on the Olympic Peninsula and graduated from the University of Washington with a degree in Anthropology. Her poems have been published in *Prairie Schooner*, among others. With guitarist Garylee Johnson, Diane co-wrote and produced *Ghost in the Garden*, a chapbook and audio tape of poetry, music, and song. Diane was a 1999 Jack Straw Writer.

David Lloyd Whited (p.54) (January 28, 1951–November 30, 2014) was a storyteller, a Trickster, and a spellbinding interpreter/reader of his work to an audience. Whited was born and raised in Oregon's Umpqua Valley. He graduated from Bowling Green State University in 1976 with an MFA in Poetry. He authored numerous poetry books, including: *Three in One* (Red Sky Press); *Shadow Dance*, and *Olde Man Coyote Goes to Towne* (nine muses books). Raven published several collaborations David created with artist Glenda Guilmet, for instance the "Shadow Dance Series," 1993. We also published numerous poems, including "Four Views of the Desert," "The Unemployment Line On Venus," and "Smart Bombs: A Euphemism For Lack Of Good Intelligence." David spent the bulk of his professional life as a planner for the Puyallup Tribe in Washington State.

Carletta Carrington Wilson: (p.135, 137) Through poetry, artist books, installations, and mixed media, Wilson discovers answers to questions she did not know to ask. This artist finds each artistic endeavor to be an act of excavation and a revelation. Her work, described as "decorative with a message," has been shown in museums, galleries, and libraries in the Seattle area and beyond. Her 2023 forthcoming artist's book, *Poem of Stone & Bone: The Iconography of James W. Washington Jr. in Fourteen Stanzas and Thirty-One Days*, documents her 2011 site-specific installations on the Seattle property of noted African American sculptor James W. Washington in 2011.

Koon Woon: (p.115, 203) Born in a village near Canton, China, Koon Woon immigrated to Washington State in 1960. He earned a BA from Antioch University Seattle and studied at Fort Hays State University. He is the author of the poetry collections *Rice Bowls: Previously*

Uncollected Words of Koon Woon (2018); *Water Chasing Water* (2013), winner of the 2014 American Book Award from the Before Columbus Foundation; and *The Truth in Rented Rooms* (1998), winner of a Josephine Miles Award from PEN Oakland. His poetry appears in *Premonitions: The Kaya Anthology of New Asian North American Poetry* (1995), among others. He has also published a memoir, *Paper-son Poet: When Rails Were Young* (2016). Woon is the publisher of Goldfish Press, and he lives in Seattle.

Bill Yake: (p.161) Although largely blessed with good fortune, Bill has experienced—as have most of us in imagination, dreams, life, or blues—confinement, grief, and other hard times. His most recent collection, *Way-Making by Moonlight* (Empty Bowl Press), gathers poems from fifty years of attention to community and the wild. These poems have appeared widely in publications serving environmental and literary communities—including *Orion, Rattle, Cascadia Review, Poetry, ISLE, Wilderness Magazine, Terrain.org,* and NPR's *Krulwich Wonders.*

Maged Zaher (p.176) was born and raised in Cairo and is the author of *On Confused Love and Other Damages* (Chatwin Books, July 2022). Zaher is also the author of *The Consequences of My Body* (Nightboat Books, 2016), *If Reality Doesn't Work Out* (SplitLevel Texts, 2014), *Thank You for the Window Office* (Ugly Duckling Presse, 2012), *The Revolution Happened And You Didn't Call Me* (Tinfish Press, 2012), and *Portrait of the Poet As an Engineer* (Pressed Wafer, 2009). Maged is the recipient of the 2013 Genius Award in Literature from the Seattle weekly *The Stranger.* He now lives in Egypt.

Andrena Zawinski, (p.301) veteran teacher of writing and an activist poet, was born and raised in Pittsburgh, Pennsylvania, but makes her home in the San Francisco Bay Area. Her poetry has received awards for lyricism, form, spirituality, and social concern. Her latest book is *Born Under the Influence* (Word Tech). Others are *Landings* (Kelsay Books), *Something About* (Blue Light Press, a PEN Oakland Award), *Traveling in Reflected Light* (Pig Iron Press, Kenneth Patchen Prize). She has also published a collection of flash fiction, *Plumes & Other Flights of Fancy* (Writing Knights Press, 2022).

BIOGRAPHICAL NOTES
Artists/Illustrators

Alfredo Arreguín was born in Morelia, Michoacan, Mexico, and developed as an artist in Seattle (BA 1967, MFA 1969, University of Washington), where he has resided since 1956. Arreguín has a long and distinguished list of accomplishments that span close to four decades. In 1979, he was selected to represent the United States at the 11th International Festival of Painting at Cagnes-sur-Mer, France, where he won the Palm of the People Award. In 1980, he received a fellowship from the National Endowment for the Arts. A climactic moment in his career came in 1994, when the Smithsonian Institution acquired his triptych *Sueño* (*Dream: Eve Before Adam*) for inclusion in the permanent collection of the National Museum of American Art. A year later, in 1995, Arreguín received an OHTLI Award, the highest recognition given by the Mexican government to distinguished individuals who perform extended activities that contribute to benefit the Mexican community abroad.

Anna Bálint: (see writers bios.)

Toni Lee Bennett is both a photographer and writer. She attended the University of Washington, where she received a PhD in English, and a Certificate in Photography. Visual work has appeared in *Women Arts Quarterly* (cover), *Cimarron Review* (cover), *Nassau Review* (upcoming), *Rappahannock Review, Glassworks, Gravel, Grief Diaries, Memoir, Poetry Review, Atomic Petals,* and others. Her work is online at *tonibennett.com*.

Anita K. Boyle is a poet and artist. As an artist, she makes paper, paintings, assemblages and prints, and handmade one-of-a-kind books with her handmade paper. Her latest publication of poetry—*Why Horses*—was published by MoonPath Press in 2020.

Matt Briggs: (see writers bios.)

Michelle Brooks: has published two collections of poetry, *Make Yourself Small* (Backwaters Press), *Flamethrower* (Latte Press), and a novella, *Dead Girl, Live Boy,* (Storylandia Press). A native Texan, she has spent much of her adult life in Detroit.

Manit Chaotragoongit was born in Bangkok, Thailand, and earned a BA in Political Science and Public Administration. Currently he works for the Port Authority of Thailand, and studies photography. "I prefer conceptual photography and street life. My artwork is all about life. [In my photos] I stopped the movement of story around myself before it changed or [was] lost in time. I took a photo and collected a moment of something or somewhere that impressed me and had meaning. I could not live without a memory, experience, or feeling from [an] event . . . The memory is important for the present and the future."

Joel A. Derefield: Served on the Roy, Washington, City Council and was Mayor of Roy for six years. He designed the cover for the South Sound [Tacoma] Edition of Raven, *Vol. 9, No. 3.*, and created illustrations for coloring books and commercial companies.

Nancy D. Donnelly taught anthropology and sociology, and published extensively on refugee issues. She is the author of *Changing Lives of Refugee Hmong Women* (University of Washington Press, 1994). Nancy illustrated many short stories for Raven in the 1990s and early 2000s.

Anita Endrezze: (see writers bios.)

Glenda J. Guilmet received a first-place award in Warhol's World Community Gallery Competition, Ovation TV, 2008, and a First Place Award for "Shadow Dance #1" in the 1988 *Crosscurrents* Arts Contest. Her images have been reproduced in *Native America in the Twentieth Century: An Encyclopedia, Sojourner's Truth and Other Stories, The Seattle Times, Seattle Post-Intelligencer, Seattle Weekly, Tacoma News Tribune, Peninsula Daily News, Raven Chronicles, Gatherings, Reflex, Arches, Aristos, Art Access,* and *Russian Morning*. Her work has been shown in the Bibliotheque National de France, Institute de Cultura Puertorriqueña (Puerto Rico), Westfälische Museum fur Naturkunde (Münster, Germany), Seattle Art Museum, Bainbridge Island Museum of Art, Sacred Circle Gallery of American Indian Art (Seattle), Park Avenue Armory (New York), and University of Arizona Museum of Art, among others. See more of Glenda's visual art at https://www.glendaguilmet.com.

Kathleen Gunton's second collection of poetry has just launched with one of her photos chosen for the cover image. *Putting Words Next To Silence* is published by Paragon and can be found at (www.specialbooks. com). Her photography continues to appear in literary journals such as *Thema* (Spring 2023). She lives in Southern California.

Jeff Niles Hacking was raised in Utah by a pack of excommunicated Mormons. He graduated from the University of Utah with a degree in Geophysics, hence his love of rocks. In prison, he learned to draw, paint watercolors, and found a love for writing.

Mike Hess is a multidisciplinary craftsman who, after 35 years in Seattle, took to the road in 2010 for three years. Since then, he's lived in AR, AZ, OR, and FL. Currently back in Oregon, in a woodshop he makes little pieces out of big ones. He's stringing words together one after another: the latest is up to 60 thousand. He's passionate about chestnut and monkey puzzle trees, the beauty in the ordinary, feeding crows and wood storks, a good night's sleep, sharp pencils, anything osseous, and the unforeseen shift.

Judy Horn is an award-winning professional photographer and electronic imaging artist. She began her art career at the University of Washington and continued training at Weber State University in Ogden, Utah. With this background in oil and watercolor painting, she has developed a process to combine art techniques with photography and free hand electronic painting. Much of her work is privately commissioned projects, portraits, and commercial work.

Paul Hunter: (see writers bios.)

Irene H. Kuniyuki's photography before art school was mostly landscapes, birds, plants, dogs, cats, urbanscapes. She then expanded to photographing dancers and performing artists, and graffiti— documenting the changing urban areas of Seattle. "The challenge for me has been re-examining nature photography with my particular vision that I used for art photos. Photographing fast-moving birds such as osprey, bald eagles, crows, and seagulls became my primary objective between 2007 and 2010." To see more of her work and products, visit www.zazzle.com/kuniyuki.

Clare McLean: Seasoned communications professional who creates pitch-perfect written and visual work. Thrives on nurturing connections between people, ideas, resources, and organizations. Avid citizen scientist, with a passion for birds, native plants, and fungi. Photographer and digital assets manager at UW Medicine Strategic Marketing & Communications (2006-2019). Commissioner: City of Mountlake Terrace Recreation & Parks Advisory Commission (2019-2021).

Scott Martin grew up in Normandy Park, in the Pacific Northwest. He is an artist and illustrator, and proprietor of Tin Hat Novelties, the originators and makers of National Waffle Association products (which can be found from Tulsa to Timbuktu), and a host of other original novelty items. A former sign painter, he now works as a freelance designer and graphic artist. He has been *Raven Chronicles'* art director for many years, wrote and produced a *Raven* online column, "Art Is Where You Find It," and interviewed many Seattle-area artists, including Terry Turrell, Patti Warashina, and Abe Blashko for Raven.

Claudia Mauro is a poet photographer, science writer, and the founding director of the nonprofit literary publisher Whit Press. She is the recipient of two Seattle Arts Commission City Artist Grants, and a Wyoming Arts Council Creative Writing Fellowship in Poetry. She is a voting member of the National Book Critics Circle, PEN America, and The Council of Literary Magazines and Presses. An alumna and former board member of Hedgebrook Writers Retreat, she has also served as a judge for the Lambda Book Awards. Her books include *Stealing Fire* and *Reading the River* (Whiteaker Press 1999, 2004), both Lambda Book Award finalists. Claudia also has extensive experience as a backcountry pilot in Alaska and was employed for over twenty years as a field science tech for the Alaska Dept. of Fish & Game, and for NOAA as Marine Science Tech crew on their research and survey vessels.

Whitney Pastorek (see writers bios.)

Joel Sackett: In the summer of 1968, Sackett got his first camera and hit the streets of New York City. In 1970, he studied and lived at the Praestegaard Experimental Film and Photography School in Alborg, Denmark. He transferred to the San Francisco Art Institute (SFAI) and graduated in 1974. He stayed on at SFAI as a staff member until

1979, when he was hired as a civilian photography instructor on board the USS San Jose. Several months and ports of call later he decided to stay in Japan. During his decade there he worked as an editorial photographer for numerous magazines around the world. He published several books, most notably, *Rikishi, the Men of Sumo*, and *Backstage at Bunraku*. In 1990 he moved to Bainbridge Island with his family with the intention of staying for one or two years. That was over 30 years ago. In 2000, he received the first Island Treasure Award in the Arts. He has produced three books about Bainbridge Island: *An Island in Time* (with Candace Jagel); *In Praise of Island Stewards*; and the forthcoming *Dave's Brainbox*.

Stephanie Shachat still lives in Seattle Washington. She has returned to photography after taking several years off to focus on fiction writing. Her love of macro photography continues. She is learning to play with different editing techniques to create digital images, and she uses both her photographs and digital images in her crafting. You can see her work on Instagram *@stephanieshachat*.

Judith Skillman is interested in feelings engendered by the natural world. Her medium is oil on canvas. Works range from seascape to still life to abstract. Her art has appeared in *Windmill*, *Artemis*, *The Penn Review*, and elsewhere. She has studied at McDaniel College, Pratt Fine Arts Center, and the Seattle Artist's League. Shows include Galvanize, and Pratt. Visit *https://www.etsy.com/shop/JkpaintingsStore*.

Martha Studt lives in Custer, South Dakota, where her work is exhibited in local galleries and online. She works in oils, pastels, and graphite, and her portraits include Native Americans, Russian immigrants, and other settlers to the area.

Peggy Sullivan lives in Seattle, steeped in music, wine, and science. She is a casual photographer of things that catch her eye.

Mark Sullo is a collage artist with a lifelong interest in photography, various visual art media, and music. Born in Boston, he has been based in Seattle for several decades. During that time he has been fortunate to have had the influence from multiple directions of the local arts community. Some of the resulting activity has included helping to establish the Apex Belltown Housing Co-op, working on and editing the *Belltown Rag*, co-founding and operating Wall of Sound Record Store, buying/selling anonymous vintage photography for collectors, and engaging with creative photography for exhibit, documentation, and publication. Eventually he began working with collage. The technique utilized for this artwork involves lifting printed media with transparent tape and recombining the source material with the aim of creating narrative impressions. The process is a chance unfolding of detail with attention to composition and ideas based on the coincidence of conjoining elements. Each piece creates its own adventure.

Gail E. Tremblay: (see writers bios.)

Carl Van Vechten: (June 17, 1880–Dec. 21, 1964, New York City), US novelist, music and drama critic, an influential figure in New York literary circles in the 1920s. He worked as assistant music critic for *The New York Times* (1906–08), then as that paper's Paris correspondent. After publishing his autobiography, *Sacred and Profane Memories* (1932), he vowed to write no more and to devote his time to photography. His extensive collection of books on Black Americana, the James Weldon Johnson Memorial Collection of Negro Arts and Letters, is now at Yale University. He also established the Carl Van Vechten Collection at the New York City Public Library and a collection of music and musical literature at Fisk University, Nashville, Tennessee.

Andrew Wesner is a professional print photographer living in Seattle. His work is displayed in commercial buildings and private residences. He believes in the principles of traditional film photography and image development as they can be applied to digital capture. Edits are minimal and limited to work that can be performed in a darkroom. He distributes his work in print format only to preserve the integrity of classic photography. Examples of his work can be seen at www.apwesner. smugmug.com, or by appointment.

Gloria White Calico: Although she calls herself an "Urban Indian," she maintains strong ties to both the Blackfeet culture of her grandfather, and the Alaskan heritage of her grandmother, an Athabaskan Indian whose tribe fished along the Yukon River. White Calico's dual heritage is reflected in her rich variety of subject matter and has influenced her love of bright colors and her experiments of adding media such as buttons, beads, and feathers to her paintings. "Color and texture," she says, "are strong sensory and tactile media, and my interpretations of life revolve around them. As an only child who frequently moved, sometimes to a new school every year, art became a source of escape into a world of imagination. Painting and drawing became my means of survival."

Carletta Carrington Wilson: (see writers bios.)

Bill Yake: (see writers bios.)

BIOGRAPHICAL NOTES
Editors

Kathleen Alcalá (see Writers Bios).

Phoebe Bosché is a cultural activist, and has been managing editor of The Raven Chronicles literary organization/Raven Chronicles Press since 1991. Since 1984, she has organized literary events and readings in the Pacific Northwest. In 1985, she co-founded, along with poet Roberto Valenza, "Alternative To Loud Boats," a literary and musical festival which ran for ten years in various venues in Seattle. She was co-editor of *Swale Magazine* (with Valenza) and *Sky Views*, a monthly literary publication of Red Sky Poetry Theater, in the mid-1980s to early 1990s. Her spoken word poems appear in various publications, including the anthology *Durable Breath, Contemporary Native American Poetry*, Salmon Run Publishing Co., Anchorage, Alaska, and *Open Sky*. She is a full-time editor and book designer. Her favorite poet is Archy, the cockroach, whose muse is Mehitabel, the alley cat.

Paul Hunter (see Writers Bios).

Anna Odessa Linzer: "My home waters are the Salish Sea. My childhood summers were spent along the beaches and my life since has been lived along these same beaches. All my writing comes from my deep and life-long connection to the Northwest. It comes from the generations of people I have known, stories I have heard, from the homes and gardens I have tended, the waters I swim in year around.

"My novel *Ghost Dancing*, published by Picador USA of St. Martin's Press, received an American Book Award in 1999. In this novel, both my Lenape heritage and my life on the Suquamish Port Madison Reservation are intertwined. These elements are also expressed in each of my three novels, *Blind Virgil, Dancing on Waters*, and *A River Story*. *A River Story* was performed as a two-person play. The three novels were published as a limited hand-bound trilogy, *HOME WATERS*, by Marquand Books. With this work I was able to bring together my 20-year designer/binder experience as the owner of The Watermark, a hand bookbindery. My poetry and short fiction have appeared in literary magazines, anthologies, and text books, and have also been part of installations in galleries and museums in the US and Canada."

PERMISSIONS AND
PUBLICATION CREDITS

Kathleen Alcalá, "A Woman Called Concha," from *The Desert Remembers My Name: On Family and Writing* (University of Arizona Press, 2007). Published in *Raven Chronicles* in 2000. Reprinted by permission of the author.

Bobby Anderson, "Writing a Place in the City," was presented at Richard Hugo House, in October 1998, at the *Power of Place Symposium*. Published in *Raven Chronicles* in 1999.

Amontaine Aurore, "Letter to Myself," published in *Raven Chronicles* in 2003, under the name Amontaine Woods. Reprinted by permission of the author.

Anna Bálint, "Terror," published in *Raven Chronicles* in 2003. Reprinted by permission of the author.

Camincha Benvenutto, "An Angry Requiem," translation of "Un Requiem Furioso," by Lara Stortoni, published in *Raven Chronicles* in 2005. Reprinted by permission of the author/translator.

Jim Bodeen, "Letter To Leo Tapia In Kuwait Near The Iraqi Border," published in *Raven Chronicles* in 2004. Reprinted by permission of the author.

Natalie Pascale Boisseau, "Entre deux langues/Between Tongues," published in *Raven Chronicles* in 2005. Reprinted by permission of the author.

Margot F. Boyer, "Cathexis," published in *Raven Chronicles South Sound Edition* in 2000. Reprinted by permission of the author.

Matt Briggs, "Seattle is a Vortex," published in *Raven Chronicles*, 2001. The essay, in another version, was presented at the *Third Annual Hugo House Inquiry: Disappearances*, October 7, 2000. The essay was published in a booklet for a set of booklets handed out at The Stranger Genius Award, 2003. Reprinted by permission of the author.

Ronda Piszk Broath, "Grace Baking," published in *Raven Chronicles* in 2003. Reprinted by permission of the author.

Rebecca Brown, "Breath" from *The End of Youth* (City Lights Books, 2003). Published in *Raven Chronicles* in 1998. Reprinted by permission of the author.

Polly Buckingham, "Hickory Dickory Dock," published in *Raven Chronicles* in 2003. Reprinted by permission of the author.

Eric Lee Christensen, "The Mind of the West," published in *Raven Chronicles* in 1997. Reprinted by permission of the author.

Glenna Elizabeth Cook, "The Peeler," from *Thresholds* (MoonPath Press, 2017). Published in *Raven Chronicles* in 1998. Reprinted by permission of the author.

Victor Hernández Cruz, "Problems With Hurricanes" from *Maraca: New and Selected Poems 1965-2000* (Coffee House Press, 2001). Copyright © 2001 by Victor Hernandez Cruz. Reprinted with the permission of The Permissions Company, LLC on behalf of Coffee House Press, www.coffeehousepress.org. Published in *Raven Chronicles* in 1999.

Michael Daley, "Climate & Currency." The full text of "Climate & Currency," first published in *Raven Chronicles Magazine* (2001), can be found in *Way Out There: Lyrical Essays* (Aequitas Books, 2006) and in *Reinhabited: New & Selected Poems* (Dos Madres Press, 2022). Reprinted by permission of the author.

Suzannah Dalzell, "Suspend," first published in *Raven Chronicles* in 2003. Reprinted by permission of the author.

Pamela Moore Dionne, "Orogeny," first published in *Raven Chronicles* in 1997. Reprinted by permission of the author.

Qwo-Li Driskill, "For Matthew," first published in *Raven Chronicles* in 2005. Reprinted by permission of the author.

Pat Duggan, "I Open My Mouth But No Words Come Out," published in *Raven Chronicles* in 2005.

Taha Ebrahimi, "Into the Hills," first published in *Raven Chronicles* in 2001. Reprinted by permission of the author.

Keith Egawa, "Another Cousin," first published in *Raven Chronicles* in 2004. Reprinted by permission of the author.

Anita Endrezze, "The Medicine Bundle," first published in *Raven Chronicles* in 2004. Reprinted by permission of the author.

Joan Fitzgerald, "Procession," first published in *Raven Chronicles* in 2004. Reprinted by permission of the author.

Waverly Fitzgerald, "The Cross/La Crusada," first published in *Raven Chronicles* in 2005. Reprinted by permission of her executor Shaw Fitzgerald.

Avita Gad-Cykman, "The Cycle of Seasons," first published in *Raven Chronicles* in 2003. Reprinted by permission of the author.

Murray Gordon, "Get to know your jacket," first published in *Raven Chronicles* in 1999. Reprinted by permission of his executor Susan Sheridan.

Robert Gregory, "At the Reading," published in *Raven Chronicles* in 2003. Reprinted by permission of his executor Karah Stokes.

Glenda J. Guilmet. Her three photographs are from *Shadow Dance*, Glenda J. Guilmet and David Lloyd Whited (nine muses books, 2004). Used by permission of the artist.

Stephen D. Guiterrez, "Jackpot Mexican" first appeared in *Raven Chronicles* (2005) and portions of it were reprinted in *The Mexican Man in His Backyard: Stories & Essays* (Roan Press, 2014). Reprinted by permission of the author.

Paul r. Harding, "Didn't It Rain," first published in *Raven Chronicles* in 2002. Reprinted by permission of the author.

Sharon Hashimoto, "The Mushroom Man" was first published in *Home To Stay, Asian American Fiction by Women*, edited by Sylvia Watanabe and Carol Bruchac (Greenfield Review Press, 1990). Published in *Raven Chronicles* in 1997. Reprinted by permission of the author.

Paul Hunter, "Homecomings" and "House Dressing," first published in *Raven Chronicles* in 2000. Reprinted by permission of the author.

Marion Kimes, "On Spilling Paint," first published in *Raven Chronicles* in 2003. "Called" was translated into French, "Interpellée," by Martha Linehan, with the support of Natalie Pascale Boisseau (traduction de Martha Linehan avec l'aide de Natalie Pascale Boisseau). Published in *Raven Chronicles* in 2005. Reprinted by permission of the translator.

Don Kunz, "A Parade on June 25th," published in *Raven Chronicles* in 2004. Reprinted by permission of the author.

Susan Landgraf, "Latecomers," published in *Raven Chronicles South Sound Edition* in 2002. Reprinted by permission of the author.

Larry Laurence, "Double Take," published in *Raven Chronicles* in 2002. Reprinted by permission of the author.

Mercedes Lawry, "Crime or Something Like It," published in *Raven Chronicles* in 2003. Reprinted by permission of the author.

James R. Lee, "Voting for the First Time," published in *Raven Chronicles* in 2002.

Stacey Levine, "Frances Johnson," published in *Raven Chronicles* in 1999, was an excerpt from her novel, *Frances Johnson* (Verse Chorus Press, 2010). Reprinted by permission of the author.

Jeanne Ruth Lohmann, "Northwest Woodcarver," published in *Raven Chronicles, South Sound Edition* in 1998. Reprinted by permission of her executor Karen Lohmann.

Priscilla Long, "Mrs. Morrissey." "Thanks to my friend Saul Slapikoff whose ten-minute play, *Mrs. Zaslovsky*, based on this short story, was produced in July 2002, in the Hovey Theater Summer Shorts, in Waltham, Massachusetts." Reprinted by permission of the author.

Peter Ludwin, "Duckabush River," published in *Raven Chronicles* in 1997. Reprinted by permission of the author.

Kevin Miller, "The Heart of Displace," published in *Raven Chronicles South Sound Edition* in 1998. Reprinted by permission of the author.

Deborah Miranda, "Repatriation," published in *Raven Chronicles South Sound Edition* in 1998. Reprinted by permission of the author.

Anna Mockler, "Painting Wallpaper" from *Burning Salt* (StringTown Press, 2004). Published in *Raven Chronicles* in 1998. Reprinted by permission of the author.

Jo Nelson, "Salmon Beach," published in *Raven Chronicles South Sound Edition* in 1999.

Paul Nelson, "Keeping Alive the Sense of Ceremony, An Interview with Victor Hernández Cruz," published in Raven Chronicles in 1999. This was an edited version of a forty-five minute, on-the-air interview (KJR-FM, KSRB-AM and other stations), conducted by Nelson, on November 22, 1998. Reprinted by permission of the author.

Doug Nufer, "Trade Tastings," published in *Raven Chronicles* in 2000. Reprinted by permission of the author.

John Olson, "Lifestyles of the Rich and Berserk," published in *Raven Chronicles* in 2004. Reprinted by permission of the author.

Sue Pace, "I Do Not Cry," published in *Raven Chronicles* in 2001. Reprinted by permission of the author.

Deborah Parks-Satterfield, "Lula," published in *Raven Chronicles* in 1998.

Whitney Pastorek, "After" and "The Momento," published in *Raven Chronicles* in 2003. Reprinted by permission of the author. Her photos were taken in New York City in September, 2001. Reprinted by permission of the artist.

David Warren Paul, "A Better Way," published in *Raven Chronicles* in 2003. Reprinted by permission of his executor Nancy Jacobs.

Peter Pereira, "Alice Alone," published in *Raven Chronicles* in 2000. Reprinted by permission of the author.

Cynthia R. Pratt, "Rodeo Clown," published in *Raven Chronicles South Sound Edition* in 1999. Reprinted by permission of the author.

Jan Priddy, "The Scar Map," published in *Raven Chronicles* in 2003. Reprinted by permission of the author. [Note: In her story, "The Scar Map," the names and some aspects of the story are from her family.]

Lois J. Red Elk-Reed, "A Force They Could Not Control," published in *Raven Chronicles South Sound Edition* in 1999. Reprinted by permission of the author.

Nancy Redwine, "The Accident," published in *Raven Chronicles* in 1997. Reprinted by permission of her executor George Merilatt.

Judith Roche, "Marie Antoinette's Last Supper," published in *Raven Chronicles* in 2000. Reprinted by permission of one of her executors Sibyl James.

Danny Romero, "P/V," published in *Raven Chronicles* in 2002. Reprinted by permission of the author.

Cat Ruiz, "A Skin You Shed" and "Warm Springs, Oregon," published in *Raven Chronicles South Sound Edition* in 1999. Reprinted by permission of the author.

Joel Sackett, photograph "Untitled," from *Tokyo: A View of the City* (Donald Richie, Reaktion Books, London, 1999). Reprinted by permission of the artist.

Mary Lou Sanelli, "Miami," published in *Raven Chronicles South Sound Edition* in 2000. Reprinted by permission of the author.

Mark Sargent, "Geoglossa, Listening to Greece" and "Jerry and the Mick," published in *Raven Chronicles* in 2002 and 2004. Reprinted by permission of the author.

Janet Sekijima, "Her Instructions" from *Pontoon 5* (Floating Bridge Press, 2001). Reprinted by permission of the author.

Martha Silano, "This is Not the Last Poem about Pears," from *Blue Positive* (Steel Toe Books, 2006). Published in *Raven Chronicles* in 2001. Reprinted by permission of the author.

Kathleen Walsh Spencer, "Army Nurses, Vietnam, 1966," published in *Raven Chronicles* in 2004. Reprinted by permission of the author.

Ann Spiers, "Listening Only," published in *Raven Chronicles* in 2005. Reprinted by permission of the author.

Virgil Suárez, "Song for the Sugar Cane," published in *Raven Chronicles* in 1998. Reprinted by permission of the author.

Mark Sullo, The source material for Mark Sullo's two collages is *My First Ten Years with the Leica* by Dr. Paul Wolff, published 1930. The title of the piece "Decade" is in reference to the book title as the artist wishes to acknowledge the original work.

Mario Susko, "The All," published in *Raven Chronicles* in 2004.

Mark Svenvold, "The Buffalo Shoe Factory" and "[Cloudy Bright]" from Svenvold's chapbook *Death of the Cabaret Hegel*, (Wood Works Press, 1997). All the poems in the chapbook were also published as a section in his book *Soul Data* (University of North Texas Press, 1998), winner of the Vassar Miller Prize in Poetry, 1997. Published in *Raven Chronicles* in 1999. Reprinted by permission of the author.

Joan Swift, "The Readings at Richard Hugo House," published in *Raven*

Chronicles South Sound Edition in 2000. Reprinted by permission of her executor Lisa Swift.

Stephen Thomas, "America, A True Story," published in *Raven Chronicles* in 2004. Reprinted by permission of the author.

Gail Tremblay, "Days," published in *Raven Chronicles* in 1998. Reprinted by permission of the author.

Carl Van Vechten, "Portrait of Jacob Lawrence," from the portfolio '*O, Write My Name': American Portraits, Harlem Heroes,* 1941. Printed 1983, photogravure, Smithsonian American Art Museum. Transfer from the National Endowment for the Arts, 1983.63.155. Photograph © Van Vechten Trust; Compilation/Publication © Eakins Press Foundation.

Suzanne A. Villegas, "Recipe for Great Aquante," published in *Raven Chronicles* in 2000. Reprinted by permission of the author.

Connie K. Walle, "Dying Wish," published in *Raven Chronicles South Sound Edition* in 1998. Reprinted by permission of her executor Charles J. Walle.

Diane Westergaard, "Stone Gardens," published in *Raven Chronicles* in 2002. Reprinted by permission of the author.

David Lloyd Whited, "Tracking Indian Creek," published in *Raven Chronicles South Sound Edition* in 1998. Reprinted by permission of the author's executor Marian Whited.

Carletta Carrington Wilson, "Jacob Lawrence: Our Beauty is Not Complete Without Your Hands . . ." and "this light called darkness," published in *Raven Chronicles* in 2000. Reprinted by permission of the author.

Koon Woon, "Forum" from *The Truth In Rented Rooms* (Kaya Press, 1998), published in *Raven Chronicles* in 1999, and reprinted by permission of the author. "From the streets at dawn," published in *Raven Chronicles* in 2001. Reprinted by permission of the author.

Bill Yake, "Prison," published in *Raven Chronicles South Sound Edition* in 2000. Reprinted by permission of the author.

Maged Zaher, "Intersections," published in *Raven Chronicles* in 2001. Reprinted by permission of the author.

Andrena Zawinski, "The New Gold Rush," published in *Raven Chronicles* in 2004. Reprinted by permission of the author.

Raven, photograph by Bill Yake

Corvids, Seattle, Washington, photographs by Alfredo Arreguín

ACKNOWLEDGMENTS

Raven is indebted to our 2022-2023 co-sponsors for partial funding of our programs: the Seattle Office of Arts & Culture (Civic Partners); 4Culture/King County Lodging Tax (Arts Sustained Support Program), and the Washington State Arts Commission/ArtsWA, with National Endowment (NEA) funding for project support. And to all Raven subscribers and donors over the past thirty-two years; this year our special thanks to: Anne Bálint, Minnie A. Collins, Kathleen Alcalá, Larry H. Laurence, Katherine Ayars, Paul Hunter, Carletta Carrington Wilson, Lawrence Matsuda, Koon Woon, henry 7. reneau jr., Susan Sheridan, Anonymous, Sally Malloy, Rachel Beatty, Susan Pace, Susan Noyes Platt, Anna O. Linzer, Sibyl James, Frances McCue, and many others, for their generous donations in support of Raven publications and programs.

Publisher
Raven Chronicles Press
Founded in 1991
A NON-PROFIT, 501(C)(3) ORGANIZATION
© 2023 The Raven Chronicles

Managing Editor
Phoebe Bosché, Seattle

Founders
Kathleen Alcalá
Phoebe Bosché
Philip Red Eagle

Anthology Editors
Kathleen Alcalá
Phoebe Bosché
Paul Hunter
Anna Odessa Linzer

Anthology Copy Editors
Phoebe Bosché, Paul Hunter,
Dana Gaskin Wenig, Carolyne Wright

Anthology Typist
Shelley Minden

ALL QUERIES
THE RAVEN CHRONICLES

MAILING ADDRESS:
15528 12TH AVENUE NORTHEAST
SHORELINE, WASHINGTON 98155-6226

TEL: 206.941.2955
HTTPS://WWW.RAVENCHRONICLES.ORG
EDITORS@RAVENCHRONICLES.ORG

TWITTER: @RAVENCHRONIC
FACEBOOK: HTTPS://WWW.FACEBOOK.COM/RAVEN.CHRONICLES
HTTPS://WWW.YOUTUBE.COM/C/RAVENCHRONICLESPRESS